JOHNSON AND BOSWELL

A Survey of Their Writings

RIVERSIDE STUDIES IN LITERATURE

RIVERSIDE STUDIES IN LITERATURE

General Editor · Gordon N. Ray

JOHNSON & BOSWELL

A Survey of Their Writings

E. L. McAdam, Jr.
New York University

HOUGHTON MIFFLIN COMPANY • BOSTON
New York • Atlanta • Geneva, Ill. • Dallas • Palo Alto

Printed in the U.S.A.

To George Milne

Preface

WHEN Dr. Gordon Ray suggested a single book on the literary careers of both Johnson and Boswell, the idea struck me as unorthodox and interesting. Johnson was older in years, and younger in some of his approaches to ideas, in contrast with Boswell's romantic feudalism. Boswell, on the other hand, was more open to the impact of new writers like Gray, and to some of the new revolutionary movements, like those in Corsica and in America. Yet they had numerous points of contact—their almost gluttonous love of life, particularly that of metropolitan London, their deep concern with morality and religion, their sportive playfulness, and a surrogate father-son relationship which provided disagreement and excitement wholly different from the sycophantic connection of the modern official or "kept" biographer.

For both men were basically and primarily writers, and therefore wrote because they were compelled to do so. Johnson, indeed, pretended to write only for money—"No man but a blockhead ever wrote, except for money"—but this is just a piece of conversational bravado. We need only to look at the wide disparity between Johnson's contracts and the resulting books. One example will do: In 1777 a group of booksellers hired him to write prefaces for a collection of English poets, for three hundred guineas. This might have been adequate for a few weeks' work, but Johnson spent years on the project, and produced ten volumes. No one demanded this but himself. Likewise, Boswell's journalizing was the result of an inner need to record himself, year after year, volume after volume. And his *Life of Johnson*, conceived as a single volume, was published as two large quartos.

Neither man is easy to classify. To describe Johnson as a neoclassicist is so gross an oversimplification as to be useful only on a very elementary level of examination. He is allied to the Age of Pope in his insistence on the moral basis of literature, and wholly opposed in his rejection of the rules. Boswell is neither a belated Augustan nor an early Blake. I have tried therefore to approach each man chronologically through his writings, with no reference to other critics, however distinguished, in the belief that before we evaluate we need to listen.

Editions Referred To in the Text

JOHNSON

Journey to the Western Islands and Boswell's *Tour*, ed. R. W. Chapman, 1924.

Lives of the Poets, 4 v., 1783, Johnson's last revision.

A Johnson Reader, ed. E. L. McAdam Jr. and George Milne, 1964, for *Rasselas* and Preface to Shakespeare.

Works, Oxford, 9 v., 1825.

BOSWELL

Journals, ed. F. A. Pottle et al., 1950– .

Life of Johnson, ed. G. B. Hill, rev. L. F. Powell, 6 v., 1934–50.

Tour of the Hebrides, ed. R. W. Chapman, 1924.

Pottle, F. A., *James Boswell, The Earlier Years*, 1966.

Contents

Preface vii

Editions referred to in the text viii

JOHNSON

I Early Years: *London;* the *Dictionary* 3

II Poet, Playwright, Essayist 26

III *Rasselas* 50

IV *Shakespeare* 61

V *Political Tracts* 70

VI *Journey to the Western Islands* 83

VII *Lives of the Poets* 92

BOSWELL

I Early Career: *Journals* 187

II *Corsica; Tour of the Hebrides* 203

III *Life of Johnson* 217

Critical List of Editions and Studies

Johnson 253

Boswell 255

Index 259

SAMUEL JOHNSON

I

Early Years: *London*, the *Dictionary*

In the eighteenth century a writer either learned his craft quickly or starved. "Slow rises worth, by poverty depress'd," Johnson wrote in *London* as he was beginning his apprenticeship to Grub Street. The line is applied to the life of a scholar, but it comes in fact out of Johnson's own career. He did not move from a dazzling precocity to early fame: his youth was dogged by poverty, and his name did not appear on a book until his fortieth year.

His talents appeared early: he composed verses at four, though their quality would perhaps not have pleased any relatives more distant than parents. He was sent to the excellent local grammar school at Lichfield, where he went through the usual course, learning Latin and some Greek, translating Latin verse and prose into English, English into Latin, and doing original exercises. Another school at Stourbridge followed, where one of Johnson's exercises, a translation into English of Addison's Latin "Battle of the Pygmies and the Cranes," shows him varying the original by slight expansions. Literal translation was evidently not encouraged—a healthy sign that his masters wanted the boys to think about the poems enough to transfer them, to a degree, into their own terms if not into their own experience.

After an interval in which Johnson worked and read in his father's bookshop—it is not safe to assume that he did not read everything which may have been in that shop—he went on to Oxford in 1728, where there was more Latin and Greek, more translating, more original exercises. But after thirteen months, funds ran out, and Johnson returned to the shop to work and to read. At twenty, his formal education was ended. He was perhaps saved from despair for his future by the lively intellectual Whig society of Lichfield, which welcomed the awkward, brilliant young man.

In 1731 one of his college exercises, a translation into Latin of Pope's *Messiah*, was published in an anthology of college poems. It is principally interesting because it was his first publication and a translation, for translations and some original verse were all he had learned to write—these and essays. In 1732 a school friend, Edmund Hector, invited him to spend a winter in Birmingham, and introduced him to Thomas Warren, the printer of the *Birmingham Journal*, for whom Johnson wrote his first series of essays. Unfortunately, no issue of the paper containing one of these essays has been discovered, but the pattern of Johnson's early work has emerged: verse, translations, and essays.

In the summer of 1734, perhaps still under Hector's stimulus, Johnson issued proposals for an edition of the Latin poems of the Italian humanist Politian, with a biography and a history of Latin poetry from the time of Petrarch to that of Politian. But subscribers were not forthcoming, and Johnson dropped the project. He did not try an edition again until his Shakespeare.

Johnson's first book appeared in London in the following year: *A Voyage to Abyssinia. By Father Jerome Lobo, A Portuguese Jesuit. Containing, A Narrative of the Dangers he underwent in his first Attempt to pass from the Indies into Abyssinia; with a Description of the Coasts of the Red-Sea. An Account of the History, Laws, Customs, Religion, Habits, and Buildings of the Abyssins; with the Rivers, Air, Soil, Birds, Beasts, Fruits and other natural Productions of that remote and unfrequented Country. A Relation of the Admission of the Jesuits into Abyssinia in 1625, and their Expulsion from thence in 1634. An exact Description of the Nile, its Head, its Branches, the Course of its Waters, and the Cause of its Inundations. With a Continuation of the History of Abyssinia down to the Beginning of the Eighteenth Century, and Fifteen Dissertations on various Subjects relating to the History, Antiquities, Government, Religion, Manners, and natural History of Abyssinia, and other Countries mention'd by Father Jerome Lobo. By Mr. Joachim Le Grand. From the French.*

This, like the essays, was printed at Birmingham for Warren, and Boswell tells the story that Johnson was so slow in getting copy to the printer that Hector persuaded him to dictate while lying in bed (*Life*, I.87). How much Johnson actually dictated of this 416-page book is not clear, but the report of dictation is worth noting: this is the first but by no means the last such report. Johnson later dictated law lectures to Robert Chambers, several poems, including several meters of Boethius, to Mrs. Thrale, and a number of legal briefs to Boswell. There appear to be two related reasons for this. Once Johnson had his materials in his mind, and had mulled them over adequately, he composed rapidly, though he wrote slowly. Boswell prints rough jottings for a *Rambler* and for an *Adventurer* essay, showing that Johnson was thinking about a subject, but we are told that sometimes he composed the whole essay while the printer's boy was waiting below stairs. Likewise, *Rasselas* was composed in a single week, though he had been considering the ideas in the book, as well as its locale, for many years.

His crabbed and difficult handwriting suggests that he wrote slowly, and there is ample evidence that he disliked the physical task of writing. Dictating was easier and faster.

Dictation also suggests a characteristic of Johnson's prose: it is particularly interesting when read aloud. It seems to be modeled in considerable part upon the *spoken* styles of the great writers of sermons of the late seventeenth century. The third paragraph of Johnson's Preface to the *Voyage to Abyssinia* illustrates this:

> He appears by his modest and unaffected narration to have described things as he saw them, to have copied nature from the life, and to have consulted his senses not his imagination; he meets with no basilisks that destroy with their eyes, his crocodiles devour their prey without tears, and his cataracts fall from the rock without deafening the neighbouring inhabitants.

Here, at the beginning of Johnson's professional career, we find the outline of his style: three elements in parallel ("to have described . . . to have copied . . . to have consulted") balanced with three similar elements in the last half of the sentence, often accompanied by antithesis ("his senses not his imagination"). On this rather simple basis Johnson was to build much more elaborate structures, but the base itself persists. In addition, Johnson's skepticism, here directed at travelers' tales, is an earthy quality which never left him. His vocabulary at this point is not noticeably Latinate.

Johnson's handling of his translation is also worth mention. Perhaps because he received only five guineas for his work (about threepence a printed page), he condensed all but the sixteen dissertations (not fifteen as the title-page says) very radically. The dissertations, by Joachim Le Grand, are given with some exactness. On the other hand, Johnson and Warren may have agreed that the English public of the day would be more interested in essays on Abyssinia by a contemporary Frenchman than in an account of a Jesuit expedition to Abyssinia a century earlier. If so, it is possible that they misjudged the tastes of their public: the book was not reprinted until five years after Johnson's death, when it appeared as a supplement to an edition of his works.

One of Johnson's characteristic opinions, on the treatment of natives by invading Europeans, occurs in this work for the first time:

> This learned dissertator [Le Grand], however valuable for his industry and erudition, is yet more to be esteem'd for having dared so freely in the midst of France to declare his disapprobation of the Patriarch Oviedo's sanguinary zeal, who was continually importuning the Portuguese to beat up their drums for missionaries, who might preach the Gospel with swords in their hands, and propagate by desolation and slaughter the true worship of the God of Peace. (p. ix.)

In 1735 Johnson married, and with part of his wife's money set up a school, which soon failed. Then, with the manuscript of his tragedy *Irene* in his pocket, he set off for London to make his fortune. It was slow in coming.

In 1734 Johnson had offered his services to Edward Cave, the publisher of the *Gentleman's Magazine*, but without result. Cave had founded the magazine in 1731 in a highly successful attempt at a new publishing formula aimed at the general reader. It was "a storehouse," the original meaning of *magazine*. A typical monthly issue, March 1738, contained fifty-six double-column pages, consisting of (1) original essays on subjects ranging from sin to the refraction of light in the moon's atmosphere; (2) essays or other prose reprinted from various sources; (3) original poetry, including Johnson's Latin ode to Cave; (4) a synopsis of the month's historical events; (5) a list of births, deaths, and ecclesiastical and military promotions; stock prices; statistics of births and deaths; prices of bread, wheat, hay, and hops; (6) a single-page account of foreign affairs; and (7) a list of books published (not reviewed). Cave's formula succeeded so well that it not only brought imitations (*The London Magazine*, *The Scots Magazine*), but brought a new meaning to the word *magazine* itself: "Of late this word has signified a miscellaneous pamphlet, from a periodical miscellany named the *Gentleman's Magazine*, by Edward Cave" (Johnson's *Dictionary*).

Soon after publishing his ode to Cave, Johnson met, probably through Cave, some other authors, Richard Savage, Elizabeth Carter, and Thomas Birch, to all of whom he addressed poems in the *Gentleman's Magazine*. He appears to have been determined to break quickly into the literary world.

Within a month Cave arranged for the well-known publisher Robert Dodsley to issue Johnson's first major poem, *London*, an imitation of Juvenal's *Third Satire*. It appeared anonymously on 12 May 1738, the same day as Pope's *One Thousand Seven Hundred and Thirty Eight* (*Epilogue to the Satires, Dialogue I*), and is reported to have sold faster than Pope's poem. Pope, indeed, asked who the author was, and being told that it was a man named Johnson, said, "He will soon be detérré."

Pope had for some time been "imitating" the satires of Horace; an "imitation" in this sense had come to mean the use of a classical author's plan, and perhaps some of his material, but with contemporary matter largely substituted for classical. Juvenal's *Third Satire* is a violent denunciation of Nero's Rome, which is contrasted with a largely imaginary golden age when vice and corruption did not exist. Johnson used the basic notion of a contrast between a vicious present (the London of George II and Sir Robert Walpole) and "Alfred's golden reign," which was far enough in the past to be idyllic. After a brief introduction, the poem consists of a long speech by "Thales," who examines the decay of public and private life in the metropolis and at the end shakes the dust of the city from his feet to live in retirement in Wales. The fact that Johnson's friend Richard Savage left London a short time later to go to Wales is a coincidence which has been remarked by many, but there is no satisfactory evidence that in this respect "Thales" was modeled on Savage.

The immediate success of *London*, which went into five English editions and an Irish one within a year, was perhaps due in part to the "patriots" opposing Walpole, who may have welcomed it as propaganda. But its lasting success cannot be attributed to such a reason: when Dodsley included it in the first volume of his *Collection* in 1748, Walpole was long since out of power. It was Johnson's most popular poem during his lifetime. Not only is it a very good poem, but, as Garrick said, it is "lively and easy" (Garrick thought *The Vanity of Human Wishes* "as hard as Greek" [*Life*, I.194]). Gray described *London* as "one of those few imitations that have all the ease and all the spirit of an original." Ease and spirit it has. The heroic couplets are expertly handled, and if Johnson did not fill the poem with Popean epigram, he nevertheless shows that he had studied the master to good effect. Too much of Juvenal's Rome has seeped in, however, and Johnson's denunciation of London appears to be just a little contrived: his long love-affair with the city was beginning.

Why Johnson did not at once follow up his success with another imitation of Juvenal is difficult to guess. (He later told Boswell that he had imitations of all thirteen satires in his head, but he wrote only one more, a decade later.) Perhaps one reason lies in the wide temperamental difference between the two men. Juvenal's tone is that of an unrelieved jeremiad; his denunciation is bitter, violent, and total. Johnson's tone is more moderate, and in *The Vanity of Human Wishes* (1749) not without hope. A more immediate and perhaps more compelling reason is that he appears to have been almost at once involved in other projects for Cave, the first of which, advertised in October 1738, was "Proposals for printing the *History of the Council of Trent*, translated from the Italian of Father Paul Sarpi." (A copy of these was first discovered in 1962.) Johnson got as far as writing a brief biography of Sarpi, which was published in the *Gentleman's Magazine* for November 1738, perhaps as a puff for the larger work. But the project appears to have been slow in attracting subscribers; at any rate it was soon dropped.

Because the *Life of Sarpi* was Johnson's first biography, it should be briefly examined. Le Courayer's French biography of

Sarpi, prefixed to his translation of the *History* (1736), is Johnson's principal and only real source. He translates, paraphrases, and, in particular, condenses very sharply. Occasionally he rearranges material for a more effective presentation. Most important, he introduces comments of his own, a habit foreign to Le Courayer. Only once does he mention an author not used by Le Courayer, when he recalls that Wotton, as well as Burnet, spoke of the excellence of Sarpi as a historian. Johnson's little biography, aimed more at the general reader than at the scholar, is a skillful piece of hack work.

His *Life of Boerhaave* appeared serially in the *Gentleman's Magazine* in 1739, a few months after that learned physician's death. Inasmuch as Boerhaave was a member of the Royal Society and well known in England, topicality may be the reason for the biography, which has little interest for the modern reader. As in *Sarpi*, Johnson used a single source, adding comments and generalizations of his own.

The *Life of Admiral Blake* was written for the *Gentleman's Magazine* in 1740 to contrast the glorious career of this Commonwealth hero with the disastrous current efforts of Admiral Vernon to capture the Caribbean port of Cartagena. Basically, Johnson's method was the same as in his earlier biographies: he used one main source, the anonymous *Lives English and Forein*, 1704, condensing radically, and occasionally glancing at other books, Heath, Clarendon, Burnet, Rapin. Johnson's comments are more extensive than before and are perhaps the only parts of the *Life* of much value. But the work served its purpose for the general reader.

Johnson's *Life of Drake* followed his *Blake* in the *Gentleman's Magazine*, 1740–41, and was no doubt inspired by the same purpose, to contrast the splendid past of England's navy with the inglorious present. As in the *Sarpi* and the *Blake*, Johnson largely used a single volume, in this case a seventeenth-century reprint of four contemporary accounts of Drake's voyages. (It would have been unlike him to search out four separate volumes.) But these are primary sources, unlike those used before; nevertheless they are used in much the same way—quoted, paraphrased, sharply condensed. Again Johnson briefly glances at another book, and again his own comments are by far the most interesting feature of the biography. He had, in short, already established the method which was to shape many of the *Lives of the Poets* in the last phase of his career.

The *Life of Barretier* (or "Baretier" or "Baratier"), written for the *Gentleman's Magazine* in 1740–41, is the story of a German wunderkind, compiled from his father's letters. It would have surprised none of Johnson's contemporaries that a boy who knew German, French, Latin, Greek, and Hebrew at nine, should have received a Ph.D. from Halle at fourteen. He died at nineteen. Some corrections were printed in 1742, and the whole, revised, was separately published in 1744. Johnson describes the elder Barretier's account of his son's linguistic attainments as "almost incredible," and of the son's understanding of the Bible in the original languages, he suggests that "the fondness of a parent has transported him into some natural exaggerations." Johnson's skeptical handling of hyperbolical exaggeration thus appears early in his career; it lasted till his death.

His *Life of Peter Burman*, published in the *Gentleman's Magazine* in 1742, a year after Burman's death, celebrates another infant prodigy, and in this instance Johnson is even more skeptical than he had been in the case of Barretier: "to reduce this narrative to credibility, it is necessary that admiration should give place to inquiry" (*Works*, 1825, VI.398), and he proceeds to contrast the Dutch study of languages with the English, in order to show that according to the Dutch method, Burman could have acquired only some moderate skill in Latin and some elementary Greek in the time stated. Otherwise, Johnson stays within the formula he had found useful for these occasional pieces.

Johnson wrote the *Life of Dr. Sydenham* for a translation of that physician's works in 1742, and it was reprinted in the *Gentleman's Magazine* in the same year. It follows the pattern of the other early lives.

During the summer or autumn of 1738 Johnson seems to have begun some regular editorial work on the *Gentleman's Magazine.* In addition to the "Address to the Reader" prefixed to the year's collected numbers, Johnson probably wrote the introduction to the "Debates in the Senate of Magna Lilliputia." Since 1732 the magazine had published the debates after the end of each session of Parliament, but when the House of Commons banned the publication of its debates, Cave decided to substitute Lilliputian names for the real names of the members (as Hurgo Castroflet for Lord Chesterfield). Members were indexed under both their fictitious and their real names, but at least a gauze veil of fiction served the decencies. However, even this slight subterfuge was thrown aside in 1739, when a fake advertisement following the debates listed both sets of names. The debates were first written up by William Guthrie; some time before 1740 Johnson began to revise them; and from November 1740 to February 1743 they were wholly compiled by Johnson, on the basis of notes furnished him as to the names of speakers and the parts they took in the debate. He did not attend the sessions; his reports, then, are only a rough approximation of what a man said, or might have said, or ought to have said. But considering that the views of many members were well known through their own pamphlets or through the political journals, Johnson had really more resources than just his imagination. As usual he composed rapidly: "Three columns of the *Magazine*, in an hour, was no uncommon effort" (*Life*, IV.409). But when he found that one of the debates had been taken as authentic and translated into French, German, and Spanish, he would have no more to do with their publication. His *Debates in Parliament* were published in 1787 in two volumes, and as a supplement to Hawkins' edition of Johnson's *Works* of the same year.

The *Debates* form a substantial part of Johnson's work during the years 1740–43, and although they were hack work, they were hack work of a rather high order. The final battle between Walpole and the Whig opposition was being waged, and Johnson was forced to look closely at the issues involved. Incidentally, Johnson said later, "I took care that the Whig dogs should not have the best of it" (*Life*, I.502). But he did not let the Tory lions get the best of it either: his presentation of the debates is eminently fair. By this time he had realized that the politics of his era was much more complicated than a neat division into the "good guys" and the "bad guys," that, indeed, there were many factions, some determined by geography, some by the conflict of mercantile and agrarian interests, and some by sheer love of power. It was a superb opportunity to study parliamentary procedures. Johnson seized this opportunity, and it is no accident that his early liking for a style based on oral delivery found reinforcement here.

Cumulatively, the *Debates* are his first major prose work before his *Life of Savage* (1744). They may perhaps be regarded as the maturing point of his prose style.

Johnson's next separately published work after *London* was *Marmor Norfolciense: or an Essay on an Ancient Prophetical Inscription, In Monkish Rhyme, Lately Discover'd near Lynn in Norfolk. By Probus Britanicus,* April or May 1739. The Latin poem, "supposed to have been found in Norfolk, the county of Sir Robert Walpole, inveighs against the Brunswick succession, and the measures of government consequent upon it" (*Life,* I.141). Besides an English verse translation of his Latin, Johnson wrote an essay to make sure that no reader would miss the point of "This . . . bloody Jacobitical pamphlet," as the *Monthly Review* called it when it was reissued in 1775, after Johnson had received his pension, in the hope that its unauthorized reprinting would embarrass him while he was supporting the government against the American colonies. Its principal interest to the modern reader lies in the fact that it is Johnson's only printed attack on the House of Hanover, though he talked from time to time against the Hanoverians. His Jacobitism was of short duration, and the pamphlet seems to have aroused little notice. As political satire it is not remarkable.

Perhaps more important was the ironical *A Compleat Vindication of the Licensers of the Stage, from the Malicious and Scandalous Aspersions of Mr. Henry Brooke, Author of Gustavus Vasa. With a Proposal for Making the Office of Licenser More Extensive and Effectual. By an Impartial Hand,* published in May 1739. Walpole had been so incensed by a political attack in one of the productions at Fielding's theater in the Haymarket that he had pushed through Parliament the Licensing Act of 1737, which provided that no play could be produced which had not been approved in advance by the government. The Licensers had disapproved Henry Brooke's play, clearly because Trollio, one of the principal characters, represented Walpole. Brooke's "scandalous aspersions" are contained in the dedication of his printed play, and these Johnson ironically castigates. His pamphlet has some importance in the struggle for freedom of the stage, but, it may be mentioned, the Act was not repealed. In advocating freedom of speech, Johnson never went as far as Milton, but this pamphlet shows that he was willing to go a considerable distance.

Sometime during 1738 Cave appears to have commissioned Elizabeth Carter to translate the Swiss Abbé Crousaz' *Examen* of Pope's *Essay on Man*, and Johnson to translate the Abbé's *Commentary* on the same poem. Both works attacked Pope's religious orthodoxy. Miss Carter's book appeared late in the year, and Johnson's is dated 1739, though it seems not to have been formally published then. Cave printed both books, but made no mention of Johnson's in the *Gentleman's Magazine*. Meanwhile a rival translation of the *Commentary* had been published (1738), perhaps the reason why Johnson's was held up. Late in 1741, however, Cave decided to publish Johnson's book, and it was issued with a new title-page dated 1742. It sold slowly. In March and November 1743, Johnson printed parts of it in the *Gentleman's Magazine*, probably hoping to stimulate sales. His earlier opinion, in an undated letter to Cave, was confirmed: "as the names of the authours concerned are of more weight in the performance than its own intrinsick merit, the publick will soon be satisfied with it" (*Life*, I.137). Johnson's translation and his notes are competent, but are still hack work. He would not have undertaken the project except for money.

Roughly between 1740 and 1743, Johnson appears to have been in charge of editing the *Gentleman's Magazine*. It is noteworthy that, except for 1743, all of his known work of these years appeared in the magazine, though *Sydenham* was first printed elsewhere. To each volume he contributed a preface, and from five to ten other pieces in prose or verse, including the *Parliamentary Debates* and five out of the six "little lives." Scattered through these volumes are four or five of his poems written at least ten years earlier, put in, possibly, to fill out an issue for which there were insufficient acceptable contributions. And in 1740 he wrote for the magazine his "Essay on Epitaphs," later included in the third edition of *The Idler;* it is the best of his early literary essays. Whether he had much influence over the editorial policy of the magazine is hard to say, but Cave, the publisher, seems to have given him a fairly free hand. It is significant that Cave and Johnson remained friends until Cave died in 1754, and that Johnson not only wrote the *Life of Cave* for the magazine but memorialized him in the *Dictionary* under *magazine*.

In 1742, Johnson wrote *Proposals for Printing, by Subscription, the Two First Volumes of Bibliotheca Harleiana: or, a Catalogue of the Library of the Late Earl of Oxford, Purchased by Thomas Osborne, Bookseller in Gray's-Inn,* which were reprinted in the *Gentleman's Magazine* in the same year. That the public should be asked to *buy* a bookseller's catalogue was something of a shocking proposal in the eighteenth century, but those who bought, got their money's worth, for the library formed by Swift's friend Harley and augmented by Harley's son was a great one, and Osborne had found the right men to make a fitting catalogue: the four large octavo volumes[1] appeared in 1743–44, with a Latin dedication by the well-known bibliographer Maittaire, followed by Johnson's "Account of the Harleian Library," and then the lists of books, described by William Oldys, author of *The British Librarian* (1737) and Johnson. (The manuscripts were not included; they were later purchased for the British Museum.) The descriptions are in English for books in English, Latin for the rest. Boswell said that Johnson wrote the Latin descriptions; Johnson's earlier biographer, Sir John Hawkins, thought that Johnson helped with the first two volumes and did the third and fourth singlehanded, but he found it not easy to distinguish between the descriptions of Johnson and Oldys. If Hawkins found such discrimination difficult, no one else has even attempted it.

The task is not wholly impossible. Though many of the notes are too short to yield adequate evidence of authorship, this is not always the case. After a long Latin note on Vol. I, No. 992, for example, we read: "This Book may be of some use to such as charge Phanaticism upon the Church of Rome. The Author was certainly a good Man; I am not willing to think him a Phanatic." Surely Johnson wrote that. Any close reader of Johnson ought to be aware that there are two small idiosyncrasies which are scattered through Johnson's prose—a persistent use of "I" ("I think"), which is remarkable, especially in anonymous writings, and a repeated softening of dogmatic statements by "perhaps," or a similarly qualifying word. These idiosyncrasies not only appear in this Catalogue, where we should expect only matter-of-fact

[1] A fifth volume, under the same title, listed Osborne's regular stock.

descriptions, but they also appear *in Latin:* "puto" and "fortasse." I submit that well over half of the descriptions are Johnson's. Nor is this surprising, for Johnson was the junior partner and unknown outside the trade, since his name had not yet appeared on a single book. He would have been expected to shoulder the major share of the work.

What has this to do with the literary career of Johnson? A good deal, it can be argued. A famous, but disputed, anecdote about Johnson has him knocking down Osborne with a folio for complaining about the slowness of his work. Aside from remarking that Johnson would have killed Osborne if he had used a folio, we may take the anecdote as basically true, for Johnson was reading the books, and Osborne may be forgiven for having feared that that would take forever. The handling and sampling of these books gave Johnson an acquaintance with one of the great libraries of his time. It may well have had a decisive part to play in making him a man who "knew more books than any man alive," as Adam Smith said of him (*Life*, I.71).

During 1743, when the first two volumes of the *Harleian Catalogue* were being published, Johnson was working on another sizeable project. This was Dr. Robert James's *Medicinal Dictionary* (1743–45), three huge folio volumes comprising an encyclopedia of "physic, surgery, anatomy, chymistry, and botany," as well as a history of drugs and their preparation, and, most important for our purposes, biographies of men eminent in these fields. Johnson and James had been schoolfellows, and Johnson very likely assisted from friendship as well as from the expectation of a fee. He probably wrote part or all of the Proposals, certainly wrote the Dedication, and also compiled six or more of the biographies. The vast work has not been carefully examined by modern scholars, and there may be still more of Johnson in these entertaining volumes. (Johnson also wrote an advertisement for James's "Powders," a proprietary remedy which is supposed to have hastened Goldsmith's death).

February 1744 saw the publication of Johnson's first major biography, *An Account of the Life of Mr. Richard Savage, Son of the Earl Rivers*. It differs from all his earlier biographies in four respects: it is a full-length book; it is not based primarily on printed sources but on what Savage had told him; it is not hack work; it is the biography of a friend. Johnson had known Savage in the dark days of 1738–39—dark for both, because in November 1737 Queen Caroline had died, the source of Savage's pension and his only steady means of support, and Johnson had only begun to work on the *Gentleman's Magazine* and was still poor. Together, Johnson told Boswell, they had walked the streets of London, declared themselves for liberty, and without settled lodgings slept on bulkheads along the Thames. It is no wonder that under such circumstances Johnson should have believed Savage's story that he was the illegitimate son of Lady Macclesfield by Earl Rivers, and the cause of Lady Macclesfield's divorce. (Savage seems to have deluded himself into believing he was a changeling.)

Savage had character if not talent. He wrote much verse, some addressed to the Queen, made the acquaintance of Pope and got some money out of him, and even in his last days, spent in a debtors' prison, forced his creditor to allow him pocket money. He even survived a murder trial. Johnson had the ingredients for a good biography and used them well. He does not soften the prickly side of Savage, a man who demanded the support of every one of his acquaintance, and occasionally did so with some surliness. Johnson's quotations from Savage's poems are lengthy enough for anyone to judge of their quality, and the notes include two dedications which give an excellent notion of Savage's manner with those who helped him. The quotations and notes are so extensive, in fact, as to raise a slight suspicion that they were included in order to make up a full-length book. Johnson's later practice was to avoid notes; material for which he could find no place in the text he omitted altogether. In the first edition of his *Life of Milton*, for example, there is only one footnote, and that is short.

As usual, Johnson composed with great rapidity. He later said: "I wrote forty-eight of the printed octavo pages of the Life of Savage [about one quarter of the book] at a sitting; but then I sat up all night" (*Life*, I.166). His speed was possible because he had the material in his head, except for the long quotations and the notes, whereas with his earlier biographies he had worked from one or more printed sources and had translated, condensed, and inserted comments at the same time. Furthermore, Johnson was emotionally involved in the story as a friend and a partisan. The result is a book which moves swiftly. Johnson does not allow the reader to stand at a distance. We may not be convinced, but we are held.

The biography was relatively successful, going through six editions, alone or with other works, before Johnson added it to the *Lives of the Poets* in 1781. It was translated into French in 1767.

In 1744 Johnson also wrote an introduction for *The Harleian Miscellany, or a Collection of . . . Pamphlets and Tracts . . . found in the late Earl of Oxford's library* (eight volumes, 1744–46), the most important such collection produced in the century. It was twice reprinted. Johnson's introduction was later called "An Essay on the Origin and Importance of Small Tracts and Fugitive Pieces," and shows such a keen interest in the subject that one is tempted to suggest that he selected the pieces to be printed. After all, he had helped to catalogue the library and probably knew it better than any other man alive. We may hope that it was he to whom we owe the inclusion of the excommunicatory curse of Ernulfus which Sterne took over entire for one of the great passages of *Tristram Shandy*.

In 1743–44 the sumptuous Oxford edition of Shakespeare had appeared in six large quarto volumes, edited by Sir Thomas Hanmer, whose principal qualification for the task seems to have been that he was Speaker of the House of Commons. In February and March 1745, Johnson advertised his *Miscellaneous Observations on the Tragedy of Macbeth: with Remarks on Sir T. H.'s Edition of Shakespear*, and appended proposals for what was, in effect, a "poor man's" edition in ten pocket volumes at the moderate price of 25 shillings complete. The *Observations* were relatively brief (62 pages) but they were intended to show Johnson's qualifications for the work. They consist of forty-six notes, ranging from a long one on witchcraft, with quotations ranging from Olympiodorus and St. Chrysostom to James I, to mere glosses of two or three lines. Some propose emendations of text or clarification of punctuation. The passage of two decades did not lessen Johnson's regard for these notes: in his 1765 edition of Shakespeare he dropped only eight, retaining the rest in whole or in part. In the very long note on witchcraft, for example, he omitted only two clauses. The brief remarks in the *Observations* on Hanmer's editing tend to be contemptuous—"too trivial to deserve mention," "harmless industry" (*Works*, 1825, V.93, 94), but when Johnson mentioned Hanmer in his Preface to *Shakespeare*, he did so with good will and something approaching respect.

Within a few days after Cave published the *Observations*, the publisher Jacob Tonson wrote to him claiming perpetual copyright in Shakespeare's work, and the project was dropped. The scarcity of the proposals suggests that they were clipped off the pamphlet as soon as Tonson's letter was received.

In 1747 Bishop Warburton praised Johnson's *Observations* in the Preface to his own edition of Shakespeare as "written, as appears, by a man of parts and genius." Such praise was welcome. It will be noted that when Johnson's *Shakespeare* finally appeared in 1765, the Tonson firm headed the list of publishers. An accommodation had been reached. Their claim to perpetual copyright was at length successfully challenged by a Scottish bookseller named Donaldson, who did produce a poor man's edition in 1771 and won the lawsuit brought against him.

But in the summer of 1745 Johnson's project was dead, and his feelings may have been bitter. For the third time he had proposed a major editorial project (Politian, 1734; Sarpi, 1738), and for the third time had failed. This time his name had not even appeared on the proposals. Under the circumstances, no one could have blamed him if he had joined the troops of the Duke of Cumberland to turn back Bonnie Prince Charlie's invasion.

It is likely that at this time Cave and Dodsley had a talk about how to employ the great talents of this young man. At any rate, Dodsley suggested that Johnson undertake a large English dictionary. The precise date of this suggestion is not known, but it may have been early in 1746, for by the summer of that year Johnson was paying Francis Stewart for work as an amanuensis on the *Dictionary*, and in 1747 the *Plan* of the *Dictionary*, addressed to Lord Chesterfield, was published. In brief, Johnson proposed to compile a dictionary "by which the pronunciation of our language may be fixed, and its attainment facilitated; by which its purity may be preserved, its use ascertained, and its duration lengthened" (*Works*, 1825, V.20–21). He was aware of the extent to which customary usage determines language, but he proposed following the best English writers, basing his choice on a list of such writers prepared by Pope, from the Elizabethans to his own time. He had the general public in mind as the users of his work, not primarily scholars, and thus intended to include only such technical and scientific words as the general reader might come across. He hoped also to give satisfactory etymologies, to indicate spelling and pronunciation, and to give real definitions even of common words. He had set himself a prodigious task.

In preparing his *Dictionary*, Johnson used earlier general dictionaries to provide lists of words and to check against omissions (Edward Phillips' *New World of English Words*, 1658; Robert Ainsworth's *Thesaurus linguae Latinae, compendiarius*, 1736; Nathaniel Bailey's *Universal Etymological English Dictionary*, 1721), but he omitted many words found in these on the supposition, often correct, that they had been invented by the lexicographers. In addition, he used technical dictionaries, such as Cowell's *Interpreter*, 1607 (for legal terms), Ephraim Chambers' *Cyclopaedia*, Tusser's *Husbandrie*, Miller's *Gardener's Dictionary*, Quincy for medical terms, etc. He then read the major authors from the Elizabethans down to his own time, underlining each word he wanted to use and putting the initial letter of the word in the margin. (Several such marked volumes have survived; one volume of Bacon is at Yale.) At this point one of his six amanuenses took over and copied the word and the sentence in which it occurred onto a slip of paper.

Then Johnson made a main entry, marking the principal accent but otherwise paying less attention to the pronunciation than he had hoped to do. The etymology followed, the best that Johnson could do given the primitive state of linguistics at the time; it is the weakest part of his work, though by no means contemptible when compared with the efforts of his predecessors. The definition of the basic meaning of the word came next, with examples in chronological order in the spelling of the author quoted. Then each of the subordinate or derived meanings was handled in the same manner.

As might have been expected, Johnson collected far too much material, particularly illustrative examples, to be included even in two huge folio volumes, and he had, reluctantly, to omit much of what he had hoped would be a sort of anthology of English literature. But the examples of usage which remain are highly informative and vastly entertaining.

Johnson did not exclude any class of words, but since his sources were principally printed works, colloquial language is not very well represented. But some dialectal words, principally Scottish, are there, supplied by one of his five Scottish amanuenses, and some gambling slang, from the same sources. There are also a few words which have, until recent years, been considered indecent.

But neither the great range of words nor the inclusiveness of the examples were the reasons why the work was regarded as the authoritative one for nearly a century. The true splendor of the *Dictionary* lies in the definitions. Here Johnson's precision and his endless labor gave the English language for the first time definitions which *really* explained and delimited. Johnson was well aware, as he says in his Preface, that to define simple words, longer ones must be used, and he did not shirk this task, even defining *network* as "Any thing reticulated or decussated, at equal distances, with interstices between the intersections." Bailey defined *net* as "a device for catching fish, birds, etc."; he omitted *network*. On a few occasions Johnson gave incorrect definitions: *windward* and *leeward* with the same meanings; *pastern*, "the knee of a horse." Occasional definitions show prejudice—*excise:* "A hateful tax levied upon commodities, and adjudged not by the common judges of property, but wretches hired by those to whom excise is paid"; *pension:* "An allowance made to any one without an equivalent. In England it is generally understood to mean pay given to a state hireling for treason to his country." One prejudice Johnson does not show in the *Dictionary* is a feeling against Scotland. As has been pointed out many times, his famous definition of oats is merely repeated in substance from earlier works: "A grain, which in England is generally given to horses, but in Scotland supports the people." As a matter of fact, it takes some imagination to read any prejudice into the definition. There are scores of other places in the *Dictionary* where a Scottish expression is defined, and I do not recall one which is not wholly objective in tone. Indeed, the number of definitions without Johnsonian color vastly outweighs the number of Johnsonian definitions, though these last are naturally more famous.

When Johnson began his work on the *Dictionary* he did so

with some confidence that he could establish and fix correct usage. After all, that is what the French Academy and the (Italian) Accademia della Crusca had attempted to do, and these were his professed models. But what was at least theoretically possible in Italy in the sixteenth century and in France in the seventeenth was no longer possible, if it ever had been, in England in the eighteenth century. An authoritarian climate, and a willingness to accept authority, had existed in France under Richelieu, where even a wide-ranging genius like Corneille could be made to conform to the rules of decorum. No such spirit existed in England in 1755, at least as far as the use of words was concerned, and even as Johnson objected to the "needless" importation of French words, we find him in the *Dictionary* commending "paramour" and wishing that it might be brought into wider use. In fact, he was himself constantly introducing or re-introducing Latinisms, when he felt that they were useful or euphonious. In his last *Rambler* (14 March 1752), written while he was compiling the *Dictionary*, he says: "When common words were less pleasing to the ear, or less distinct in their signification, I have familiarized the terms of philosophy, by applying them to known objects and popular ideas. . . ." Moreover, with the growth of trade, arts, and sciences, the eighteenth century constantly required new words, as greater precision was demanded in describing the new objects and concepts. Johnson's use of technical dictionaries is his acknowledgment of the need for these new words. He does not have much to say about the spoken language, but in his Preface, talking about collecting his materials, he uses one most revealing phrase, "the boundless chaos of a living speech." One might advise the users of the English language, commend or chastise them,—"a low, cant word,"—but by the time Johnson wrote his great Preface he knew that he could do no more. It was enough.

If the imprint of Johnson's personality is plain in the pages of the *Dictionary* itself, the Preface shows Johnson speaking in every line. His involvement is complete. A work which he had expected to finish in three years had taken nine—till 1755. After initial encouragement, Chesterfield had ignored him. His wife was dead. He was childless and alone. But he knew what he had accomplished, and, in effect, dedicated his book, "the labour of years, to the honour of my country, that we may no longer yield the palm of philology to the nations of the continent." He continues:

> The chief glory of every people arises from its authors: whether I shall add anything by my own writings to the reputation of English literature, must be left to time: much of my life has been lost under the pressures of disease; much has been trifled away; and much has always been spent in provision for the day that was passing over me; but I shall not think my employment useless or ignoble, if, by my assistance, foreign nations, and distant ages, gain access to the propagators of knowledge, and understand the teachers of truth; if my labours afford light to the repositories of science, and add celebrity to Bacon, to Hooker, to Milton, and to Boyle. (*Works*, 1825, V.49–50.)

No author of the century had written a nobler piece of prose than this Preface. It is at the same time personal and general. Johnson is not afraid to use splendid language or to show emotion. And his rhetorical figures are handled with such subtle and accomplished skill that the reader is hardly aware of the mechanics underneath: triple balance ("much of my life has . . . ; much has . . . ; much has . . .") followed by longer doublets ("if by my assistance. . . ; if my labours . . .").

The *Dictionary* met with immediate success. It was reprinted at once in parts so that a purchaser could spread the cost over several months, and Johnson made a two-volume abridgment in the following year. In 1773 he revised the work for the fourth edition. Adam Smith reviewed the *Dictionary* favorably in the year of publication; some objections were made to details, but almost everyone used it. It held the field for about a century.

During the years in which Johnson was compiling the *Dictionary*, he produced other works of substantial importance. The first of these was the *Prologue* written to inaugurate Garrick's management of the Drury Lane Theatre in September 1747. In it, Johnson surveyed the state of the drama in vigorous terms:

> When Learning's triumph o'er her barb'rous foes
> First rear'd the stage, immortal SHAKESPEAR rose;
> Each change of many-colour'd life he drew,
> Exhausted worlds, and then imagin'd new:
> Existence saw him spurn her bounded reign,
> And panting Time toil'd after him in vain:

His pow'rful strokes presiding truth impress'd,
And unresisted passion storm'd the breast.
 Then JOHNSON[2] came, instructed from the school,
To please in method, and invent by rule;
His studious patience, and laborious art,
By regular approach essay'd the heart;
Cold approbation gave the ling'ring bays,
For those who durst not censure, scarce cou'd praise.
A mortal born he met the general doom,
But left, like Egypt's kings, a lasting tomb.
 The wits of Charles found easier ways to fame,
Nor wish'd for JOHNSON'S art, or SHAKESPEAR's flame;
Themselves they studied, as they felt, they writ,
Intrigue was plot, obscenity was wit.
Vice always found a sympathetick friend;
They pleas'd their age, and did not aim to mend.
Yet bards like these aspir'd to lasting praise,
And proudly hop'd to pimp in future days.
Their cause was gen'ral, their supports were strong,
Their slaves were willing, and their reign was long;
Till shame regain'd the post that sense betray'd,
And Virtue call'd oblivion to her aid.
 Then crush'd by rules, and weaken'd as refin'd,
For years the pow'r of tragedy declin'd;
From bard, to bard, the frigid caution crept,
Till declamation roar'd, while passion slept.
Yet still did Virtue deign the stage to tread,
Philosophy remain'd, though Nature fled.
But forc'd at length her antient reign to quit,
She saw great Faustus lay the ghost of wit:
Exulting Folly hail'd the joyful day,
And pantomime, and song, confirm'd her sway.
 But who the coming changes can presage,
And mark the future periods of the stage?—
Perhaps if skill could distant times explore,
New Behns, new Durfeys, yet remain in store.
Perhaps, where Lear has rav'd, and Hamlet dy'd,
On flying cars new sorcerers may ride.
Perhaps, for who can guess th' effects of chance?
Here Hunt may box, or Mahomet may dance.
 Hard is his lot, that here by fortune plac'd,

[2] A common eighteenth-century spelling of Ben Jonson's name.

Must watch the wild vicissitudes of taste;
With ev'ry meteor of caprice must play,
And chase the new-blown bubbles of the day.
Ah! let not censure term our fate our choice,
The stage but echoes back the publick voice.
The drama's laws the drama's patrons give,
For we that live to please, must please to live.
Then prompt no more the follies you decry,
As tyrants doom their tools of guilt to die;
'Tis yours this night to bid the reign commence
Of rescu'd Nature, and reviving Sense;
To chase the charms of sound, the pomp of show,
For useful mirth, and salutary woe;
Bid scenic virtue form the rising age,
And Truth diffuse her radiance from the stage.

Genest, in his *Account of the English Stage* (IV.231), called these lines "the best Prologue that was ever written." Even those who rightly admire Dryden's prologues might well agree. Johnson wrote four more prologues, to Garrick's *Lethe*, 1740, to Milton's *Comus*, 1750, to Goldsmith's *The Good Natur'd Man*, 1768, and to Kelly's *A Word to the Wise*, 1777. All are graceful and felicitous, but the *Drury-Lane Prologue* in its density, its incisive couplets, and its sharp criticism stands out above all the others.

In 1748 Johnson wrote for the *Gentleman's Magazine* a short *Life of Roscommon* later included in the *Lives of the Poets*, and a lengthy preface to Dodsley's *Preceptor . . . A general Course of Education . . . for the Instruction of Youth*, which book also contained Johnson's popular tale "The Vision of Theodore, the Hermit of Teneriffe." Dodsley's two volumes were intended not only for use in schools, but also as an aid to self-education, a matter of growing importance in the eighteenth century when very few Englishmen could afford the time or the money to prepare for the two universities, much less attempt to enter them, although the majority of the population was literate and had been so since the Elizabethan age. For such were home-study books on spelling, arithmetic, and the like being written. *The Preceptor* went a step further, branching out from "reading, speaking, and writing letters" into geometry, astronomy, chronology, history, rhetoric, poetry, drawing, logic, natural history, "ethics, or morality," trade, commerce, laws and government, and "human life and manners" (title-page). Johnson, who was so largely self-educated, heartily approved of such home study, and recommended the diversity of subjects for the boy whose attention wanders when strictly confined to one subject, or for the class where there is the usual range of students with different aptitudes:

> That, therefore, this roving curiosity may not be unsatisfied, it seems necessary to scatter in its way such allurements as may withhold it from an useless and unbounded dissipation; such as may regulate it without violence, and direct it without restraint; such as may suit every inclination, and fit every capacity; may employ the stronger genius, by operations of reason, and engage the less active or forcible mind, by supplying it with easy knowledge, and obviating that despondence, which quickly prevails, when nothing appears but a succession of difficulties, and one labour only ceases that another may be imposed. (*Works*, 1825, V.233.)

II

Poet, Playwright, Essayist

JOHNSON'S APPRENTICESHIP may, perhaps, be said to have ended when he began to work regularly on the *Gentleman's Magazine*, probably in the summer of 1738 just before he was twenty-nine. He might be described as a journeyman between that time and the first weeks of 1749, when he finally put his name to a work, *The Vanity of Human Wishes.* He was at long last, even in his own eyes, a master.

The difference between his use or handling of Juvenal's *Tenth Satire* in *The Vanity of Human Wishes* and his imitation of the *Third* in *London*, just over ten years earlier, is indicative of his development. *London* is a young man's bid for fame: it is against the government, for the generally sound reason that a work is more interesting if it opposes the Establishment rather than favors it. It is also an attack on London by a countryman who was soon to begin a love affair with the city, which was to last till his death a great many years later. It is more than a competent poem, it is a very good one. It has touches of the virtuoso. But it does not appeal to the permanent interests of mankind as does *The Vanity of Human Wishes. London* relies more on Juvenal than does the later poem; it is less deeply felt, since Johnson's knowledge of urban life in the spring of 1738 was scarcely a year old, and another decade, moreover, was to teach him a great deal about the nullity of human wishes.

Whereas *London* is only an incomplete rendering of Juvenal's Rome in eighteenth-century terms, Johnson in the later poem tries to come to grips with the universal and timeless problem of the fruitlessness of most human desires. But his concern with large problems is still firmly linked, for the most part, to actual historical examples. He begins by announcing the universality of his survey ("from China to Peru"), stating that man is betrayed by pride into seeking the common goals of position, wealth, and fame: "How rarely reason guides the stubborn choice. . . ." The first verse paragraph describes the paths of life, clouded and mazelike, as confused by man's hopes, fears, and desires, which lure him into seeking satisfaction for his pride. All of this carries an ominous overtone of fatality: "fate . . . fate . . . fatal . . . fatal" all occur within just thirteen lines. The next paragraph is built around one of the fatal temptations, "gold." The word occurs three times in five lines and in strong positions, once as a rime and twice in the first foot.

From this, in the next two paragraphs, Johnson derives his first moral: in civil wars, where "rival kings" contend and "bonny traitors" (the Scottish lords in 1746) land in the Tower, only the poor man is safe, "Untouch'd his cottage, and his slumbers sound. . . ." And the poor traveller suffers no fears of highwaymen as he walks across the wild heath. (The specific character of the imagery, the barren ground and the rustling bracken, adds much vividness to the passage, and indeed is noticeable throughout the poem.)

Now Johnson asks Democritus, the laughing philosopher of classical Greece, to comment, "With chearful wisdom and instructive mirth," on the foolishness of modern life—the use of "motley" in this passage suggests the clown's clothing which perhaps we ought to wear. And if Democritus laughed at the ills of his relatively unsophisticated era, how much more he will ridicule the "modish tribe" of the present. (As Juvenal in the reign of Nero used an imagined golden age of Rome for contrast with his degenerate times, so Johnson contrasts the age of George II with a supposedly simple period of Greek life, where "scarce a sycophant was fed by pride."

But in modern times, those who thirst for wealth and preferment are everywhere; Fortune, however, represented by the medieval symbol of the wheel, is inexorable: "They mount, they shine, evaporate, and fall." Eighteenth-century symbols of the thirst for wealth are the "weekly scribbler" and the "dedicator" (Johnson had recently addressed the Plan of the *Dictionary* to

Chesterfield), and, in politics, the average voter, whose greatest wish is to abuse the government and who gets his usual bribe every seven years to make voting in an election worth his trouble.

From general types, Johnson now turns to individuals. The portrait of Cardinal Wolsey is justly famous—"Law in his voice, and fortune in his hand." The eminence of his political position brought him so close to the pinnacle of power that he inevitably incurred the displeasure of the king, Henry VIII. His fall was swift, and even at the end, in his monastic refuge, he had not learned much about the general vanity of human wishes: "his last sighs reproach the faith of kings."

Johnson here reiterates his moral: those who are dissatisfied with their humble position should study Wolsey's fate and be content with their safer life. The Duke of Buckingham, assassinated in the reign of Charles I, Swift's friend Oxford, and Strafford and Clarendon, all fell from positions of great power because of insatiable ambition.

In the next paragraph Johnson draws on his own experience, and it is, therefore, one of the liveliest parts of the poem. The college student leaves his easy life at home in order to seek fame. Oxford, with its great library and its recollections of great scholars like Roger Bacon, receives him. With the guide of virtue, he may arrive at truth, "And pour on misty Doubt resistless day." The reader is caught up in Johnson's enthusiasm as, looking back on his own youth, he recalls the freshness and the excitement of the search for learning. But then there are the dangers: praise which may enervate, a beautiful woman who may capture him, and worst of all melancholy, Johnson's own disease. If he survives these, along with the temptations of novelty and the opiate of sloth, he has, at the end, lack of recognition to face: "Toil, envy, want, the garret, and the jail." (After the first edition of the poem, following his experience of Chesterfield's neglect of the *Dictionary*, he changed "garret" to "patron." The word, in its complete unexpectedness, gives a satiric point to the line which it wholly lacked before.)

After a brief glance at Archbishop Laud, who reached a pinnacle of political and ecclesiastical power under Charles I only to be executed by the Puritans, Johnson considers the warriors Alexander, who devastated nations, and Charles XII of Sweden, whose armies swept across Europe into Russia only to be pulverized and who met an obscure death in Norway: "He left the name, at which the world grew pale, / To point a moral, or adorn a tale." This couplet, by the way, is the only one in Johnson's poetry to achieve independent fame. Its ironic antithesis between contemporary terror and trivial after-fame epitomizes the vanity of military pride and of the desire to make war in order to achieve fame and power. The hope of praise has a motivating power not equalled by that of mere virtue.

Another ancient and modern pair is next. Xerxes, the only example Johnson used from Juvenal, and Charles Albert, Elector of Bavaria, illustrate the same revolutions of fortune shown by Alexander and Charles XII, and the same kind of vanity, in desiring short-lived power, which they achieved through military victories.

Other human wishes are examined and deflated. The elderly who once wished for long life find that "life protracted is protracted woe," of which dotage, arthritic attacks, the loss of family and friends, and the dreaded knowledge that one is superfluous make up a chilling variety of possibilities. A mother's wish for beauty in her daughter may, if fulfilled, result only in the daughter's ruin.

Johnson's final paragraph contains his most striking difference from Juvenal, who as a Stoic gave the stoic answer to the seeming helplessness of man, the victim of fate: extirpate your desires, and you will not be disappointed. Johnson's solution is, not unexpectedly, Christian: seek divine guidance and ask only for those things which are compatible with both religion and human happiness—love, patience, and faith. "With these celestial wisdom calms the mind, / And makes the happiness she does not find."

So the poem comes to rest in affirmation and serenity. It has a unity much more impressive than that of *London*, since its structure is much more complex. The earlier poem relies on the relatively simple device of the speaker's departure from London, shaking the dust of the wicked metropolis from his heels. Now Johnson has looked sharply at some of the hopes of men, has found them hollow, and has come up with a solution. He does not, however, assert anywhere in the poem that *all* is vanity, and at no time in his life did he do so. Love, patience, and faith are realities, not nullities, when they are directed to the proper objects. But in this poem he, as a satirist, confines himself quite properly to an emphasis on attacking evil, rather than proposing schemes for reform. In *Rasselas,* which is not primarily a satire, we will find Johnson, through his characters, examining both sides of a question (marriage versus single life, for example). His own involvement is much more evident in *The Vanity of Human Wishes* than in *London*, particularly in his sketch of the life of the scholar. His handling of the heroic couplet provides vigorous and effective support for his ideas.

In January 1749 when *The Vanity of Human Wishes* appeared, Johnson's only play, *Irene*, was in rehearsal. It was produced in February and published in the same month with his name on the title-page. I do not believe it has been suggested that there may be a connection between the writing of *The Vanity of Human Wishes* and the production of *Irene*. It looks as though someone had decided, once the play was scheduled for Drury Lane, to put on a campaign to get Johnson known in the literary world. Dodsley published both these works, and he was also, significantly, the prime mover of the *Dictionary*, well under way at this time.

Johnson had written a draft of *Irene* before he came to London in 1737. He had been interested in amateur dramatics in Lichfield to the extent of writing an epilogue for a local production of Philips' *Distrest Mother*, an adaptation from Racine. He had read a great many plays, but he was not a habitual theater-goer. If a motive must be found for his venturing into tragedy, it is simple: money. There was no way for an author to make a substantial sum of money more *quickly* than to write a successful play. (The same thing was true a generation later when Goldsmith's and Sheridan's plays were produced, and the same motivation can be found behind the plays of Wordsworth, Coleridge, Keats, and probably Shelley and Byron.) *Irene* must have seemed a symbol of his delayed fame. He had tried to get it performed and failed, and then had tried to get it printed and failed again. Meantime, he had improved it here and there, as surviving manuscripts show. Johnson made more money from *Irene* than from the *Lives of the Poets*, even though, from a critical aspect, *Irene* had failed whereas the *Lives of the Poets* resoundingly succeeded.

The story of the play, taken largely from Knolles' *General History of the Turks*, must have seemed ready-made for the stage.

The sultan Mahomet II after the conquest of Constantinople in 1453 fell in love with a Greek Christian, Irene, and found his love returned. In the original version of the story, he lives with her in happy amorous dalliance, oblivious of his military and governmental duties until his subjects bring him to his senses. With a fine Oriental gesture, he cuts off Irene's head at a banquet, thereby signifying his return to his royal duties.

Johnson modifies this crude story of the preference of duty over love by making its elements more sophisticated. Mahomet offers to make Irene his empress, giving her the opportunity of benevolence to thousands of her countrymen. This possibility, and her ambition, attract Irene to the position. A contrasting pair of lovers, Demetrius and Aspasia, who are Greeks and revolutionaries, are added to the story. They try to persuade Irene to cast her lot with her compatriots against the conquerors. The revolution of the Greeks fails, but Demetrius and Aspasia escape. Irene, however, through irresolution and ineptness, is fatally compromised. By means of the machinations of a xenophobic Turkish officer, she is murdered and the tragedy ends.

When Garrick accepted the play for Drury Lane, he asked for some changes, including having Irene killed on-stage. This was no doubt an attempt to introduce some action to support the long love-versus-honor debate, but it was misguided: the first-night audience cried "Murder" at that point. In subsequent performances and in the published version, Irene was dispatched off-stage. In order to give the play every advantage, Garrick mounted it with an impressive cast. He played Demetrius, Barry played Mahomet, Mrs. Pritchard was Irene, and Mrs. Cibber was Aspasia. The run of nine nights was enough to give Johnson his third night's benefit performance three times. The play was not revived, though it was reprinted twice in Johnson's lifetime.

As was more or less the convention for tragedy, Johnson wrote his play in blank verse. His use of that form was unfortunate. His lines tend to be end-stopped; out of the first ten, for example, only one is run-on. The hearer, or reader, soon finds that he is waiting for a rime-word, which does not come. Johnson's lines at best have weight, but they are relatively undecorated and the movement of each speech tends to be slow. The dialogue, therefore, tends to be a series of set speeches, some of them very impressive, but, nevertheless, essentially declamatory in nature.

A modern reader finds *Irene* difficult to like because its characters are not convincing enough to involve him emotionally in the play. The heroine, divided between love for Mahomet and love for her country, ought to be the most interesting character, but her love for either one is not convincing. She is not *torn* between the one and the other, but merely *swayed* between two possibilities. We are told that she is beautiful, but we can see that she is stupid. Not even passages of impressive verse can outweigh this lack. Mahomet, Demetrius, and Aspasia are more credible and are therefore more interesting; unfortunately, they are also less important in the play.

To be fair, one ought to compare *Irene* with other English tragedies of the period: between Addison's *Cato* in 1713 and Sheridan's *Pizarro* in 1799, *Irene* is among the best—better, I think, than *Cato*. But the era is not noted for producing any truly great English tragedies.

Johnson's next major work, *The Rambler* (1750–52), is a series of separately published, semi-weekly essays in the tradition of *The Tatler* and *The Spectator* of almost forty years earlier. The convention of a commentator upon society and literature who has some sort of persona distinct from that of the author was established by Addison and Steele, though they did not invent it. It was a radical departure from Montaigne's familiar essays, or Bacon's, which are inseparable from the most intimate habits of thinking of Montaigne and Bacon. In contrast, the first number of Steele's *The Tatler* begins, "Though the other papers, which are published for the use of the good people of England, have certainly very wholesome effects, and are laudable in their particular kinds, they do not seem to come up to the main design of such narrations, which, I humbly presume, should be principally intended for the use of politic persons, who are so public-spirited as to neglect their own affairs to look into transactions of state." A point of view, gently mocking, urbane, is here at once established. Steele continues through his first essay in the same vein, until his persona is clear. But the persona was not Steele, a sentimental, romantic ne'er-do-well, though they did have some traits in common. Nor, to be sure, is there later on any characteristic identifiable as one of Addison's, who afterwards joined Steele in the anonymous series of essays.

Similarly, the first number of *The Spectator* begins: "I have observed that a reader seldom peruses a book with pleasure, till he knows whether the writer of it be a black or a fair man, of a mild or a choleric disposition, married or a bachelor, with other particulars of a like nature, that conduce very much to the right understanding of an author." Here we have again a persona with a light touch, about whom we are subsequently given a dozen autobiographical details, not one of which has any connection with Addison, who wrote this essay, or with Steele, who was his collaborator in the series.

Johnson begins his first *Rambler* quite differently from the first number of either *The Tatler* or *The Spectator:* "The difficulty of the first address on any new occasion, is felt by every man in his transactions with the world, and confessed by the settled and regular forms of salutation which necessity has introduced into all languages." The difference is immediately evident: there is no "I" and there is no reader mentioned, but rather a generalization on beginning a new venture. When Johnson is almost three-quarters of the way through his essay, he comments that such essays, being short, need not detain the reader long. This is his first attempt to speak directly to his reader. It is followed immediately by a sentence not calculated to seduce the reader into genial acceptance: "But whether my expectations are most fixed on pardon or praise, I think it not necessary to discover; for, having accurately weighed the reasons for arrogance and submission, I find them so nearly equiponderant, that my impatience to try the event of my first performance will not suffer me to attend any longer the trepidations of the balance." There are two more paragraphs, verging almost on truculence.

If any persona has begun to emerge at this point, it is that of a sour old codger who has managed to put two Latin quotations and a Greek one into a single essay. This picture was surely unintended, as Johnson's title, *The Rambler,* must indicate. But the relaxed, casual tone of a rambler is nowhere evident. The series sold slowly, which is perhaps not surprising inasmuch as Johnson and the publisher seem to have depended wholly on word-of-mouth promotion.

Johnson's synopsis of the second essay is unattractive: "The necessity and danger of looking into futurity. Writers naturally sanguine. Their hopes liable to disappointment." He is writing about himself and his professional problems, but does not yet much involve the reader. One sentence, however, suggests better things to come. Speaking of Don Quixote, he says, "When we pity him, we reflect on our own disappointments; and when we laugh, our hearts inform us that he is not more ridiculous than ourselves, except that he tells what we have only thought." Here Johnson has moved momentarily out of his book-lined study into human life. He does this more often later.

The third essay Johnson described as an allegory on criticism. (These descriptions did not appear until the original numbers were collected and bound.) It tells nothing about Johnson, and nothing about criticism except that it is sometimes flattering and sometimes malevolent.

The next essay, on fiction, is remarkably better. For one thing, the topic was most timely; within a three-year period, 1747–49, the three greatest contemporary novelists—Richardson, Fielding, and Smollett—had published their major works, *Clarissa*, *Tom Jones*, and *Roderick Random.* At this particular moment, the romances of the marvelous had gone out of style, as Johnson observes, and a new, realistic type of novel had been established. Standards of criticism for the new kind of novel had not yet been formed, however, and Richardson had chosen to class his works as biographies, not wishing them to be debased into the romance category. Fielding, also wishing to use a more respectable form than the old romance, had invented the "comic epic poem in prose," and in the Preface to *Joseph Andrews* and the essays interspersed in *Tom Jones* discussed what he had intended.

Johnson is well aware that the new novel had to come out of "accurate observation of the living world," but he does not think it should be a transcript of life. He believes that the novel is written "to the young, the ignorant, and the idle," and must therefore be instructive; its purpose is "to initiate youth" into life "by mock encounters . . . and to increase prudence without impairing virtue." The mixture of virtue and vice in heroes is particularly to be avoided: "as we accompany them through their adventures with delight, and are led by degrees to interest ourselves in their favour, we lose the abhorrence of their faults, because they do not hinder our pleasure, or, perhaps, regard them with some kindness, for being united with so much merit." Johnson is probably talking about Tom Jones, though he mentions no names anywhere in the essay. When he is talking about villains, he seems to have Richardson's Lovelace in mind: "Vice, for vice is necessary to be shown, should always disgust. . . . Wherever it appears, it should raise hatred by the malignity of its practices, and contempt by the meanness of its stratagems: for while it is supported by either parts or spirit, it will be seldom heartily abhorred." This is Johnson's first important essay on literature.

Perhaps fearing to frighten away the general reader with too much seriousness, Johnson turns in the next essay to something lighter, spring. Here we have a brief sketch of a character of Micawberish disposition who is confident that everything will be better when spring comes, and, when it comes and goes, remains confident that the next spring will be better. There is just a suggestion here of the lightly sardonic tone, almost avuncularly indulgent, which Johnson later used very effectively in *Rasselas*. He appears to be experimenting with this tone, in contrast with the sharp satiric tone of both *London* and *The Vanity of Human Wishes*, but in this essay he goes no further.

In essay No. 18, published six weeks later, the point of view of the Rambler begins to assume definition. He is, of course, a moralist, not primarily a philosopher or literary critic. After a few years, when a work was identified as by the author of *The Rambler*, it was expected to be written from the point of view of the moralist. This point of view had been basic to Johnson's two imitations of Juvenal, and it permeates *Irene*. As we have just seen, it directs Johnson's attitude toward the novel.

This eighteenth essay is on marriage, with an inquiry into some causes of its frequent failure. Johnson suggests that readers may have been given a biassed notion of this institution from the accidental fact that most writers have been men. He proposes looking at several different marriages to see whether men or women are at fault for their frequent failure. He describes his own character as one "in the cool maturity of life, arrived at . . . command" over his passions. The reader who knows anything at all about Johnson will recognize that this is a wholly fictional description of himself. It is apparent from this fact that Johnson has begun to see the need of adopting a personality different from his own in order to give direction and effect to what he has to say.

He then gives little vignettes, showing how some men have chosen wives for the wrong reasons: Prudentius wanted a rich wife and found that he had married a fury; another mistook coquetry for wit and cheerfulness; a third, spending a summer in an isolated village, finds a wife whose apparent love of the simple life turns into an uninhibited pursuit of frivolity once she reaches the city; and so on. Unfortunately for Johnson's purpose, he spends much more space on the follies of the women than on the poor reasons why the men chose them. The effect, therefore, is somewhat misogynic. His conclusion in consequence, "that marriage is the strictest tie of perpetual friendship," built upon confidence and integrity, comes too late: the reader in all probability has already decided that Johnson thinks women the cause of failed marriages. But such a deduction results from his imperfect technique in presenting the essay, not from an incorrigible antipathy to women. Johnson had no such antipathy whatever.

In No. 21, Johnson considers some of the problems of a writer, all of which have professional interest, though it may be questioned whether he considered how many of his readers in May 1750 could be expected to share this interest. To be more blunt, Johnson does not seem to have thought much at this point about what audience he was trying to reach, and a certain hit-and-miss or scattering of effect is the result. Even so, one sentence contains a point of interest to the general reader: "Our juvenile compositions please us, because they bring to our minds the remembrance of youth; our later performances we are ready to esteem, because we are unwilling to think that we have made no improvement. . . ."

In No. 31, Johnson analyzes a psychological problem, the resistance of the ego to contradiction or criticism: "those who break out into fury at the first attacks of contradiction, or the slightest touches of censure, conceive some injury offered to their honour, some antient immunity violated, or some natural prerogative invaded . . ." (first edition, later modified). Johnson is not sure of the precise reason for this behavior, but he is aware of the essential irrationality of such a reaction against an attack: it is as though the secret center of being is threatened, and all forces are summoned in defense. Johnson does not long continue his essay at this level, but he has sketched out a vital insight.

No. 60, one of the best-known of Johnson's essays, is another important discussion of literature. In it he examines "the usefulness of biography," by which he means biography's ability to involve us to such an extent "that we feel, while the deception lasts, whatever motions would be excited by the same good or evil happening to ourselves." Johnson points out that biographies which describe those things "naturally incident to our state of life" involve us to a much greater extent than those which describe the careers of kings and emperors, who are distant from us. He is thus saying farewell to the heroic and welcoming the domestic life as a subject for writing. He then restates the classical norm of Sir Philip Sidney, that literature should teach and delight—no other kind of literature "can be more delightful, or more useful," than biography. Johnson thus stresses the importance of biography as example.

Further on in the essay, he recommends that the writer pay less attention to great events in the life of a man than to "the minute details of daily life, where exteriour appendages are cast aside. . . ." Boswell was only ten when this was written, but he later applied this lesson carefully when he wrote the *Life of Johnson*, in which he quoted all of the passage (I.32). (For the most part, Johnson ignored his own precept when he came to write the *Lives of the Poets:* such minute details were not readily at hand for most of his subjects, and he was unwilling to spend the time or effort required to dig such details out of the midden heap of history.) Johnson comments that most biographies contain little that cannot be gathered from "publick papers" and therefore show less of a man's real character than could be gathered from a short talk with one of his servants. A good biography will accordingly be written as soon as possible after the death of the subject: "If a life be delayed till interest and envy are at an end, we may hope for impartiality, but must expect little intelligence; for the incidents which give excellence to biography are of a volatile and evanescent kind, such as soon escape the memory, and are rarely transmitted by tradition." And Johnson anticipates the objection that many persons will wish to hide the failings of their friends: "If we owe regard to the memory of the dead, there is yet more respect to be paid to knowledge, to virtue, and to truth."

In this essay Johnson has again projected his ideas, as he did in the earlier one on fiction, with clarity and force. He has chosen an emerging literary form, related it to his basic thinking, and taken an original position with regard to it (i.e., that intimate and domestic details rather than spectacular incidents should be included in biographies). I may point out also that in the last sentence quoted there is not a single learned or unusual word. When he chose, Johnson could write with great simplicity.

In writing some two hundred numbers of *The Rambler*, Johnson never established a persona wholly separate from himself, as Addison and Steele had done. The Rambler and Johnson tend often to merge, since the most obvious characteristic of each is that of the moral commentator on life. On the other hand, Johnson does not commonly, in this periodical, speak out in his own person. He is therefore following more or less in the *Spectator* tradition. That this was intentional is clear when he quotes Castiglione in the last number: "A mask confers a right of acting and speaking with less restraint, even when the wearer is known to the whole company."

In this final number, 208, published on 14 March 1752, Johnson speaks throughout in his own person, quite fittingly for his farewell. The tone tends to be gloomy, perhaps in part because his wife was ill and indeed died three days later. ("He that condemns himself to compose on a stated day, will often bring to his task an attention dissipated, a memory embarrassed, an imagination overwhelmed, a mind distracted with anxieties, a body languishing with disease.") But Johnson's independence is also plain; all of his struggles had not yet achieved fame, yet he would not stoop to get it: "Having laboured to maintain the dignity of virtue, I will not now degrade it by the meanness of dedication." At the end the reader is won to sympathy and admiration as Johnson hopes to be "numbered among the writers, who have given ardour to virtue, and confidence to truth."

About eight months after Johnson concluded *The Rambler*, his friend John Hawkesworth began a similar essay-periodical, *The Adventurer*, to which Johnson was a major contributor, if he was not, indeed, a prime mover of the enterprise. Of Johnson's twenty-nine essays, a series of four letters signed Misargyrus ("Money-hater"), Nos. 34, 41, 53, and 62, are the most interesting. They purport to come from a once-rich spendthrift now in debtors' prison, and the first two relate a kind of rake's progress to his present abode, with especial attention to exorbitant money-lenders. In the third, the "club" of jailed spendthrifts is described, and in the last a group of men who went surety for friends who subsequently defaulted. These letters are in some places made vivid by characteristic Johnsonian comments: "there are among us many . . . that owe their present misery to the seductions of treachery, the strokes of casualty, or the tenderness of pity; many whose sufferings disgrace society, and whose virtues would adorn it . . ." (No. 53). But we are not told enough about any of the characters to become really interested in them, and their sufferings are not given in the detail needed to arouse our pity. As for the other twenty-five numbers, there is no distinctive point of view, no single "adventurer"; the essays have a random character which has not left a mark on literature at all comparable to that of the *Rambler* essays. They are accomplished, agreeable, and somehow not especially memorable.

Johnson's last major series of essays, *The Idler* (1758–60), was written for inclusion in the *Universal Chronicle*, a newspaper just beginning, published by a friend. (The motive of friendly assistance, here as with *The Adventurer*, is significant.) In the 104 weekly numbers, Johnson managed for a second time to establish a distinct persona, perhaps because he was largely working alone, instead of contributing a charitable bit to another man's series. The series, then, has a satiric bite largely missing from *The Adventurer*. Indeed, in No. 22 on the subject of warfare, Johnson felt so deeply that he produced an essay so bitter it was not reprinted in his lifetime.

The essay begins on a deceptively serene tone, talking about the supposed ability of animals to communicate their thoughts to each other; dogs, hens are adduced. So far, the essay sounds like some of the arid letters in the *Philosophical Transactions* of the Royal Society, which printed not only important scientific papers but also the hazy and superficial observations of amateur naturalists. Then Johnson reports, in the words of a Bohemian shepherd, the conversation of a mother vulture with her young on how to get along in the world: they have seen her seize a fowl or kid and bring them aloft. "But you remember the taste of more delicious food; I have often regaled you with the flesh of man." The young birds naturally want to know how this superior food is to be found, and why their mother has not brought whole men instead of mere tidbits to the nest. She mentions their formidable size, which puzzles her children since they know that she does not meddle with wolves or bears. But nature, she says, has "devoted" man "to our uses," having endowed him with "a strange ferocity" not shared by any other being: the urge to destroy one another in herds, which "meet and shake the earth with noise, and fill the air with fire."

The young pursue the discussion: why don't the men eat those whom they have killed? Their mother has no answer, since she has observed that all other animals eat their kill. But this reminds her of the profound deduction of an old vulture-philosopher of Carpathia: "His opinion was, that men had only the appearance of animal life, being really vegetables with a power of motion; and that as the boughs of an oak are dashed together by the storm, that swine may fatten upon the falling acorns, so men are by some unaccountable power driven one against another, till they lose their motion, that vultures may be fed." The bird admits another opinion, that there may be a mischievous man in each herd who is "eminently delighted with a wide carnage"—one who is neither particularly big nor swift, but is, by his eagerness and diligence, more than the rest "a friend to vultures." The Swiftian note of controlled but violent anger is rare in Johnson. It is present here.

In the next number of *The Idler*, Johnson looks at debtors' prisons, a humanitarian problem of concern to large numbers of his contemporaries, and one which he had already discussed in *The Adventurer*. He opens the essay with a picture unusually vivid for him: "As I was passing lately under one of the gates of this city, I was struck with horror by a rueful cry, which summoned me *to remember the poor debtors*." He comments on the folly of a law obliging able-bodied men to beg, and the injustice of submitting the liberty of one man to "the passions" of another. Only a few debtors are suspected of concealing assets; the rest "are imprisoned by the wantonness of pride, the malignity of revenge, or the acrimony of disappointed expectation." And he follows up this typical resounding generalization with a lively series of bourgeois excuses: "his debtor once lived better than himself . . . his wife looked above her neighbours, and his children went in silk cloaths to the dancing school. . . ." After this surface view, Johnson turns to a more mordant and deeper analysis: "Some will confess their resolution, that their debtors shall rot in jail; and some will discover, that they hope, by cruelty, to wring the payment from their friends."

In addition to the humanitarian view, Johnson presents economic arguments against debtors' prisons: "The prosperity of a people is proportionate to the number of hands and minds usefully employed. To the community sedition is a fever, corruption is a gangrene, and idleness an atrophy." He elaborates upon this argument, in a way which Adam Smith would have approved (*The Wealth of Nations* was published in 1776), and ends the essay with an observation that might be termed businesslike: "We have now learned, that rashness and imprudence will not be deterred from taking credit; let us try whether fraud and avarice may be more easily restrained from giving it." This conclusion reflects Johnson's developing belief that the increasing complexity of commercial relations was not being accompanied by a commensurate coverage of law, and that the average man was therefore in ever increasing danger of fraud.

Two *Idlers* of a different sort are Nos. 61 and 62 on a fictional character, Dick Minim, the hanger-on of critics and habitué of coffeehouses, who had learned enough of the right literary attitudes and the right critical adjectives to gain a moment's attention from those even lazier than he. He talks about copying "nature," and of the fact that all great authors had beauties and defects. (Johnson is not invulnerable here inasmuch as he himself was rather inclined to balance beauties and defects in his accounts of authors.) Our pleasure in this extended portrait lies in its timelessness. Change the clichés and we are in London, Greenwich Village, or Berkeley in the 1960's. Moreover, Johnson is not out to destroy but only to laugh rather indulgently at this pseudo-critic. At the end, Minim ("little-note," we might translate the musical term) becomes a teacher and happily transmits his bloodless ideas to "a youth of promising parts." After receiving the word, the boy "retires illuminated, resolves to follow his genius, and to think how Milton would have thought; and Minim feasts upon his own beneficence till another day brings another pupil."

During the 1750's while Johnson was finding a distinctive voice as an essayist and establishing himself as a lexicographer, he continued as a poet. His first important poem after *The Vanity of Human Wishes* was a prologue for a performance of Milton's *Comus* in 1750 for the benefit of Milton's granddaughter, who had been discovered living in near poverty. Johnson had once before shown his admiration of Milton when, at Oxford, he made a Latin translation of Dryden's lines comparing Milton with Homer and Vergil. Now Johnson offers the audience "this prelude of perpetual praise!" and suggests that Milton's present triumph will give hope for the future of "slighted arts." He then moves gracefully to the object of the Prologue, the relief of Milton's granddaughter, "Hers the mild merits of domestic life, / The patient suff'rer, and the faithful wife." He concludes with charging the fair, the wise, and the brave to "crown desert—beyond the grave!" The poem admirably fulfils its charitable purpose.

A large amount of Johnson's occasional work from this time forward arose from either friendship or compassion. His next prologue was written for his old friend Goldsmith's first comedy, *The Good-Natur'd Man* (1768). The lines seem to have been composed during one of Johnson's periods of depression, and the opening is gloomy: "Prest by the load of life, the weary mind / Surveys the general toil of human kind." But he states next that the dramatist shares the "epidemic" cares of politicians facing an election (one was approaching). This neat topical allusion lightens the tone enough so that the actor speaking the prologue can talk about the heckling of "loud rabbles" without being offensive. The tone, however, does not rise to the jocular level, as might be expected in an introduction to a comedy, and the lines end on a note of surly virtue: the bard, "confident of praise, if praise be due, / Trusts without fear, to merit, and to you."

Johnson's last prologue was written for a performance of Hugh Kelly's *A Word to the Wise* for the benefit of the playwright's widow and children. Johnson had no very high opinion of Kelly, but this harmless sentimental comedy had suffered at the hands of political opposition and Johnson's object was twofold, to aid a widow and to provide a quiet hearing for the play. He succeeded, partly by touching in his resounding fashion on "Th' oblivious grave's inviolable shade," and partly by pointing out the "harmless merriment" of the play. He concludes with the suggestion that the audience will be pleased with an occasion when "mirth was bounty with a humbler name." The tone is just right: he does not claim that the play is a piece of deathless art, and his sympathy is handled with tact.

Much of Johnson's other poetry of this period is occasional. He translated dozens of mottoes for *The Rambler* and *The Adventurer*, and in doing so found the short space of a couplet or two congenial. He added lines to poems of Goldsmith, Crabbe, and Hannah More which were submitted to him for criticism, and wrote whole poems to fill out a volume published for the benefit of his blind friend Miss Williams.

Other poems were impromptus called forth by a spirit of ridicule. Much as he believed in the unearthing and publishing of old literary works, such as the ballads in Percy's *Reliques*, he thought that imitating antiquity was puerile. Hence, when Percy himself wrote a full-length poem, *The Hermit of Warkworth*, in what he conceived to be a medieval manner, Johnson volunteered two parodies:

> The tender infant meek and mild
>   Fell down upon a stone;
> The nurse took up the squealing child
>   But yet the child squeal'd on.
>
> I put my hat upon my head
>   And walk'd into the Strand,
> And there I met another man
>   Who's hat was in his hand.

The second of these found an unexpected immortality when Wordsworth attacked it in his famous Preface to *Lyrical Ballads* (1800), under the mistaken impression that Johnson had been attacking traditional ballads rather than modern imitations.

Johnson wrote another poem of ridicule on the appearance of his friend Thomas Warton's *Poems* (1777):

> Wheresoe'er I turn my view,
> All is strange, yet nothing new;
> Endless labour all along,
> Endless labour to be wrong;
> Phrase that time has flung away,
> Uncouth words in disarray:
> Trickt in antique ruff and bonnet,
> Ode and elegy and sonnet.

Toward the end of his life, in 1780, Johnson wrote his only personal satire, on the coming-of-age of Thrale's nephew, Sir John Lade, who had once been silly enough to ask Johnson whether he ought to marry. "A Short Song of Congratulation" is the deadly prediction of Sir John's future career. Here are the fifth and the last stanzas:

> Wealth, Sir John, was made to wander,
> Let it wander as it will;
> See the jocky, see the pander,
> Bid them come, and take their fill.
>
> If the guardian or the mother
> Tell the woes of wilful waste,
> Scorn their counsel and their pother,
> You can hang or drown at last.

Sir John, who could scarcely have seen these lines in Johnson's lifetime, since they were sent in a private letter, at least carried out their spirit by marrying a whore and squandering his fortune.

A very different poem is Johnson's elegy on Robert Levet, the pensioner-surgeon who ministered to the needs of Johnson's household for many years. In the last three stanzas Johnson captures very effectively the modest powers and qualities of this man:

> His virtues walk'd their narrow round,
> Nor made a pause, nor left a void;
> And sure th' Eternal Master found
> The single talent well employ'd.
>
> The busy day, the peaceful night,
> Unfelt, uncounted, glided by;

His frame was firm, his powers were bright,
Tho' now his eightieth year was nigh.

Then with no throbbing fiery pain,
No cold gradations of decay,
Death broke at once the vital chain,
And free'd his soul the nearest way.

There is no gilding of his subject, no sentimentality. The simple verse form is right and the diction fitting. Johnson knew the effect he wanted and he knew how to get it. This is true of the great bulk of his verse; his failures are few, his successes frequent.

The personal note which is present here and in so much of Johnson's writing also turns up in the book reviews he contributed to the *Literary Magazine*, a new journal which he began to edit in 1756. Most of these were uncontroversial, but one took issue with Jonas Hanway's *Essay on Tea*, in which that solemn philanthropist attacked Johnson's favorite beverage. Hanway replied and, for the only time in his life, Johnson answered an attack in print. His essay is characteristic in its formal structure and fully impregnated with the Johnsonian spirit: "Of tea, what have I said? That I have drank it twenty years, without hurt, and, therefore, believe it not to be poison; that, if it dries the fibres, it cannot soften them; that, if it constringes, it cannot relax. I have modestly doubted, whether it has diminished the strength of our men, or the beauty of our women; and whether it much hinders the progress of our woollen or iron manufactures. . . ." (*Works*, 1825, VI.33.)

Much of Johnson's occasional writing during his last twenty years was done at the house of his friends the Thrales, and Mrs. Thrale was well informed about his writings. In one of her diaries she says, "Dr. Johnson was liberal enough in granting literary assistance to others, I think; and innumerable are the Prefaces, Sermons, Lectures, and Dedications which he used to make for people who begged of him." All of these have one quality in common, anonymity. They were to be thought Percy's (*Reliques*), or Joshua Reynolds' (*Discourses*) if they were dedications, and the authors of the books so dedicated or prefaced generally kept quiet about Johnson's help: Reynolds seems to have feared that if Johnson's help had been known it would have been thought that he had also written the *Discourses*. In any case, Johnson's style is so different from that of most of his contemporaries that once his authorship is suspected, one familiar with his style is usually able to ascertain it with some confidence. Mrs. Thrale was able to do so, and Boswell. In modern times these prefaces and dedications of which Johnson is the suspected author have been brought together by Professor Allen Hazen, who has convinced virtually all scholars in the field that Johnson was indeed the author.

These dedications are remarkable for the fact that Johnson avoids the common temptation of the dedicator to pour on praise, whether for love or money. He is able to compliment a patron of a book with grace and with dignity, whatever his rank or power. This is no mean feat, and to have accomplished it scores of times is really noteworthy. I do not know of any failures. One of the best is the dedication written to the Earl of Shaftesbury in *The English Works of Roger Ascham*, which was nominally edited by James Bennet, with much help from Johnson:

> My Lord,
>
> Having endeavoured, by an elegant and useful edition, to recover the esteem of the publick to an authour undeservedly neglected, the only care which I now owe to his memory, is that of inscribing his works to a patron whose acknowledged eminence of character may awaken attention, and attract regard.
>
> I have not suffered the zeal of an editor so far to take possession of my mind, as that I should obtrude upon your Lordship any productions unsuitable to the dignity of your rank or of your sentiments. Ascham was not only the chief ornament of a celebrated college, but visited foreign countries, frequented courts, and lived in familiarity with statesmen and princes; not only instructed scholars in literature, but formed Elizabeth to empire.
>
> To propagate the works of such a writer will be not unworthy of your Lordship's patriotism: for I know not what greater benefit you can confer on your country, than that of preserving worthy names from oblivion, by joining them with your own. . . .

This is simpler than most of Johnson's dedications, but it is especially noteworthy in its emphasis on Ascham rather than the editor, and in its delicacy in pointing out how proper it is for a man of Shaftesbury's rank to associate himself with the cause of literature.

It is unfortunate that Chesterfield could not foresee around 1750 that Johnson would become the most skillful dedicator of the century, and that he did not pay more attention to him while the *Dictionary* was in progress. As it happened, Chesterfield received the most famous anti-dedication in English literature in a private letter later published by Boswell:

> Is not a Patron, my Lord, one who looks with unconcern on a man struggling for life in the water, and, when he has reached ground, encumbers him with help? The notice which you have been pleased to take of my labours, had it been early, had been kind; but it has been delayed till I am indifferent, and cannot enjoy it; till I am solitary, and cannot impart it; till I am known, and do not want it. I hope it is no very cynical asperity not to confess obligations where no benefit has been received, or to be unwilling that the publick should consider me as owing that to a Patron, which Providence has enabled me to do for myself.

Johnson's prefaces are less distinctive than his dedications. They are either good summaries of the book to follow, or satisfactory introductions. They are hack work done with style.

Of Johnson's anonymous sermons—he told Sir John Hawkins that he had done about forty—some twenty-six or twenty-seven have been tentatively or positively identified. Twenty-four were written for Johnson's former schoolmate John Taylor, and posthumously published as Taylor's own; one Johnson wrote for the funeral of his wife, and one for his good friend Henry Hervey. Unlike the prefaces and dedications, none of these were written for publication, and only one, that for Hervey, was in fact published during Johnson's lifetime. The circumstances of the delivery of the sermons account for differences among them—Hervey's was an anniversary sermon given in St. Paul's Cathedral before the dignitaries of the church, those written for Taylor were delivered in his parish church at Ashbourne or at Westminster, the sermon on his wife was given at a burial which must have been almost private. However, they have a degree of uniformity in their dignity, their appropriateness, and their occasional sonority.

The lectures mentioned by Mrs. Thrale in her diary were hidden, for good reason, and were not identified until twenty-five years ago. They were composed by Johnson to help his young friend and protégé Robert Chambers, who suddenly found himself, at the age of twenty-nine, successor to Blackstone as Vinerian Professor of Law at Oxford. Most endowed professorships at Oxford or Cambridge could have been handled without effort, or even without lectures, by any eighteenth-century incumbent. But not this one. Blackstone himself had drawn up the statutes for the endowment, and with a thoroughness unprecedented in the century had stipulated not only the number of lectures to be given, but also the penalties for failing to lecture. These in aggregate would exceed the annual salary.

Composing a series of lectures was not necessarily onerous. Blackstone had originated them as commentaries on the law for the undergraduate, with the purpose of explaining what any young man ought to know who might succeed to an estate or one day enter Parliament. They were not in any sense aimed at training a lawyer. The four volumes made up from Blackstone's lectures were in the process of being published, and they met with great success in Great Britain, and later in America, because their purpose was clear, their handling direct, and their organization practical.

Nevertheless, Blackstone's very success must have been intimidating to the young man who was his assistant. Blackstone left Oxford to become Solicitor General to the Queen, and Chambers, paralyzed by stage fright, appealed to Johnson, who responded at once. At Oxford, and later at London, Johnson dictated the lectures to Chambers, leaving him to fill in references and to expand where desirable.

Johnson did not do this out of sheer bravado. For years he had considered a legal career, but neither of the two paths to the law looked feasible—a university degree if he wanted to practice civil law, or a long residence at the Inns of Court in London if he wished to pursue the common law. He had read in law books for years and had about seventy in his library. In 1765 he had still thought of studying professionally and perhaps of entering Parliament. So his opportunity to help Chambers must have appealed to him greatly.

In the course of time, fifty-six lectures were written; about a third, I think, with Johnson's style clearly visible. They are numerous enough to constitute a major work. None were published until Johnson and Chambers had been long dead, when one section was published over Chambers' name (1824). An official copy of the whole series is deposited in the British Museum. The lectures bear a striking resemblance in their clarity, their sensible organization, and their directness to other Johnsonian work done on behalf of his friends. As a sample, the two paragraphs introducing the first lecture show Johnson giving appropriate attention to the law, to Blackstone, and a good deal more subtle attention to Chambers, who, in effect, is urged to get down to work:

> If I commence with diffidence and timidity the employment to which I am now advanced, it is not merely because I consider the law, which I am to profess, as by its extent difficult to be comprehended or by its variety difficult to be methodized; for obstacles like these must be encountered in all studies, must be encountered with vigor and surmounted by diligence.
>
> My fears proceed from discouragements peculiar to myself. Professors like princes are exposed to censure not only by their own defects, but by the virtues of their predecessors. I am to read and explain the laws of England, from a place just vacated by a man equally eminent for extent of knowledge and elegance of diction, for strength of comprehension and clearness of explanation. That by the choice of this learned University I am called into his office, as it depresses my hopes, must excite my diligence. Abilities no man has the power of conferring on himself, but fidelity and industry are always attainable. I hope to erect such a fabric of juridical knowledge as may stand firm by its solidity, though it should not please by its elegance, and shall think it sufficient to mould those materials into strength, which only the genius of a Blackstone could polish into lustre. (*Dr. Johnson and the English Law*, p. 81.)

Perhaps the general virtuosity of Johnson has been illustrated enough in this discussion of his prologues, prefaces and dedications, his sermons and law lectures. Without undue disarrangement of chronology, we may turn to Johnson as a novelist.

III

Rasselas

In 1759 Johnson wrote *The History of Rasselas, Prince of Abissinia* in one week to defray the funeral expenses of his mother—he did not even have enough ready cash to go to Lichfield for the service. But the novel bears no marks of this origin, nor does it bear any marks of hasty composition. In a sense, Johnson had been composing it in his head for many years: it is the fruit of his long musing on the choice of a career and on the pursuit of happiness. (The location and the name of the hero were suggested by his translation of Lobo's *Abyssinia.*) The book appealed to the public from the beginning, and it has been reprinted in English and translated into all major European languages some two hundred times. It may be worth inquiring why.

For one thing, *Rasselas* was new. It was the first full-length Oriental tale in English. A French version of the *Arabian Nights* had been previously translated into English, so some foundation existed for public interest, but these tales were short situation stories with a minimum of characterization and very few ideas of any complexity. Johnson had earlier tried two short Oriental tales in *The Rambler;* except as experiments, they are not very interesting. The reading public had been accustomed to think of the Near East as exotic but approachable, Greece through Homer and Palestine through the Bible. Therefore Abyssinia, a step farther into the unknown, involved not the incredible but the willing suspension of disbelief (as Coleridge later called it). *Rasselas* succeeded not only because of the novelty of its exotic setting, but also because of the popular liking for escape literature, probably no less common in the eighteenth century than it is now. Opportunities for actual escape, of course, were limited to the rich who could go on the Grand Tour, or to the desperate adventurers who went to the American colonies or India and risked everything for a fortune. Reading romances or travel books was the more ordinary way to relieve boredom. Johnson was devoted to both types of books: he knew romances such as *Amadis of Gaul* and books like Norden's *Travels in Egypt and Nubia*, which appeared two years before he wrote *Rasselas*.

The first appeal of this novel, then, was its exotic setting—a remote, mountainous kingdom where the heir to the throne was sealed off from the world of politics in a Happy Valley in which every imaginable pleasure and luxury was provided to amuse him. The young man, however, experiencing the typical unrest and unhappiness of the adolescent, is dissatisfied with his "paradise." The exotic is thus closely linked to the recognizably human and familiar. The key phrase, which Johnson introduces early and reiterates frequently, often with ironic emphasis, is "the choice of life." The hero, prince though he is, must experience the universal adolescent self-discovery: for this is an initiation novel.

The remote insulated setting gives the work an aura of the unfamiliar. The somber grandeur of Johnson's opening sentence, with its total absence of the colloquial tone, is admirably in keeping with the distance of his setting: "Ye who listen with credulity to the whispers of fancy, and pursue with eagerness the phantoms of hope; who expect that age will perform the promises of youth, and that the deficiencies of the present day will be supplied by the morrow; attend to the history of Rasselas prince of Abissinia." Our hero does not appear in the first chapter, but Johnson prepares us for his point of view by remarking that the entertainers admitted to the valley to amuse the princes are "competitors for imprisonment."

In the second chapter the young prince Rasselas is introduced; he is dissatisfied with the diversions of the gilded cage and indulges in "solitary walks and silent meditation." He observes his difference from the rest of the animal creation: the birds and the beasts are contented; he alone is "burthened" with himself; he, unlike them, fears pain, and he both recollects evils and anticipates them. This discovery naturally gives him pleasure "in his own perspicacity," and to this he is able to add his awareness of the fineness of his feelings, and, not least, his eloquence in verbalizing them.

No wonder that with this series of self-discoveries he is able to join cheerfully in the evening's usual (unintellectual) diversions. In the awakening of an innocent egotism, Rasselas shows himself to be a fairly typical young man, and Johnson describes him from the half-amused but indulgent point of view of middle age. It is a subtle and sophisticated portrait.

Chapter Three introduces a foil to the youth and a plot-device, an old teacher who tells Rasselas that if he knew the bad world outside, he would know how to value *the happy valley*. (Johnson uses italic to underline his irony.) This is fresh water to Rasselas' parched lips: "you have given me something to desire"—the sight of the world beyond the valley. He then gives himself over to imagining what lies beyond the hitherto impassable mountains and seeing himself as a rescuer of maidens in distress. In due time —Rasselas thinks very slowly—he discards fantasy in favor of attempted escape over the mountains. No easy route exists, but he meets an inventor who is building a flying machine and is thus exposed to the enthusiasm of a visionary. Rasselas' intelligence is of a rather practical sort, or perhaps it should be described as rudimentary. Indeed, Johnson uses his hero more than once to deflate the hyperbolic rhetoric of another character. Rasselas, then, points out the difficulties in the way of the inventor's plan and receives the sturdy reply, "Nothing . . . will ever be attempted, if all possible objections must be first overcome" (Ch. VI). The flying machine fails, but Rasselas' disappointment is brief inasmuch as his involvement was slight.

The coming of the rainy season ends outdoor activity. In the palace, the poet Imlac's recitation of verses on the "various conditions of humanity" induces Rasselas to ask "a thousand questions" about life on the outside, and, eventually, to inquire why Imlac chose to retire to the happy valley. Imlac responds with the story of his life, and begins with a resoundingly Johnsonian statement: "Sir," he says, "my history will not be long: the life that is devoted to knowledge passes silently away, and is very little diversified by events. To talk in publick, to think in solitude, to read and to hear, to inquire, and answer inquiries, is the business of a scholar. He wanders about the world without pomp or terrour, and is neither known nor valued but by men like himself" (Ch. VIII).

The content of this remark is similar to Johnson's description of the life of the scholar in *The Vanity of Human Wishes*, without the bitterness of the earlier passage. Here, moreover, Johnson is beginning to develop the character of Imlac, who, though he is frequently the mouthpiece of the author, is by no means identical with him. There is a slightly pompous tone in much of what Imlac says, and a good deal of self-admiration.

When Imlac speaks of the rapacity of the governors of the province where he was born, Rasselas reacts with virtuous indignation, and Imlac replies with a statement on human relations which Boswell would have recognized instantly as Johnson speaking: "Subordination supposes power on one part and subjection on the other; and if power be in the hands of men, it will sometimes be abused." The prince lacks the experience necessary to understand this piece of political wisdom, and urges Imlac to go on. Imlac moves quickly over another aphorism which is, in fact, of greater psychological interest to Rasselas, that "some desire is necessary to keep life in motion." Johnson thus uses Rasselas' brief interruption to show a little more about his protagonist and at the same time to break up a long speech and give it variety of movement.

However, when Imlac describes his being abused by his companions in a caravan, Rasselas interrupts again: in his innocence he cannot imagine depravity which does not involve profit. Imlac allows himself only a passing remark on pride, unwilling to stop his story for a close analysis of motive. He moves quickly on to tell of an emperor who flattered him with questions about his travels. Imlac, of course, does not see that he was being flattered, but the reader does, as Johnson intended him to.

Having revealed something of his character, Imlac launches into his famous exposition of the function of the poet, in which he glorifies his own profession. "To a poet nothing can be useless": he gratifies his reader with "remote allusions and unexpected instruction" (Ch. X). "The business of a poet," he goes on, "is to examine, not the individual, but the species; to remark general properties and large appearances: he does not number the streaks of the tulip, or describe the different shades in the verdure of the forest." Moreover, he must "divest himself of the prejudices of his age or country," arrive at an understanding of "general and transcendental truths," and, at the last, acquire "every delicacy of speech and grace of harmony." Johnson no doubt agreed with much of this, if perhaps not quite all. Nevertheless, for dramatic purposes he at once deflates Imlac's "enthusiastic fit" with the prince's "Enough! Thou hast convinced me, that no human being can ever be a poet." Imlac lamely concedes that it is "indeed very difficult" and goes on with his story.

His fondness for sententious remarks is revealed when he comments on the pilgrims he met in Palestine during his travels: "Pilgrimage," he says, "may be reasonable or superstitious, according to the principles upon which it is performed. . . . Truth, such as is necessary to the regulation of life, is always found where it is honestly sought" (Ch. XI). He is just launched into a comment on the holy places of Palestine when Rasselas stops him again: characteristically of his youth, he wants short, categorical answers. Are the Europeans (whom Imlac knew in Palestine), with all their knowledge, happier than the Abyssinians? To this Imlac gives a subtle answer: "Ignorance is a mere privation, . . . a vacuity," and he is inclined to conclude that "we grow more happy as our minds take a wider range." Rasselas does not comment on this, but states that the good roads and bridges which facilitate communication between absent friends must make Europeans happy. Imlac will not accept this simplistic deduction, but insists that happiness is relative and ends the chapter somberly: "Human life is everywhere a state in which much is to be endured, and little to be enjoyed" (Ch. XI).

Rasselas is not satisfied with this gloomy view; he is sure that if he had "the choice of life," he could live with pleasure, virtue, and generosity. Imlac ignores this youthful optimism and concludes his story by telling of his discontent with the world and his leaving it for "perpetual confinement" in the "*happy valley*" (Ch. XII).

For Imlac, however, the "happy valley" has not turned out to be the solution to the unhappiness of life: community of possessions there may be, but not "community of love or of esteem." To "the natural malignity" of the imprisoned, insupportable boredom is added. Every part of Imlac's description is pejorative, and Rasselas is thus convinced that he may safely open to the poet his own hope of escape. Imlac is willing to go along, and Rasselas is at once more comfortable: he has a friend, his first, in whom he can confide.

They decide to dig their way through a cave going into the mountain barrier. They are soon tired, but Johnson gives Imlac one of his own favorite devices for attacking a large project: split it into manageable pieces and you will not be discouraged. Do a little and a sense of accomplishment will carry you forward to tackle the next piece. With this technique they make good progress until, one day, they are discovered by Rasselas' favorite sister, Nekayah, who declares that she will accompany them. Rasselas agrees, regretting only that he had not shown his confidence in her by "a voluntary communication," a nice touch on Johnson's part which shows the young man's growing sensitivity to others.

At length they escape. The princess is apprehensive of the unknown and so is Rasselas, though he thinks it "more manly" to conceal the fact. He has taken one more step, emotionally as well as literally, into the world of maturity. They reach Cairo, where Rasselas is disturbed to find himself unhappy in the midst of cheerful crowds. Imlac suggests, with some shrewdness, that he look into his own mind to find out what may go on in the minds of others—that they may be unhappy also and only counterfeiting cheerfulness. Imlac also tells him, in his function as Johnson's mouthpiece, that solitude is to be dreaded since it delivers one to "the tyranny of reflection" (Ch. XVI). Unable to speak from experience on that point, Rasselas returns to his main idea and replies that a proper "choice of life" should lead to happiness. Again Imlac answers in the Johnsonian mode: choose something even if it cannot be absolutely proved to be the best: "he who would fix his condition upon incontestable reasons of preference, must live and die enquiring and deliberating" (Ch. XVI).

Rasselas now begins to look at the choices that others have made. He ventures into the diversions of the rich young men of the city, but he finds their pleasures mindless and superficial, and when he lectures these new friends they laugh at him, his first experience of "the horrour of derision." He survives this, of course, and next finds a venerable philosopher teaching a stoic indifference to the vicissitudes of life. Imlac warns Rasselas that professors "discourse like angels, but they live like men" (Ch. XVIII). He is unwilling to believe this, but in a few days he finds the stoic abandoning his philosophy to grieve the death of his daughter. Rasselas, increasing in stature as his contact with people is broadened, is humane enough to refrain from rebuking the old man for inconsistency.

He investigates the pastoral life as well; he quizzes the shepherds to find out whether their life holds more good than bad, but they are unused to verbal distinctions and cannot give him clear answers. The princess, however, is shallower than her brother and given to snap judgments: she would not live among such rude savages but would be quite willing to live, in storybook fashion, in a rustic glade with her elegant companions and a few clean sheep. For contrast, the party then visits the palace of a rich man, who lives in constant fear that the governor will confiscate his property. (Again, this is a theme repeated from *The Vanity of Human Wishes.*) In further contrast, they visit a hermit. The princess at first sight dislikes him; when she hears his cheerful discourse, however, she repents her hasty judgment. With such small touches Johnson slowly builds up his characterizations. As soon as Rasselas begins to find the hermit's way of life attractive, because there is no evil in it, the man says that he is about to return to society, the advantages of which may outweigh its disadvantages. Moreover, he feels that "the life of a solitary man will be certainly miserable, but not certainly devout."

While in Cairo, Rasselas visits an "assembly" of the learned which bears a remarkable resemblance to Johnson's Club. It contains disputatious egotists, detractors, and a young man who is sure that the hermit is a hypocrite. An older philosopher suffering from delusions of certainty declares that if one will cooperate with the universe, all will be well. Rasselas, stupefied with this flatulent banality, is silent; this the sage interprets as assent. (Throughout the novel the reader will be reminded of Candide and his "best of all possible worlds." Voltaire's hero and Johnson's have a certain innocence in common. By a coincidence which rules out influence, the two books appeared almost simultaneously, in 1759.)

The princess, who is looking for happiness in domestic life, finds that the poor do not easily forgive a Lady Bountiful; she also discovers something more generally interesting, that domestic discord is more common than domestic bliss. There is rivalry between children and parents, between children themselves, and even between parents. This report makes Rasselas think for a moment of remaining single, but the princess, reflecting Johnson's own views, is firm on this matter: "Marriage has many pains, but celibacy has no pleasures."

Rasselas begins to realize now that as a king his power to do good and allay discontent will be limited. He has become realistically aware that fewer subjects can be rewarded than will be disappointed, and that affection will sometimes sway justice. The princess, in her turn, has a moment of insight, and realizes that natural and political evils usually touch good and bad persons equally. The characterization at this point seems to be subordinate to Johnson's presentation of his philosophy.

The same may be said of the end of the next chapter. (Johnson likes to close with a witty remark, almost in the way each act of a Restoration comedy ends in a verse tag.) Rasselas in another discussion of marriage with his sister utters the fatuous observation that the world "must be peopled" by marriage or without. Nekayah replies: "I see no danger that the present generation should omit to leave successors behind them: we are not now enquiring for the world, but for ourselves" (Ch. XXVIII). The wit is more characteristic of Johnson than of Nekayah.

When this subject is temporarily exhausted, Imlac points out that in discussing the choice of life they are neglecting to live. He suggests that they should do some sight-seeing. Rasselas sturdily objects: "my business is with man," but Imlac corrects him, saying that the monuments show the progress of the human mind, the most "useful" part of history, and so the next day they visit the Pyramids. Pekuah, the companion of the princess, is afraid to enter and remains outside. Imlac lectures the party on the vacuity of these monuments—royal power, satiated with pleasure, has found nothing better to do with life. Properly impressed, they go back outside and find that Pekuah and her two maids have been kidnapped by a band of Arabs.

Months pass, the princess despairs of seeing Pekuah again and thinks of retiring from the world. Imlac gives her some advice on how to meet bereavement: "Do not suffer life to stagnate; it will grow muddy for want of motion: commit yourself again to the current of the world" (Ch. XXXV). And Rasselas persuades her to postpone her retirement for a year. Within that time not only does her grief become bearable but Pekuah is discovered and ransomed. She has found captivity an educationally rewarding experience: she has learned some astronomy from her captor, who was surprised to find that some women have brains; she has learned a little about men; and she has found that harem life is uninspiring.

Rasselas had meantime discovered the pleasures of learning and begins to think of a life of literary retirement. Imlac, however, knows an astronomer whose forty solitary years of observation and calculation have addled his mind so that he thinks he can control the sun and the weather. His story is used by Johnson to show the different degrees of maturity of the three young people: Rasselas, who has developed most in his understanding of people, heard it soberly; the princess, who is a cultivated lady, smiled; and Pekuah, whose reactions tend to be visceral, was convulsed with laughter. Johnson is speaking through Imlac when he observes that the astronomer's knowledge and virtues are both great and rare; unfortunately, insanity may come to anyone. "Of the uncertainties of our present state, the most dreadful and alarming is the uncertain continuance of reason." Thus Johnson's fear for his own stability surfaces, and once again he measures his characters: the princess stops smiling, since illness is not amusing to a lady; Pekuah is abashed, since she has been rebuked; and Rasselas wants to know more about mental illness.

Johnson now comes to his most profound point of psychological analysis, a total rejection of the concept of the normal. Mental disorders, Imlac says, are much more common than it is commonly believed. Indeed, "if we speak with rigorous exactness, no human mind is in its right state" (Ch. XLIV). If the "right state" does not exist in any given individual, it does not, for purposes of comparison, exist at all. This is a far cry from Dryden's "Great wits are sure to madness near allied / And thin partitions do their bounds divide," for there are no partitions and no boundaries; the norm does not exist. Johnson's experience with melancholia is familiar to readers of his life, but it may be worth mentioning that this statement in *Rasselas* comes close to the nadir of his own life, almost exactly between the death of his wife in

1752 and his meeting Mrs. Thrale, an anchor of his later years, in 1765.

As Rasselas and his party are walking along the Nile, they meet an elderly sage who is still in full possession of his faculties. Although he had neither mother nor wife to rejoice in his accomplishments (nor, then, did Johnson) he has reached a sort of middling serenity—he is neither wholly triumphant nor wholly dejected. Once more Johnson uses a character to point up the relative maturity of the three young people, and the order is the same as before: Rasselas is satisfied that "the noon of life might be bright, if the evening could be calm." He does not demand more than some "ease" in the decline and weakness of old age. This attitude is, however, too complex for the two women. The princess dismisses old age as querulous, and Pekuah thinks the sage must be older than he looks. Johnson, as often, ends the chapter on a lighter note. Everyone is tired, and the ladies hope that Imlac will delay the sunrise.

This comment on controlling the sun leads naturally to a visit to the half-mad astronomer, whose confidence they gradually obtain. Their friendship brings him back to the ordinary world, and he admits that he has chosen the wrong course. Even now he fears the chains of solitude, and he has some vague notions of guilt that he may be letting the sun and the weather run along without his necessary guidance. This impels Imlac to give him some good advice on superstition, melancholy, and the illusion of guilt, and he ends with a ringing affirmation of reason, coupled with the most down-to-earth prescription for dealing with his problem: "Open your heart to the influence of the light, which, from time to time, breaks in upon you: when scruples importune you, which you in your lucid moments know to be vain, do not stand to parley, but fly to business or to Pekuah, and keep this thought always prevalent, that you are only one atom of the mass of humanity, and have neither such virtue nor vice, as that you should be singled out for supernatural favours or afflictions" (Ch. XLVI).

As the novel approaches its end the party visits the catacombs where they talk about the nature of the soul, particularly whether it can inhere in matter. Nekayah, practical to the last, sees no great use in the question. Rasselas turns the discussion to the idea of the immortality of the soul, in which he believes, as did Johnson, in contrast to the shortness of human life, commenting that the dead lying in front of them were perhaps snatched away while thinking of the choice of life.

The last chapter is headed "The conclusion, in which nothing is concluded." Johnson will not let Pekuah head a convent, or the princess a college of intellectual women, or Rasselas a state, as they wish, or marry them off, as the eighteenth-century reader probably expected. No loose ends are tied up. Instead, in the last sentence, they decide to go back to Abyssinia.

This is, then, a novel of beginnings, of initiation. Its characters learn something of the world outside of the womb (the Happy Valley), and they return to their home country, though not to the Valley. To the exotic novel, and the novel of initiation, Johnson has added something else, the novel without an ending. It is the first one in English. *Tristram Shandy* and *A Sentimental Journey* soon followed.

IV

Shakespeare

In 1765, after twenty years of frustrated, delayed, and sporadic preparation, Johnson published the eight thick volumes of his edition of Shakespeare. We might pause for a moment to look at his predecessors, in order to evaluate his accomplishment. In the seventeenth century there were no *edited* editions of Shakespeare, in the modern sense of the word. The four folios, each very expensive, were *compiled*, rather, from whatever manuscript or printed sources were available, and were without notes. In 1709, the year of Johnson's birth, Rowe, the dramatist, brought out an annotated and emended edition which also contained the first biography of Shakespeare. Pope followed suit in 1725 with an edition marked in its emendations more by enthusiasm than by knowledge of Elizabethan language or by concern for what Shakespeare actually wrote. But Pope's preface is an important landmark in Shakespearean criticism. Lewis Theobald's attack on Pope's edition is soundly based on superior learning, but his own edition of 1734 shows more pedantry than judgment. Editions by Sir Thomas Hanmer and by William Warburton in the 1740's were amateurish and of little scholarly significance.

In comparison with all of these, Johnson's edition is scholarly in the best sense: he applies the same standards long demanded of editions of the Greek and Latin classics. By virtue of his work on the *Dictionary*, he knew more about the language of Shakespeare's time than any of his predecessors. He owned a copy of the First Folio and used it as his basic text, but he was also aware that the quartos had, in some cases at least, an important and independent authority. He had borrowed those that Garrick owned and had at least glanced at them. He did not, however, collate them carefully against the Folio texts. He was thoroughly familiar with all of the earlier eighteenth-century editions and quoted from them freely, so that his is sometimes known as the first variorum edition.

The chief virtues of Johnson's edition are a reasonably reliable text, supported by enough variants to give an ample range of critical conjecture; next, considerable background information on Shakespeare's sources from Charlotte Lennox's *Shakespear Illustrated*, for which he had written a dedication; and, probably by far the most important, an analysis of a great many characters in the notes on the plays, in which he displays his sound common sense, his sensitive and sympathetic reading of the plays, and his remarkable absence of crippling preconceptions.

He begins his Preface by outlining the basis for his critical approach, remarking that when we are dealing with matters not capable of scientific proof, we handle them by comparison with other works of the same kind. We appeal to "observation and experience." The effect of a long lapse of time is important in such attempts at evaluation, since frequent comparison will have confirmed to us the value of a work of art. He observes that Shakespeare had been dead long enough for the influence of any chance topicality in his plays to have vanished, as well as the temporary influence of friendship or enmity.

The first of Shakespeare's particular excellences in Johnson's view is his just representation of "general nature": his characters are "the genuine progeny of common humanity, such as the world will always supply. . . . (*A Johnson Reader*, p. 317.) It is interesting to note that this is almost a paraphrase, or restatement, of one of Johnson's fundamental ideas, that human nature is always and everywhere basically the same. Although the basis of Shakespeare's characterization is general, he is nevertheless able to keep his personages distinct. In this connection, Johnson makes the more radical statement that "Shakespeare has no heroes; his scenes are occupied only by men, who act and speak as the reader thinks that he should himself have spoken or acted on the same occasion." (p. 319.) (Luckily perhaps for Johnson's argument, he adduces no examples: we are not required to put ourselves in the place of Lear or Cleopatra.) He notes that Shakespeare's sentiments are in accord with real life and that his dialogue is "determined by the incident" and "seems . . . to have been gleaned . . . out of common conversation, and common occurrences." (p. 318.) (The use of "seems" is just right here: Johnson is saying that Shakespeare gives us the sense of actuality, which is more important than any transcription of actuality.) Furthermore, Shakespeare shows the variety of passions found in life itself, unlike other dramatists, who use love as the universal motivation. In short, Johnson finds in the plays "human sentiments in human language. . . ." (pp. 319–20.) The objections of Dennis and Rymer that the Romans are not Roman enough and of Voltaire that it is improper to represent Hamlet's uncle as drunk, Johnson sweeps aside as "the petty cavils of petty minds": Shakespeare was dealing with "general nature," not with the merely Roman or the ideally royal. (p. 320.) The recurrence of the word "nature," one of the most chameleon of eighteenth-century critical terms, is significant; it stands here for life as observed by any competent person.

The compilers of the First Folio, Johnson says, considered a comedy to be a play which ended happily, and a tragedy, a play which ended unhappily, but which was not necessarily more dignified nor more elevated than comedy. "History was a series of actions" not clearly distinguished from tragedy. (p. 322.) But in all three types designated in the Folio, Shakespeare's method was the same—"an interchange of seriousness and merriment, by which the mind is softened at one time, and exhilarated at another." (p. 322.) Moreover, Shakespeare succeeded: "as he commands us, we laugh or mourn. . . ." (Parenthetically, I might note that when Johnson needs monosyllabic words he uses them to great effect.)

Shakespeare's plays are thus compositions of a distinct kind, exhibiting real life, "which partakes of good and evil, joy and sorrow, mingled with endless variety of proportion and innumerable modes of combination; and expressing the course of the world, in which the loss of one is the gain of another; in which, at the same time, the reveller is hasting to his wine, and the mourner burying his friend; in which the malignity of one is sometimes defeated by the frolick of another; and many mischiefs and many benefits are done and hindered without design." (p. 320.) Johnson therefore dismisses the classical objection to mixing tragic and comic scenes, declaring it irrelevant since the plays are not either comedies or tragedies. Such intermingling is indeed "contrary to the rules of criticism . . . but there is always an appeal open from criticism to nature." (p. 321.) It is plain that Johnson was bent on analyzing what Shakespeare had done, instead of legislating what the drama ought to be.

Johnson makes clear his preference for Shakespeare's comedy, which, he believes, arose out of Shakespeare's "natural disposition." As is Johnson's habit, he summarizes in an epigram: "His tragedy seems to be skill, his comedy to be instinct." (p. 323.) The comedies had endured to Johnson's time because their characters were motivated by "genuine passion" and were very little influenced by the superficialities of time and place. Moreover, the dialogue of the comic characters, Johnson points out, belongs to the level of speech "above grossness and below refinement," which tends to remain unchanged with the passage of time, a language which "is probably to be sought in the common intercourse of life, among those who speak only to be understood. . . ." (p. 324.) This is very close to what Wordsworth, thirty-three years later, defined as the proper language of poetry.

Johnson's discussion of Shakespeare's faults makes clear to the modern reader a basic disagreement of critical judgment between his time and ours. Shakespeare seems to Johnson to have written "without any moral purpose" (p. 324): he made "no just distribution of good or evil." In other words, good is not uniformly rewarded nor evil always punished. Furthermore, his plots are loosely constructed, his dialogue sometimes "reciprocations of smartness," and the jests of his comic characters "commonly gross." (p. 325.) Johnson does not seem to have realized that a reader might appeal all of these judgments to Johnson's own statement earlier in the Preface that Shakespeare was looking at life and reflecting what he found there. Had any reader so objected, Johnson's answer would no doubt have been prompt: Shakespeare was right to reflect life up to a point, but he had above all a duty to serve the higher aim of writing, which was to teach.

Johnson also thinks that there is too much "pomp of diction" in Shakespeare's narration, but he is more seriously disturbed by what he considers Shakespeare's failure to maintain a consistent tone in his "soft and pathetick" passages without "some idle conceit, or contemptible equivocation." (p. 326.) That word-play, like the alternation of comic and tragic, might be derived from life, seems never to have occurred to him. He accordingly now brings into action the full force of his powers of rhetoric against an object hardly worth it, the pun.

Johnson never really thought of play as a rewarding sort of human activity. That it should occasionally or frequently involve adults, he could not really believe. Hence, when he had decided that Shakespeare had spent a good deal of his genius on word-play, he was outraged to a degree which is hard to understand. But there is no doubt whatever as to his position:

> A quibble is to Shakespeare, what luminous vapours are to the traveller; he follows it at all adventures, it is sure to lead him out of his way, and sure to engulf him in the mire. It has some malignant power over his mind, and its fascinations are irresistible. Whatever be the dignity or profundity of his disquisition, whether he be enlarging knowledge or exalting affection, whether he be amusing attention with incidents, or enchaining it in suspense, let but a quibble spring up before him, and he leaves his work unfinished. A quibble is the golden apple for which he will always turn aside from his career, or stoop from his elevation. A quibble, poor and barren as it is, gave him such delight, that he was content to purchase it, by the sacrifice of reason, propriety and truth. A quibble was to him the fatal Cleopatra for which he lost the world, and was content to lose it. (p. 327.)

If the reader is inclined to put this barrage down to a temporary blindness in Johnson, I can only refer him to Boswell's *Life*, where over and over again Johnson rejects the claim that Burke is witty, on the ground that verbal play cannot be wit.

The application of the classical requirements of the unity of time, place, and action to Shakespeare's plays is Johnson's next concern. He is satisfied that in the comedies and tragedies the unity of action is adequately observed, and he considers it irrelevant in the histories. Those of time and place, he says, had been thought necessary to make the drama credible. But like Dryden before him and Coleridge later, he denies that this is needed by the spectator, who is never actually deceived by what happens on the stage or at a loss to supply with his imagination what is needed. In other words, Johnson gives more credit to the audience than the usual classical critic was willing to do. He concludes that an observation of these unities is "not essential to a just drama."

Rather uncharacteristically, Johnson is not sure that he has persuaded the reader to his point of view. Nevertheless, he has no more to say about the unities, and now turns to the question of how, in general, we should approach an appraisal of Shakespeare's performance. We should judge Shakespeare in the light of the culture of his own time, which "was yet struggling to emerge from barbarity." He comments on the general Elizabethan taste for the marvelous as continuing from an older tradition and indicates that Shakespeare naturally had to write for a relatively unsophisticated audience. This leads to a discussion of Shakespeare's sources. Sometimes they looked backward to the medieval, as in *As You Like It*, sometimes they were familiar from tradition, as in the English history plays, and sometimes, as in the Roman plays, the source was a contemporary translation of Plutarch. Whatever his sources, Shakespeare surpassed all authors but Homer in achieving "the first purpose of a writer, by exciting restless and unquenchable curiosity, and compelling him that reads his work to read it through." (p. 334.)

Johnson has observed that all of Shakespeare's known sources were English, and this leads him to agree with Ben Jonson's report that Shakespeare "had small Latin and less Greek." Whatever he may have lacked in formal learning, however, was more than compensated for by his perspicacious observation of people and of the inanimate world. But the Shakespearean trait which Johnson most admires is originality, the same trait which he uses as a principal touchstone in *The Lives of the Poets:* "Perhaps it would not be easy to find any authour, except Homer, who invented so much as Shakespeare, who so much advanced the studies which he cultivated, or effused so much novelty upon his age or country. The form, the characters, the language, and the shows of the English drama are his." (p. 340.)

He also praises Shakespeare's versification, ascribing to him, "unless Spenser may divide it with him," the discovery of how much the English language could be softened into "smoothness and harmony," qualities which Johnson always admired in English poetry. He delighted to see the hand of a master subduing some of the natural roughness of the language.

After this high praise, Johnson again looks at one of Shakespeare's faults: his failure to do the best he was capable of. Here Johnson condemns him for being willing only to satisfy his audience without going beyond that point to satisfy himself. Furthermore, says Johnson, he did not care enough for future readers to go to the trouble of publishing his works, but, indifferent to their fate, left them to be collected posthumously. A modern scholar would perhaps suggest that Shakespeare wished to keep his plays out of the hands of the rival company and therefore did not publish them.

Johnson now gives a short history of the editions, with which he has worked enough to be certain that the First Folio is the only folio with textual value. For the most part he is generous to the eighteenth-century editors, particularly to Pope and Warburton, both of whom had praised him when he was struggling and unknown. When Johnson turns to contemporary critics of Shakespeare, he is less gentle. Of Thomas Edwards and Benjamin Heath he writes almost in the tone of *The Dunciad:* "The one stings like a fly, sucks a little blood, takes a gay flutter, and returns for more; the other bites like a viper, and would be glad to leave inflammations and gangrene behind him." (p. 348.) Another has been "unable to restrain the rage of emendation, though his ardour is ill seconded by his skill." A fourth has made "some useful observations." (p. 349.)

Johnson's editorial principles are conservative: the original editors, with some sort of genuine copy before them, are more to be trusted than a modern editor relying upon intuition. He has an amusing remark on how to make footnotes which tear one's enemies apart and yet seem to promote genuine criticism. Then he offers every student some excellent advice: First "read every play from the first scene to the last, with utter negligence of all his commentators" (p. 357), since stopping at the notes will chill one's interest.

At last Johnson comes to a discussion of his own editorial procedures. In addition to explanatory and textual notes, he has a third sort not common in twentieth-century editions; these are "judicial, by which faults and beauties are remarked." As one looks through the volumes, the "judicial" are relatively infrequent; there are probably enough, however, to provide a reader with some guide-posts to Johnson's tastes. There are more such notes on some plays than on others; not from design, he says disarmingly, but from chance and caprice. This remark almost allows us to see him in his study, where one day, reading and writing with excitement, his comments come quickly and easily, whereas on the next day torpor may have intervened.

He does think of his reader, who will want to make his own judgment and form his own opinion: "it is natural to delight more in what we find or make, than in what we receive." (p. 351.) As a good teacher, he will partly point out the way and partly let the inexperienced student find it, neither dictating his own judgment nor leaving the student wholly to his own devices.

Johnson appended to most plays short general comments on faults and excellences. Perhaps the reader will welcome a sample from one of these since they are highly characteristic of Johnson and show, in a short space, a relaxed and appreciative attitude. He used a single such comment for both parts of *Henry IV*. There is perhaps nothing particularly noteworthy in what he says about the two plays or about the character of Hal or Percy. What he says about Falstaff, however (about a quarter of the whole comment), is pure Johnson. He shifts suddenly and unexpectedly into the familiar and affectionate "thou":

> But Falstaff unimitated, unimitable Falstaff, how shall I describe thee? Thou compound of sense and vice; of sense which may be admired but not esteemed, of vice which may be despised, but hardly detested. Falstaff is a character loaded with faults, and with those faults which naturally produce contempt. He is a thief, and a glutton, a coward, and a boaster, always ready to cheat the weak, and prey upon the poor; to terrify the timorous and insult the defenceless. At once obsequious and malignant, he satirises in their absence those whom he lives by flattering. He is familiar with the prince only as an agent of vice, but of this familiarity he is so proud as not only to be supercilious and haughty with common men, but to think his interest of importance to the duke of Lancaster. Yet the man thus corrupt, thus despicable, makes himself necessary to the prince that despises him, by the most pleasing of all qualities, perpetual gaiety, by an unfailing power of exciting laughter,

which is the more freely indulged, as his wit is not of the splendid or ambitious kind, but consists in easy escapes and sallies of levity, which make sport but raise no envy. It must be observed that he is stained with no enormous or sanguinary crimes, so that his licentiousness is not so offensive but that it may be borne for his mirth. (*The Plays of William Shakespeare*, 1765, IV.356.)

Johnson's comments on the character of Falstaff are a noteworthy example of the development and liberalization of his critical ideas. Fifteen years earlier, he had expressed strikingly different ideas in his *Rambler* essay No. 4 on a hero of fiction (Tom Jones, perhaps) who had both good and bad traits. In the earlier statement, Johnson's position is clear—and inflexible: such a hero should not be permitted in fiction, inasmuch as the reader is seduced by the attractive qualities of the hero into accepting his vices also as an inseparable part of his character. On a point to point comparison, it might be difficult to prefer Falstaff, morally, to Tom Jones. Indeed, many of us would condone in a thoughtless youth what we would condemn in thoughtless middle age. Johnson does not, like one or two eighteenth-century critics, particularly Maurice Morgann, deny Falstaff's vices. He just accepts them.

The Preface is a major statement of Johnson's views. It is noteworthy for its remarkable freedom from critical bias, for an enthusiastic salute to Shakespeare's originality, for an acute analysis of his language, and for a concise statement of his differentiation of characters. The edition itself is so full of information and suggestive comment that it has been mined by successive editors down to the present.

V

Political Tracts

THE NUMBER of political tracts of the eighteenth century which are still remembered today is not large because the issues which produced them have become obscure. Defoe and Swift, Addison and Steele occasionally wrote political pamphlets, but these are not widely read today. Who now cares about the War of the Spanish Succession or the War of Jenkins' Ear? However, those pamphlets written on larger conflicts and greater issues, such as the American and French revolutions, are still of interest to modern readers. All of Johnson's four political tracts are of this kind.

They were suggested to him by Lord North's Ministry, but Johnson was sufficiently interested in the disputes he was asked to write about to enter wholeheartedly into the battle. The granting of his government pension was far enough in the past, eight years, that he was able to think of himself as independent of governmental commands, though he was not oblivious of a minister's wish for a changed sentence or two—a nice distinction.

In political controversy, as in any kind of fighting without benefit of rules or referee, strict fairness or accuracy is not to be expected, and Johnson was neither entirely fair nor always accurate. The political controversialist is, after all, out to win.

The first pamphlet, *The False Alarm* (1770), is an attempt to show that the excitement raised by barring John Wilkes from the House of Commons was without merit, even though the action deprived the voters of Middlesex of "a Briton's birthright —representation in parliament." (*Works*, 1825, VI.156.) (This is an interesting echo of the Colonial battle cry, "Taxation without representation is tyranny.") There is a certain agreeable irony in Johnson's being asked to write on such a subject, for he thoroughly disapproved of Wilkes, even though Wilkes was a boon companion of Boswell's. The famous dinner party when Johnson had to sit next to Wilkes was still to come.

Johnson begins with a calm and typical generalization: whereas the progress of science ("philosophy") has freed men from the terrors once inspired by eclipses and meteors, political knowledge has not progressed far enough to relieve them of such equally baseless terrors as are spread by "publick faction." Wilkes as a subject is disposed of in one sentence: "Lampoon itself would disdain to speak ill of him, of whom no man speaks well," (p. 156) which neatly indicates that Johnson's pamphlet is not a mere lampoon, but a discussion of a more elevated nature.

The first point in his argument is that the Commons must be the sole judge of the qualifications of its members, or else it cannot be coordinate with the other parts of the government, but becomes subordinate. Examining the successive expulsions of Wilkes in 1769, because he had been convicted of sedition and impiety, he concludes that the Commons, having excluded Wilkes, had the power to declare by resolution the runner-up elected. The Wilkes faction had argued that the Commons in excluding Wilkes had taken to itself the power of the whole legislature in passing an act, which the lower house, by itself, cannot legally do. Johnson argues, elaborately, that the Commons passed not a law but a resolution; that a law differs from a resolution in that it is permanent, whereas a resolution dies with the dissolution of the House of Commons; a law requires the assent of both houses and of the king, and a resolution is the action of one part only, and concerns, really, only its internal affairs. All this is perhaps unobjectionable, but it is also a little more sober than is appropriate for the fight that is shaping up.

Johnson soon drops his modest and sober tone and returns to the tone of controversy. He speaks of his opponents as "puny" antagonists (he can use short and pungent adjectives, and the contempt he expresses by this means is more difficult to shout down than his arguments) and uses irony: in this "alarming crisis" if the House is thus easily able to expel members, one group may turn out all the English: "Every one knows the malice, the subtlety, the industry, the vigilance, and the greediness of the Scots." (p. 168.) Unfortunately, a substantial number of Englishmen probably misunderstood the irony and took this passage at its face value; the Earl of Bute had only recently been forced out of power by popular clamor from the fear that the Scots were gaining too much influence with George III.

But Johnson changes the tone from irony to a mild contempt as he takes up one of his favorite themes: political crises affect few people: "The sun has risen, and the corn has grown, and, whatever talk has been of the danger of property, yet he that ploughed the field commonly reaped it; and he that built a house was master of the door; the vexation excited by injustice suffered, or supposed to be suffered, by any private man, or single community, was local and temporary, it neither spread far, nor lasted long." (p. 170.)

He observes that agitators whip up apprehension among common people by the use of the usual emotive words: "pensions and places, venality and corruption, oppression and invasion, slavery and ruin," (p. 172) and describes their activities in his own more original emotive words in the next sentence: "malignity . . . folly . . . indeterminate wickedness . . . ridiculous petitions." There follows a delightful sarcastic sketch of the birth and development of petitions circulated by such agitators: an "ejected placeman" goes down to his country friends, who call a meeting, complete with food and drink. The local Cicero speaks, and as a matter of course everyone approves the petition as read: "Those who are sober enough to write, add their names, and the rest would sign it, if they could." Just the right touch of contempt. The petition goes from town to town: "One man signs, because he hates the papists; another, because he has vowed destruction to the turnpikes; one, because it will vex the parson; another, because he owes his landlord nothing; one, because he is rich; another, because he is poor; one, to show that he is not afraid; and another, to show that he can write." (p. 173.)

Johnson finally contrasts the present discontent with the action of the House of Commons with two earlier rebellions, both, in his opinion, based on disputes of genuine importance: "The civil war was fought for what each army called, and believed, the best religion and the best government. The struggle in the reign of Anne, was to exclude or restore an exiled king. We are now disputing, with almost equal animosity, whether Middlesex shall be represented, or not, by a criminal from a gaol." (p. 177.) Contempt is the weapon again. But one surprise remains: having dealt with Wilkes and his Whig friends Johnson turns to the Tories and is disturbed that they have regarded the struggle "with frigid neutrality." They, at least, should have recognized that at last they have a king "who wishes to be the common father of all his people." This is perhaps Johnson's sharpest criticism of his own party, as it is at the same time his most graceful acknowledgement of his Hanoverian king.

The pamphlet ends with direct advice: "As a man inebriated only by vapours soon recovers in the open air; a nation discontented to madness, without any adequate cause, will return to its wits and its allegiance, when a little pause has cooled it to reflection. . . . Let the court despise the faction, and the disappointed people will soon deride it." (p.178.)

Johnson's next political pamphlet was *Thoughts on the Late Transactions Respecting Falkland's Islands* (1771), which generally follows the organization of the preceding one. It opens with a splendid generalization on war: "To proportion the eagerness of contest to its importance seems too hard a task for human wisdom. The pride of wit has kept ages busy in the discussion of useless questions, and the pride of power has destroyed armies, to gain or to keep unprofitable possessions." (p. 179.) He comments on the relief of all at the recent ending of the Seven Years' War, only to have the peace threatened by "a new concussion," a struggle for "a few spots of earth" in the South Atlantic.

He continues in the grand manner as he sketches in the discovery of America, the exploitation of its mineral riches by Spain, and the belated voyages of the English in the last years of Elizabeth I when the Falklands were, apparently, first seen by Captain Davis. Their succeeding history he gives quickly: other landfalls by Hawkins, by the Dutch, French, and Spanish, and by Captain John Strong, who "probably" gave them their present name. (Johnson refers to Strong's unpublished journal in the British Museum, which is surprising inasmuch as original research is most unusual for him in such ephemeral work as this.)

The casual international attitude toward the islands changed sharply when in George Anson's *Voyage* it was suggested that the islands had a strategic value in any British attack on Chile.

Johnson acutely observes: "Scarcely any degree of judgment is sufficient to restrain the imagination from magnifying that on which it is long detained" (p. 182); he has concluded that the navigator, frustrated by the ill-success of his voyage, inflated the importance of the islands out of all proportion.

The Falklands, says Johnson, are "a bleak and gloomy solitude, an island, thrown aside from human use, stormy in winter, and barren in summer; an island, which not the southern savages have dignified with habitation; where a garrison must be kept in a state that contemplates with envy the exiles of Siberia; of which the expense will be perpetual, and the use only occasional; and which, if fortune smile upon our labours, may become a nest of smugglers in peace, and in war the refuge of future bucaniers." (p. 198.)

That settlement of the islands might be useful in wartime, Johnson admits. "But war is not the whole business of life; it happens but seldom, and every man, either good or wise, wishes its frequency were still less." (p. 183.) And warlike preparations, he adds with considerable subtlety, "generate malignity" and are therefore dangerous in themselves. In times of peace, the islands would be of use only to those British merchants penetrating Spanish South America, "the triumphant robber and successful cheat" (the two adjectives are in Johnson's best and briefest manner, defining his position without further argument). Such a merchant-brigand, moreover, will bring home as a product of his commerce something Britain does not need, "a mind hardened in evil, too proud for reproof, and too stupid for reflection. . . ." (p. 184.)

Johnson presents a detailed account of the events leading to an encounter between an English garrison and some Spanish vessels which forced the English to evacuate the islands in 1770. When that news reached England, the fleet was readied for war, but the Spanish government made concessions in time, disavowing the mission of its own vessels and restoring the port to the British. Thus the determination of prior right to the islands was put off to the indefinite future.

The patriots, however, wanted Spain to acknowledge England's sovereignty over the islands, and Johnson attacks "the feudal gabble" of Pitt, without naming him, a man whose "splendour of character . . . once illuminated the kingdom, then dazzled, and afterwards inflamed it. . . ." (p. 197.) For one of the "patriots," however, Johnson shows some respect—Junius, the anonymous writer of letters to the *Public Advertiser* now thought to be Sir Philip Francis, a minor politician who carried his secret to his grave. Johnson calls him "one of the few writers of his despicable faction, whose name does not disgrace the page of an opponent." (p. 198.) He is, to be sure, only setting up Junius in order to pummel and flay him, but for the moment he delays.

For the legal title to these barren islands, the patriots were ready to wage war, "the last of remedies . . . the extremity of evil. . . ." And Johnson's indignation mounts as he considers "with what coolness and indifference the greater part of mankind see war commenced." (p. 199.) He is chilled with horror at the incidental causes of death in a war: "Of the thousands and ten thousands, that perished in our late contests with France and Spain, a very small part ever felt the stroke of an enemy; the rest languished in tents and ships, amidst damps and putrefaction; pale, torpid, spiritless, and helpless; gasping and groaning, unpitied among men, made obdurate by long continuance of hopeless misery; and were, at last, whelmed in pits, or heaved into the ocean, without notice and without remembrance." (p. 199.) He is indignant at the thought of businessmen at home growing rich from military contracts, and when he considers the greedy hopes for an easy conquest of South America, he is contemptuous: "We shall throw brass and iron out of our houses, and nothing but silver will be seen among us." (p. 202.) (So much for Johnson's supposed dependence on big words, by the way.)

He reinforces his opposition to waging war for such a place, and for such reasons, by describing the disastrous English forays against the Spanish in the Americas from Elizabethan times to his own day, ending poignantly with an expedition in which his dear friend Dr. Bathurst was lost: "In the last war the Havanna was taken; at what expense is too well remembered. May my country be never cursed with such another conquest!" (p. 203.)

He now turns with some zest to Junius, a spokesman for the patriots: "out of the reach of danger, he has been bold; out of the reach of shame, he has been confident." (p. 205.) As to his rhetoric and his power, "Let us abstract from his wit the vivacity of insolence, and withdraw from his efficacy the sympathetick favour of plebeian malignity; I do not say that we shall leave him nothing; the cause that I defend, scorns the help of falsehood; but if we leave him only his merit, what will be his praise?" Nothing.

Johnson is equally effective in attacking less important members of the patriotic faction and shows his skill in picking out single abusive words—"the inferiour bellowers of sedition." (p. 211.) In that same paragraph in the first edition of the pamphlet occurred his famous abuse of George Grenville: "Let him not, however, be depreciated in his grave. He had powers not universally possessed: if he could have got the money, he could have counted it." (*Falkland's Islands*, 1771, p. 68.) After the pamphlet had been printed, Johnson was persuaded, either by the ministry or by his own judgment, to soften the passage thus: "He had powers not universally possessed: and if he sometimes erred, he was likewise sometimes right." (*Life*, II.135.) A final revision removed the last trace of sarcasm: "Let him not, however, be depreciated in his grave. If he was sometimes wrong, he was often right." (*Works*, 1825, VI.211.)

When Johnson considers the justice of Britain's agreement with Spain to put aside the question of prior right to the Falklands, he insists that the settlement was equitable and examines the pros and cons dispassionately. It is impossible for a modern reader to disagree that the flag-waving jingoists were both irrational and dangerous.

In the last pages of the pamphlet Johnson brings the argument to a relatively quiet close: the superpatriots have been discredited, he believes, and their warlike demands for sovereignty over the Falklands will be disregarded. The reputation of the nation is greater in Europe than it had been before the dispute with Spain. The vipers have turned out to be harmless, "and may, therefore, quietly slink into holes, and change their slough, unmolested and forgotten." (p. 214.)

The Patriot (1774), "addressed to the electors of Great Britain," is headed by an epigraph from Milton's second sonnet "On the detraction which followed upon my writing certain treatises":

> They bawl for freedom in their senseless mood,
> Yet still revolt when truth would set them free;
> License they mean, when they cry liberty,
> For who loves that must first be wise and good.

This is a rather curious choice for a man with a reputation as a sturdy Tory, but there are points of contact between Johnson's common sense and Milton's which might be remembered in connection with Johnson's not wholly sympathetic *Life of Milton* written a few years later. This short pamphlet is very similar in tone to Johnson's angry remark in 1775, "Patriotism is the last refuge of a scoundrel." (*Life*, II.348.) The focus of his attack in this pamphlet is, to some extent, the same as that of the two previous pamphlets, a group of politicians who have arrogated the word "patriot" to themselves as though they were the only ones who deserved it—implying, of course, that all of their opponents are unpatriotic—and who are using it as a shibboleth, hoping that their motives and their actions will be approved because of the label.

This pamphlet was occasioned by an approaching Parliamentary election. As usual, Johnson begins with a ringing generalization: "To improve the golden moment of opportunity, and catch the good that is within our reach, is the great art of life." (p. 214.) In this "saturnalian season" of choosing representatives everyone wishes to select patriots, but how can they be known? Some claim to be so "by an acrimonious and unremitting opposition to the court." (p. 215.) But this badge is not enough: "Patriotism is not necessarily included in rebellion. A man may hate his king, yet not love his country." A disaffected man may growl about "arbitrary power . . . to gratify his malice." Such a man, soon quieted by getting a place, is less dangerous than one who fills the newspapers "with sly hints of corruption and intrigue" from base motives, or tries to raise fears of Popery because Catholicism is allowed in Quebec, which had recently come under British control. Johnson, a Protestant, is quick to point out that "persecution is not more virtuous in a protestant than a papist" and that "in an age, where every mouth is open for *liberty of conscience*, it is equitable to show some regard to the conscience of a papist, who may be supposed, like other men, to think himself safest in his own religion; and that those, at least, who enjoy a toleration, ought not to deny it to our new subjects." (p. 218.)

A patriot loves the people, but if a politician looks principally to the poor and the profligate, he may be a "hearty fellow" but not necessarily a patriot. (p. 219.) A true patriot stirs up the "reasonable hopes" of the people, a false one deludes them with lavish promises. This last point leads Johnson once more to the subject of war, and he refers, by implication, to the Falkland Islands dispute: "As war is one of the heaviest of national evils, a calamity in which every species of misery is involved; as it sets the general safety to hazard, suspends commerce, and desolates the country; as it exposes great numbers to hardships, dangers, captivity, and death; no man, who desires the publick prosperity, will inflame general resentment by aggravating minute injuries, or enforcing disputable rights of little importance." (p. 220.)

Conversely, no patriot "wishes to see his country robbed of its rights," and this brings him to briefly discuss the American colonies: he observes that since they have accepted Britain's protection, "we may, therefore, subject them to government." Parliament may enact a law of capital punishment for the colonies; it can likewise impose taxes. He concedes that some innocent Bostonians have been injured along with the guilty (as when Parliament closed the port of Boston in retaliation for the Boston Tea Party), but this is unavoidable in acts of rebellion.

Johnson concludes the pamphlet rather abruptly by congratulating the recent Parliament for passing a law by which disputed elections will be tried with "scrupulousness and solemnity," and with the hope that the next House of Commons will act on the same principles as the last, but more consistently, and that the nation will reject those who "by deceiving the credulous with fictitious mischiefs, overbearing the weak by audacity of falsehood, by appealing to the judgment of ignorance, and flattering the vanity of meanness, by slandering honesty, and insulting dignity, have gathered round them whatever the kingdom can supply of base, and gross, and profligate; and 'raised by merit to this bad eminence,'[1] arrogate to themselves the name of patriots." (pp. 223–24.)

The pamphlet is noteworthy for two things: Johnson's reiterated abhorrence of war and his almost curt rejection of the American claims. He returns to the colonists in his next pamphlet.

Taxation no Tyranny; An Answer to the Resolutions and Address of the American Congress (1775), begins with a broad general statement quite moderate in tone: "In all the parts of human knowledge, whether terminating in science merely specu-

[1] *Paradise Lost,* II, 5–6, referring to Satan (slightly misquoted by Johnson).

lative, or operating upon life, private or civil, are admitted some fundamental principles, or common axioms, which, being generally received, are little doubted, and, being little doubted, have been rarely proved." (p. 224.) Of these, one is that "the supreme power of every community" has the right of taxation for "publick safety or publick prosperity." (p. 225.) (If we substitute "publick welfare" for "publick prosperity," the phrase has a very familiar ring, as it actually anticipates some of the most famous words of the United States *Constitution.*) Johnson, however, quickly drops the tone of sweet reasonableness as he turns on "those zealots of anarchy" who have denied Parliament's right to tax the Colonies. (p. 225.)

He finds that love of one's country has been supplanted by a new perversion, hatred: "These antipatriotick prejudices are the abortions of folly impregnated by faction, which, being produced against the standing order of nature, have not strength sufficient for long life. They are born only to scream and perish, and leave those to contempt or detestation, whose kindness was employed to nurse them into mischief." (pp. 225–26.)

Before discussing the constitutional question, Johnson deals with some practical matters and decides that taxation is not hurting American trade. Moreover, threats from three million Americans, who may "multiply with the fecundity of their own rattlesnakes," might induce England to attack before it is too late. (p. 227.) Using, ironically, the language of tragedy, Johnson comments that pity and terror unite with admiration in viewing the stance of the Bostonian heroes, who had been reported ready to abandon the city if the Stamp Act had not been repealed. He is contemptuous of the notion that those solid burghers would have preferred the liberty of starving in the forests to remaining in their comfortable houses.

Now he turns, more soberly, to the subject of the tax, by definition "a payment, exacted by authority, from part of the community, for the benefit of the whole." (p. 230.) (This is worse than commonplace, it is dull.) The Americans, he goes on, have not denied their obligation to help pay for their safety, but they have insisted that they themselves shall determine how they shall pay and how much. To show that there is no basis for the American position, he now analyzes the two different kinds of colonies, and here his discussion picks up greatly in liveliness. In the earliest times, he says, a restless adventurer gathered a band of fellow-spirits and, cutting off all ties to the homeland, set off to found a new society. But during the Age of Discovery the Spanish, Portuguese, and English colonies were extensions of the main body and did not sever themselves from it. (Characteristically, Johnson regrets that Columbus found the Spanish court cordial to him: "nor has any part of the world yet had reason to rejoice that he found, at last, reception and employment.")

A supporter of the American cause had pointed out that it was once considered illegal for the British Parliament to tax Ireland, and had insisted that the cases of Ireland and the American colonies were alike. Johnson counters with the reminder that in 1719 Parliament affirmed its right to legislate for Ireland, in spite of the fact that there was a legislature in Dublin. Johnson has already mentioned that a colony far distant from the central government must inevitably be granted greater power to regulate itself than a dependency closer to home. But he does not carry out this reasoning in a comparison of Ireland and the American colonies. Having stated the importance of distance, he does not pursue its implications and mentions it only once more. He is actually more interested, at the moment, in the legal aspects of the case not the practical ones, and in this respect his position is radically opposed to Burke's, whose point of view was regularly that of the politician, the practitioner of the art of the possible. Johnson therefore spends some time discussing the nature of the charters under which the colonies were founded; but, however interesting this is as seventeenth-century history, it has a dated and unreal air when applied to the situation existing in 1775.

Much more interesting is Johnson's argument that in any representative government power has been delegated by the electors. Moreover, only a tiny percentage of the inhabitants of the British Isles actually vote; the rest are nevertheless represented by the members of Parliament, and in any election the losing voters are in fact represented by those men they voted against. Nevertheless, the system works, and Johnson feels that the same "virtual representation" is as valid for the American colonials as for some new industrial town in England which has no direct representative at all. Finally, Johnson points out with some acerbity that the Americans have not asked for representation and do not want it: rather than pay taxes with representation, they want to govern themselves.

One of the liveliest parts of this pamphlet is the "Address" from an imaginary congress met in Cornwall to declare that county's independence from Great Britain. It consists of fifteen paragraphs of parody of the Congressional Address from Philadelphia; the parody is occasionally very close, elsewhere it departs from the original wildly enough to give zest to the performance. After a sonorous opening full of splendid ideas like "universal happiness," he continues, "But since, having long indulged the pleasing expectation, we find general discontent not likely to increase, or not likely to end in general defection, we resolve to erect alone the standard of liberty." (p. 255.) As to the presumptive original compact between the Cornishmen/Americans and the English, "We gave our ancestors no commission to settle the terms of future existence. They might be cowards that were frighted, or blockheads that were cheated. . . ." (p. 256.) And in reference to the American resolution to prohibit trade with Britain, "we will, after the tenth day of September, keep our tin in our own hands: you can be supplied from no other place, and must, therefore, comply, or be poisoned with the copper of your own kitchens." (p. 256.) The concluding sentence has the full Johnsonian roar: "If any Cornishman shall refuse his name to this just and laudable association, he shall be tumbled from St. Michael's mount, or buried alive in a tin-mine; and if any emissary shall be found seducing Cornishmen to their former state, he shall be smeared with tar, and rolled in feathers, and chased with dogs out of our dominions."

As Johnson returns to his direct attack he reiterates his belief that sheer greed is at the bottom of the American demands: "That any obligations should overpower their attention to profit, we have known them long enough not to expect." One English friend of the Americans has proposed that Britain grant all their demands, after which trade will continue much as before. Johnson has a typical retort: "One wild proposal is best answered by another. Let us restore to the French what we have taken from them. We shall see our colonists at our feet, when they have an enemy so near them. Let us give the Indians arms, and teach them discipline, and encourage them, now and then, to plunder a plantation." (p. 260.) Johnson pauses for breath, hoping that the trouble will end without bloodshed, but in a moment returns to the attack, mentioning that someone had proposed that the slaves should be set free (they had been set free in England); perhaps they might be given firearms for defense. . . . The reader is allowed to imagine the blacks attacking their former masters.

Johnson now turns angrily on the politicians at home who are encouraging the Americans, from low motives, he believes. Their pretended fears are baseless: "We are told, that the subjection of Americans may tend to the diminution of our own liberties; an event, which none but very perspicacious politicians are able to foresee. If slavery be thus fatally contagious, how is it that we hear the loudest yelps for liberty among the drivers of negroes?" (p. 262.)

Taxation No Tyranny ends weakly. Johnson supposes the dreadful possibility of Britain's being beaten by the Americans, who, he hopes, will then let in British goods on the same terms as those of other foreigners and allow an occasional Englishman to become a citizen without making him abjure his opinion of England. However dreadful this may have sounded to Johnson, it does not move a modern reader at all.

In general the four political pamphlets are successful: they effectively and forcefully present a comprehensible, mildly conservative position. Johnson is particularly good in his castigation of those who would go to war over unimportant disputes or consider war without exhausting every means of accommodation. Sometimes his contempt of the opposite view is expressed in sharp, biting wit; sometimes he boils over in anger. Throughout, he is readable.

VI

Journey to the Western Islands

The form of *A Journey to the Western Islands of Scotland* (1775) is loosely that of a topographical report on Boswell and Johnson's tour in the autumn of 1773; on the framework of this report are arranged Johnson's comments on life in that northern country. Before this trip Johnson had never been out of England, and he seized this opportunity to satisfy his curiosity about a civilization which had been foreign until 1707. He arrived in Scotland on 14 August, and returned to England on 22 November, having at the age of sixty-four survived one hundred days of very rugged travel. Since no map accompanied Johnson's book, I may mention that Johnson begins his account with their leaving Edinburgh; they continue counterclockwise up the east coast through St. Andrews and Aberdeen, then north and west near the coast to Inverness, down to Fort Augustus, west through the Islands, back to the mainland, to Glasgow, and return again to Edinburgh, after a side-trip to Boswell's home, Auchinleck. There are few entries characteristic of a diary and almost no reported conversations, except in the third person. In these two respects the *Journey* contrasts sharply with Boswell's *Tour to the Hebrides,* which is primarily a diary and famous especially for its reports of direct dialogue.

The beginning is characteristically Johnsonian: a personal remark, "I had desired to visit the Hebrides," and a compliment to his companion, "whose acuteness would help my inquiry, and whose gaiety of conversation and civility of manners are sufficient to counteract the inconveniencies of travel, in countries less hospitable than we have passed." (Johnson always prided himself on his command of the social graces, somewhat to the amusement of his friends.) He was in a mood ready to be pleased, and he comments at once on the absence of toll-gates and the hospitality of a professor at St. Andrews. However, the few remnants of the cathedral left standing, once the seat of the archbishop of the kingdom, roused Johnson to remark on the violence of the Reformation in Scotland, a theme to which he returns more than once. And a college chapel, disused except as a kind of greenhouse, led him to hope that shame would lead to the restoration of its proper function. The moralist is never far behind the topographer. Johnson was even more affected by the poor state of the University, the oldest in Scotland, which had only a hundred students.

Bishop Percy once remarked that "Johnson's invectives against Scotland, in common conversation, were more in pleasantry and sport than real and malignant" (*Johnsonian Miscellanies*, 1897, II.216), and the reader should be aware that Johnson's jocularity is sometimes boisterous. For example, he expressed himself this way on the subject of large trees, which he repeatedly insisted were scarce in Scotland: "A tree might be a show in Scotland as a horse in Venice." (p. 9.) In this particular case, though, the attitude behind the remark is serious and complex: he would like more "variety of sun and shade," and he is aware from large stumps seen on occasion that such trees have existed. Knowing the country to be poor, especially in the Highlands and in the Islands, he is exasperated that a cash crop of such value as timber should be neglected by the present generation.

On occasion, however, Johnson's comments on the Scots are so hyperbolical that they approach violence. For example, he contrasts the excellence of the literary culture of Scotland before the Union with what he considers the squalor in which the Scots had lived and concludes, "their tables were coarse as the feasts of Eskimeaux, and their houses filthy as the cottages of Hottentots." (p. 24.) The sting of this insult lies not merely in Johnson's saying that their food was coarse and their houses dirty, but rather in his comparing them to the food and houses of savages.

But Johnson's praise could be great also. The ruined monastery at Aberbrothick impressed him so greatly that he thought it alone almost worth the journey. The inn at Montrose, at the opposite end of the scale, Johnson thought unworthy of "the commercial opulence" of the town until "Mr. Boswell desired me to observe that the innkeeper was an Englishman, and I then defended him as well as I could." (p. 11.) On this light note we proceed. The travelers visit Lord Monboddo, attracted by "the magnetism of his conversation." Such compliments are frequent in the book, and another follows at once at Aberdeen, where Johnson praises not only several of the present professors at King's College but also its first president, Hector Boece, one of the leaders of the Renaissance and friend of Erasmus. Johnson admires the "elegance and vigour" (p. 13) of Boece's history and gently excuses his credulity on the grounds that at first the revival of learning generally relayed the knowledge of the ancients, whereas a critical appraisal was reserved for a later generation. The climax of Johnson's visit to Aberdeen came, perhaps, when he was presented with the freedom of the city, and he returns a delicate compliment: "I found no petty officer bowing for a fee" (p. 16), unlike the English custom.

The travelers then visited Slanes Castle, high on a rock lashed by the North Sea, and Johnson allows himself to wish "without violation of humanity" that as storms "will sometimes happen" (pp. 16–17) he might see one from the castle. This eagerness for experience, however violent, is a little surprising in that elderly citizen of London; it recurs several times in the *Journey*. Indeed, Johnson and Boswell explore a great break in the cliff nearby, first from the top, and then, by boat, from the bottom. Johnson describes it in almost Gothic terms, touched a little by jocosity: "The interception of all lateral light caused a dismal gloom. Round us was a perpendicular rock, above us the distant sky, and below an unknown profundity of water. If I had any malice against a walking spirit, instead of laying him in the Red-sea, I would condemn him to reside in the Buller of Buchan." (p. 18.) But pleased as he is with all this wild scenery, he comments that he has seen only one tree older than himself.

Johnson observes that windows in Scotland are not equipped with weights but are merely propped up with a stick (no stick, no fresh air). He justifies this attention to minutiae on the ground that life consists not in great events or "elegant enjoyments" (p. 19), but in small improvements: "As they approach to delicacy a nation is refined, as their conveniencies are multiplied, a nation, at least a commercial nation, must be denominated wealthy." (p. 20.)

There is nothing Spartan about Johnson's morality; rather, his appreciation of creature comforts is constant and vocal. So, the fact that only once was he displeased with a Scottish meal is highly remarkable, especially since he was traveling in districts so unfrequented by travelers that there were sometimes no inns.

The ruins at Elgin reminded Johnson that the cathedral had been stripped of its lead roof after the Reformation to pay the Scottish army, but he also remembers, with indignation suddenly turning into fury, that contemporary England is no better: "Let us not however make too much haste to despise our neighbours. There is now, as I have heard, a body of men . . . longing to melt the lead of an English cathedral. What they shall melt, it were just that they should swallow." Johnson cancelled this harsh passage after the book had been printed and substituted an innocuous one. (p. 21.)

Soon, however, on property belonging to the Duke of Gordon, Johnson saw a happier sight—an orchard, some large trees, and a plantation of oaks. This pleasure was surpassed at Fort George by the elegant conversation of Sir Eyre Coote, which "left us no attention to the delicacies of his table." (p. 23.) It is hard to imagine higher praise from Johnson.

A little later he saw his first Highland cottage, and, "as our business was with life and manners," the party went in. (p. 27.) Johnson's description is now wholly objective; there is scarcely a pejorative expression in 400 words.

After the party left Fort Augustus, they heard of a gentleman who "fells his timber," and, another surprise, in the tiny village of Anoch the innkeeper's daughter, educated at Inverness, turned out to be "gentle and pleasing." (p. 32.) Johnson, as usual, capitulated at once to feminine charm and presented her with a book which he happened to have about him. In writing up the incident he added, "I . . . should not be pleased to think that she forgets me." (p. 32.) Along the way to Anoch, the party had given a tip to some soldiers repairing the road, and now, in a barn beside the inn, the soldiers were drinking up their money. Johnson and Boswell added some more coins to make the party worth-while, and a superb little vignette appears: "All that we gave was not much, but it detained them in the barn, either merry or quarrelling, the whole night, and in the morning they went back to their work, with great indignation at the bad qualities of whisky." (p. 32.)

A few pages later there is another vignette, in which Johnson is the central figure. The mood is so unusual that the passage is perhaps worth quoting in full: "I sat down on a bank, such as a writer of Romance might have delighted to feign. I had indeed no trees to whisper over my head, but a clear rivulet streamed at my feet. The day was calm, the air soft, and all was rudeness, silence, and solitude. Before me, and on either side, were high hills, which by hindering the eye from ranging, forced the mind to find entertainment for itself. Whether I spent the hour well I know not; for here I first conceived the thought of this narration." (p. 35.)

For the past week the party had traveled through some very wild country, rather than nature tamed into gardens and parks; now Johnson allows himself to imagine that he is alone and without provisions or a guide. In such a situation want, misery, and danger are near, and man must acknowledge his weakness. Yet Johnson realizes the wildness of Scotland is nothing to what the Taurus mountains or "the desarts of America" might threaten. (p. 36.) His companions soon bring this romantic reverie to an end, but the modern reader may relish it as showing a side of Johnson usually hidden—the undramatic man, the city-dweller, opening his mind to the romantic wilderness he is in.

Shortly after this, benighted deep in the Highlands, they were sent some rum and sugar by one of the neighboring gentry, who was told of their plight by a servant. Cheered by this courtesy, Johnson had a bundle of hay brought into the room "and slept upon it in my riding coat. Mr. Boswell being more delicate, laid himself sheets with hay over and under him, and lay in linen like a gentleman." (p. 43.) Next morning, they took a boat to the Isle of Skye, where Johnson found the men downing a glass of whiskey before breakfast. He does not express disapproval, and later tasted it "for experiment." Nevertheless he did not enquire how it was made, and this was unlike him. The reason soon appears, as the moralist speaks: "What was the process I had no opportunity of inquiring, nor do I wish to improve the art of making poison pleasant." (p. 50.)

On the Isle of Raasay, the party was elegantly entertained by the laird and his family, and Johnson compliments them gracefully. However, Johnson again has occasion to attack Presbyterianism; he notes that even there "the malignant influence of Calvinism" had destroyed the Catholic churches. Moreover, the Presbyterians had not replaced them, for there was not one place of public worship. (p. 58.) But if the state of the churches was worse than before the Reformation, the passage of time had brought some benefits: in the Isle of Muck the laird had innoculated eighty people for smallpox, a great boon in an age when the disease might devastate an isolated area like the Hebrides.

At Kingsborough the party was entertained by Flora Macdonald and her husband, and Johnson compliments her for courage and fidelity in rescuing Bonnie Prince Charlie in the Rebellion of 1745. At Dunvegan, entertained by Macleod, chief of the clan, Johnson thoroughly enjoyed himself: "At Dunvegan I had tasted lotus, and was in danger of forgetting that I was ever to depart, till Mr. Boswell sagely reproached me with my sluggishness and softness." (p. 63.) At Ulinish they were shown an old fort reputed to be Danish, caves supposed to be the homes of primeval natives (Johnson is skeptical), and a shattered fortress of the time of James VI, where a Macdonald who had plotted to kill his chief was left to starve in a dungeon. They visit a cave to hear a famous echo, which does not perform. Boswell borrows a rod from a boy and catches a fish, which leads Johnson to remark on the place of fish in the Hebridean economy as both food and illuminating oil. He notes that it is scarce in winter when the sea is too rough for fishing and later wonders why some inland lochs have not been stocked with fish.

At Talisker they were so agreeably entertained that they stayed late in the day and had to travel "almost without light, thro' naked solitude . . . among the craggs and hollows. . . ." Johnson allows himself to think that the descriptions in Gothic romances of travelers who "might very suddenly pass from the gloom of woods, or the ruggedness of moors, to seats of plenty, gaiety, and magnificence" (p. 69) were not entirely without basis in fact.

Storms now forced the party to halt for a few days before taking a boat to the Isle of Col, and Johnson's narrative also pauses for some forty pages of observations on Highland life. He comments on economic matters and describes the use of seaweed for manure and seashells for liming fields, the lack of useful minerals, the price of cattle, and the lack of interest in breeding up a good stock. (He had learned something of this from his schoolboy friend Dr. Taylor, whose talk was "of bullocks." [*Life*, III.181.]) These topics lead naturally to the subject of the people, and Johnson finds no evidence that a life with few luxuries produces longevity. So much for Rousseau's primitivism. At best, he observes, one might avoid corpulence. Johnson next considers the economic structure of Highland society. Below the laird is the tacksman, something more than a steward in that the post and the land that went with it were originally hereditary. Johnson decides that the man occupies a useful function, in opposition to those Scots living nearer England who had told him that they would abolish all middlemen as drones.

He goes on to discuss politics. While conceding that the law disarming the clans after the Rebellion of '45 was harsh to the loyal clans, he argues that it was politically expedient, a point of view often held by Johnson. However, later in the book he urges the repeal of the law since it is no longer needed. Johnson also discusses the more important fact that large numbers of Highlanders were emigrating to America. His opinion of this shows his usual down-to-earth approach: nothing can be done to moderate the harshness of the Highland climate, but local grievances and ill-treatment can be alleviated. He is so radical as to suggest that if tenants' rents are too high, landlords be subsidized by the state to keep them low. (Later on, Johnson returns to the subject of emigration, shrewdly discerning a fact which has also been observed by modern sociologists, that an individual receives psychological support from belonging to a community: when the Scots go to America, he notes, they are dispersed, and "they must want that security, that dignity, that happiness, whatever it be, which a prosperous community throws back upon individuals." [p. 119.])

A discussion of housing follows, then an account of the disadvantages of a goods economy as compared with a money economy: "The great effect of money is to break property into small parts." (p. 92.) In town, he notes, you can buy a piece of meat with a shilling; in the Hebrides you must kill a sheep. Bagpipes, education, religion, superstitions (brownies) come under review. Johnson is glad to find that there is now a school in each parish (formerly there were none) but is disturbed that the children are taught only English, which they are unlikely to use much in the Gaelic-speaking Highlands and Islands. The religion of the Islands is Presbyterianism, but the "ancient rigour of puritanism is now very much relaxed;" furthermore, he praises the clergy very highly for both knowledge and social grace. (p. 95.) Finally, Johnson discusses second sight, which he defines as "an impression made either by the mind upon the eye, or by the eye upon the mind, by which things distant or future are perceived, and seen as if they were present." (p. 97.) Johnson's considerable interest in parapsychology had been whetted by Boswell's report that second sight was much more common in the Hebrides than in other parts of Scotland or in England, and both men hoped to find conclusive evidence that it existed. After considerable investigation, in which the witnesses were disarmed by Boswell's "frankness and gaiety," Johnson renders the verdict of many Scots juries, "not proven."

When James Macpherson published his *Fragments of Ancient Poetry* in 1760, claiming that they were direct translations from old Erse, and followed up this volume with two full-length epics for which he made similar claims, a violent controversy broke out over the genuineness of the poems. Johnson proposed to investigate the question among the Gaelic-speaking Highlanders, but he had already made up his mind before coming to Scotland that the poems were modern forgeries, and his enquiries in the Hebrides were desultory and inept. He heard Erse songs, but only on one occasion was anyone able to translate for him, perhaps, as one incident suggests, because the informants were quite unaware of any precise meaning of "translation" and told him only the subject of the poem. Moreover, he says that when the practice of a bard's recital of poetry died out, "nothing had been written in the Earse language" (p. 102), but he is wrong. He then generalizes mistakenly, on the basis of his own limited experience, that "all attempts to find traces of Highland learning" are hopeless. Yet, after damning Macpherson in very plain language, Johnson comes near the truth: "He has doubtless inserted names that circulate in popular stories, and may have translated some wandering ballads, if any can be found." (p. 107.) In addition, some manuscripts of songs did in fact exist and were used by Macpherson. Unfortunately, Johnson's irritation with Macpherson led him to insult the whole country: "A Scotchman must be a very sturdy moralist, who does not love Scotland better than truth: he will always love it better than inquiry." (p. 108.)

After such an insult to his host country, the reader will think it no more than poetic justice that two paragraphs later Johnson wrote: "I was sea-sick and lay down. Mr. Boswell kept the deck." (p. 108.) They had resumed their journey and had embarked on a very small ship for the Isle of Mull. The storm was so bad that in the morning they disembarked at the Isle of Col, where Johnson spent a few days of bad weather in making further enquiries into island economy.

When the journey is resumed, Johnson's pleasure in meeting people is repeated. The party sees the Isle of Iona and its ancient ruined churches, the sight of which moves Johnson deeply. They reach the mainland, are entertained by the Duke of Argyle, see Glasgow, and proceed to the Boswell family seat at Auchinleck, where, for once, Johnson and Boswell are agreed that the old castle is more interesting than the comfortable and elegant modern mansion. So far has Johnson allowed himself to go in the direction of romantic sensibility. They return to Edinburgh, where Johnson is much interested in a successful school for the deaf. The end of this lively book is relatively abrupt, but it has the virtue of modesty: "I cannot but be conscious that my thoughts on national manners, are the thoughts of one who has seen but little." (p. 149.)

VII

Lives of the Poets

It is curious that Johnson's *Lives of the Poets*, his greatest achievement as a critic, should have been called forth by an attempt by a publishers' cartel to crush an outsider. Edward Dilly, one of some thirty-five firms in the combine, wrote to Boswell (26 September 1777) that a "little trifling edition" of the English poets was being printed for Bell, the outsider, in "extremely small" type and very inaccurately. The real reason for publishing an elaborate edition of the poets was that the cartel considered Bell's attempt "an invasion" of their literary property. That they did not seek a court injunction against Bell may perhaps be explained by the fact the courts had thrown out their claim to perpetual copyright only four years earlier—one of their authors, Cowley, had been dead 110 years. And so Johnson had been asked to write "a concise account of the life of each authour." Johnson agreed, and set a price of £210, which the publishers raised to £315, later adding another £100 when the work was revised in 1783.

The original scheme was "to print an elegant and accurate edition of all the English poets of reputation from Chaucer to the present time" (same letter to Boswell) but at some early point it was decided, by whom it is not clear, to begin with Cowley. Goldsmith was omitted for reasons of copyright, and perhaps Churchill for the same reason. To the publishers' list, Johnson added four names, Blackmore, Watts, Pomfret, and Yalden, and perhaps also James Thomson.

Two years later (1779), Johnson published four volumes containing twenty-two *Prefaces, Biographical and Critical, to the Works of the English Poets*, along with the fifty-six volumes of the poems themselves. In 1781 the other six volumes of the *Prefaces* appeared, with thirty lives, as well as Johnson's two-volume index. None of the volumes were sold separately, but the Dublin pirates quickly remedied this disservice to the selective reader by renaming the "Prefaces" *Lives of the English Poets and a Criticism of their Works* and selling them as a three-volume set. The London publishers followed suit in 1781. That Johnson had perhaps no responsibility for the contents of any volume of the works may be guessed from the fact that he printed Gray's *A Long Story* and his *Ode to Musick* at the end of the life, inasmuch as they were not included in the volume of Gray's poems. And why were the "Prefaces" not printed as such, but collected in volumes by themselves? The first two paragraphs of Johnson's "Advertisement" give the answer:

> The booksellers having determined to publish a body of English poetry, I was persuaded to promise them a preface to the works of each author; an undertaking, as it was then presented to my mind, not very extensive or difficult.
>
> My purpose was only to have allotted to every poet an advertisement, like those which we find in the French Miscellanies, containing a few dates and a general character; but I have been led beyond my intention, I hope, by the honest desire of giving useful pleasure.

In other words, Johnson found so much to say about the major figures that, for example, the Prefaces to Cowley and Waller alone fill the first volume, 165 and 128 pages respectively. And his "Advertisement" just quoted does not even hint at his major advance beyond the original plan—the inclusion of a substantial amount of criticism of each poet.

The lives were neither written nor printed in chronological order.[1] That of Waller was in type by April 1778, and if not the first, was one of the first written. We may examine it in some detail, for if it was actually the first Johnson wrote, it may in part have determined his method; if not, it is at least typical.

[1] Johnson's *Life of Savage* is discussed in Chapter I.

Waller

1606–1687

Johnson disposes of Waller's birth, education, fortune, and election to Parliament in three short paragraphs, and quotes from the author of the biography prefixed to Waller's *Works* the following story about James I:

> He found Dr. Andrews, bishop of Winchester, and Dr. Neale, bishop of Durham, standing behind his Majesty's chair; and there happened something extraordinary, . . . in the conversation those prelates had with the king, on which Mr. Waller did often reflect. His Majesty asked the bishops, "My Lords, cannot I take my subjects' money, when I want it, without all this formality of parliament?" The bishop of Durham readily answered, "God forbid, Sir, but you should: you are the breath of our nostrils." Whereupon the King turned and said to the bishop of Winchester, "Well, my Lord, what say you?" "Sir," replied the bishop, "I have no skill to judge of parliamentary cases." The King answered, "No put-offs, my Lord; answer me presently." "Then, Sir," said he, "I think it is lawful for you to take my brother Neale's money; for he offers it." Mr. Waller said, the company was pleased with this answer, and the wit of it seemed to affect the King; for, a certain lord coming in soon after, his Majesty cried out, "Oh, my lord, they say you lig with my lady." "No, Sir," says his Lordship in confusion; "but I like her company, because she has so much wit." "Why then," says the King, "do you not lig with my Lord of Winchester there?" (*Lives of the Poets*, I.330–31.)

Johnson remarks that the biographer "seems to have been well-informed of facts, though he may sometimes err in chronology." It is typical of Johnson to give credit to a source, and also to give some suggestion as to the reliability of the source. But here he has done something both more subtle and more spectacular. By relating a single story, almost at the outset, he has given a devastating picture of the morality of the court of James I—and in a way prepared us for Waller's disgraceful political career.

Next he mentions Waller's first significant poem, *The Prince's Escape at St. Andero*, "a piece which justifies the observation made by one of his editors, that he attained, by a felicity like instinct, a style which perhaps will never be obsolete; and that, 'were we to judge only by the wording, we could not know what was wrote at twenty, and what at fourscore.'" (I.331.) Johnson then shifts abruptly from "wording" to versification, or perhaps, in his mind, they were very closely allied in poetry: "His versification was, in his first essay, such as it appears in his last performance. By the perusal of Fairfax's translation of Tasso, to which, as Dryden relates, he confessed himself indebted for the smoothness of his numbers, and by his own nicety of observation, he had already formed such a system of metrical harmony as he never afterwards much needed, or much endeavoured, to improve." (I.332.) Such extended critical comments Johnson was later to omit from the biographical section, reserving them for the critical section at the end.

Johnson then glances quickly at two more poems, and even more quickly at Waller's marriage to a city heiress, who died after bearing two children, leaving him to pursue Lady Dorothy Sidney, "Sacharissa": "His acquaintance with this high-born dame gave wit no opportunity of boasting its influence; she was not to be subdued by the powers of verse, but rejected his addresses, it is said, with disdain, and drove him away to solace his disappointment with Amoret or Phillis." (I.335.)

After mentioning Waller's second marriage, Johnson turns to his political career, quoting from his speech in 1640 on granting funds to Charles I, and giving in full his speech on Episcopacy at the beginning of the Long Parliament—a speech which, "not without great injury to his name . . . has been hitherto omitted in his Works." (I.341.) And the reader finds, rather to his surprise, Waller's closely reasoned, practical defense of Episcopacy. (Johnson has now shifted his source to Clarendon's *History of the Rebellion*, to whom, along with Whitelocke, he now gives credit.)

Johnson then gives a detailed story of Waller's plot against Parliament. The plot was discovered. Waller, according to Clarendon, confessed all that "he had heard, said, thought, or seen; all that he knew of himself, and all that he suspected of others." (I.353.) Two men were hanged; one died the night before his trial; one was imprisoned for life; several lost their estates. By public confession, lamentation, and the use of something over

£10,000, Waller procured the easy terms of a year's imprisonment and exile to Paris.

After a few years Cromwell granted Waller permission to return, and Waller's *Panegyric* to Cromwell (1655) followed—the greatest of his poetical productions, as it "has been always considered," says Johnson (I.363), commenting briefly on the contents of the poem. Brief remarks follow on the poem on the war with Spain; that on Cromwell's death "seems to have been dictated by real veneration for his memory." (I.364.) But when Waller welcomed the Restoration of Charles II with a *Congratulation*, Johnson's moral indignation is unbounded:

> It is not possible to read, without some contempt and indignation, poems of the same author, ascribing the highest degree of *power and piety* to Charles the First, then transferring the same *power and piety* to Oliver Cromwell; now inviting Oliver to take the crown, and then congratulating Charles the Second on his recovered right. Neither Cromwell nor Charles could value his testimony as the effect of conviction, or receive his praises as effusions of reverence; they could consider them but as the labour of invention, and the tribute of dependence.
>
> Poets, indeed, profess fiction; but the legitimate end of fiction is the conveyance of truth; and he that has flattery ready for all whom the vicissitudes of the world happen to exalt, must be scorned as a prostituted mind, that may retain the glitter of wit, but has lost the dignity of virtue. (I.365–66.)

Johnson describes Waller's later parliamentary career briefly, singling out especially his joining in the prosecution of Clarendon, of which "the motive was illiberal and dishonest, and shewed that more than sixty years had not been able to teach him morality." (I.369–70.) After mentioning Waller's death, Johnson gives in full Clarendon's generally unfavorable "character" of him, and concludes the biography proper with comments on Clarendon's remarks.

The critical section begins with the statement that nothing is known of Waller's reading except that "he professed himself unable to read Chapman's translation of Homer, without rapture" and that he declared that "he would blot from his works any line that did not contain some motive to virtue." (I.384.) Johnson makes no comment on either of these statements, which run without a break. The first might be regarded as extraordinary, if true; the second as commonplace, if false.

Johnson then distinguishes the two principal types of Waller's poetry—the smaller pieces, in which he seeks sprightliness and gaiety, and the larger, in which he seeks greatness and dignity. Most of the shorter group do not much please Johnson, though "Genius now and then produces a lucky trifle" (I.386) such as Anacreon's *Dove* or Waller's *To Amoret* or *On Love* ("Anger in hasty words or blows"). More are "merely pretty," and some not even "musical," as,

> Fair Venus, in thy soft arms
> The god of rage confine;
> For thy whispers are the charms
> Which only can divert his fierce design.
> What though he frown, and to tumult do incline;
> Thou the flame
> Kindled in his breast canst tame
> With that snow which unmelted lies on thine. (I.387.)

Sometimes his thoughts are "hyperbolical, and his images unnatural" (I.388), and Johnson gives examples; sometimes a good beginning is spoiled by a feeble ending; there is occasional indelicacy ("[I] banquet sometimes on thy face / But make my constant meals at home" I.389). In sum, "Of these petty compositions, neither the beauties nor the faults deserve much attention. . . . Little things are made too important; and the Empire of Beauty is represented as exerting its influence further than can be allowed by the multiplicity of human passions, and the variety of human wants. Such books therefore may be considered as shewing the world under a false appearance, and, so far as they obtain credit from the young and unexperienced, as misleading expectation, and misguiding practice." (I.391–92.) So Johnson demolished the butterfly: for the moment, both his sense of humor and his sense of proportion have deserted him. If he had been confronted with such thundering rhetorical nonsense in conversation, he might have roared: "Sir, what young man ever took a poet's praise of beauty to be literal truth?"

Johnson deals more briefly with Waller's "nobler and more weighty performances." (I.392.) Faults and virtues more or less balance out: *The Prince's Escape* has "puerile and ridiculous . . .

ridiculously mean, and . . . ridiculously tumid" parts, yet it "may be justly praised." (I.392.) Of *The King's behaviour at the death of Buckingham,* Johnson says only that Waller has "used the pagan deities with great propriety." (I.393.) In *The Navy,* "those lines are very noble, which suppose the King's power secure against a second Deluge" (I.393), but there are two errors. "The poem upon Sallee has forcible sentiments; but . . ." (I.393.) The "but" is significant in both instances: Johnson is not moved to unrestricted praise.

The only "noble" poem which Johnson praises with little reservation is the *Panegyric* on Cromwell, "for such a series of verses had rarely appeared before in the English language. Of the lines some are grand, some are graceful, and all are musical. There is now and then a feeble verse, or a trifling thought; but its great fault is the choice of its hero." (I.395.)

Turning to Waller's religious poems, Johnson makes a graceful but quite unexpected comparison: "they were the work of Waller's declining life, of those hours in which he looked upon the fame and the folly of the time past with the sentiments which his great predecessor Petrarch bequeathed to posterity, upon his review of that love and poetry which have given him immortality." (I.396.) But Johnson does not consider the Sacred Poems successful, and takes the occasion to write a short essay on religious poetry, which, he insists, "cannot often please." Poetry defending the doctrines of religion he will admit, as well as poetry praising "the Maker for his works," which would perhaps include Smart's *Song to David,* but not "contemplative piety," inasmuch as, in "the intercourse between God and the human soul," man "is already in a higher state than poetry can confer." (I.398.) In other words, hymns of praise he would admit, but not hymns of intercession.

Furthermore, "The essence of poetry is invention; such invention as, by producing something unexpected, surprises and delights." But surprise and delight can add little to devotion. And, in summary, "The ideas of Christian theology are too simple for eloquence, too sacred for fiction, and too majestick for ornament; to recommend them by tropes and figures, is to magnify by a concave mirror the sidereal hemisphere." (I.399–401.)

Johnson then examines Waller's versification, particularly its "softness and smoothness" (I.401) and its "sweetness" (I.402), which were famous. When Waller first began to write "the art of modulation" attained by the Elizabethans had been "neglected or forgotten." (I.401.) But in addition to Fairfax, Johnson suggests, Waller might usefully have studied Sir John Davies' *Nosce Teipsum*, "which, though merely philosophical, yet seldom leaves the ear ungratified." (I.401.) It is worth remarking how often Johnson uses musical terms to indicate the sound of poetry—"modulation," for example, in the passage just quoted. Johnson then mentions some flaws in Waller's versification: the frequent use of the expletive "do"; occasional use of weak rime words, particularly "so"; "double," that is feminine, rimes; and finally obsolete verb forms such as "waxeth," "affecteth," and obsolete pronunciations like "amazèd," "supposèd," on the last of which Johnson is not at all dogmatic—"I know not whether it is not to the detriment of our language that we have totally rejected them." (I.402–03.) What Johnson does not say, and what apparently he did not quite realize, is that these "abatements" to the excellence of Waller's versification were actually the principal reasons for its "smoothness" or "softness." The use of an expletive to fill out a line, reprehended also by Pope in the *Essay on Criticism*, contributes nothing to the sense, but merely an extra light syllable to the line, adding to its movement and sometimes removing hiatus between two accented syllables. As for using weak rime words, much the same may be said: the lines end with a less emphatic stop, and may even tend to run on. The use of feminine rimes softens the end of the line, and the old pronunciation "amazèd" introduces an extra syllable with virtually the same effect as that of the expletive.

Finally, Johnson appends eighteen stanzas (144 lines) from Fairfax's translation of Tasso to show the reader how much Waller's poetry surpasses Fairfax. In this specimen, Johnson does not note that there are no feminine rimes, no "so" rimes, and indeed no weak rimes at all, which may reinforce the point I have just made. Fairfax does use expletives and, when it suits him, the old "èd." But Waller moved beyond him in the free use of light syllables, with the result which so impressed his contemporaries.

In this early or earliest of the *Lives of the Poets*, Johnson has, with little trial and error, produced a formula: a biographical section chronologically arranged based principally or wholly on three or four printed sources, containing some anecdotes, critical and even adverse comments on the subject's actions, and a brief discussion of any prose works, along with mention of any poems which may be landmarks in the biography. This is followed by a much briefer section, in which Johnson examines the poems as to types, assesses their success or failure, gives some technical analysis of imagery and meter, and a very brief indication of the man's place in the history of English poetry.

In the *Life of Waller*, one will, I think, be impressed with the harshness with which Johnson judges Waller's political career, the close interest in the softness or smoothness of his metrical effects, and Johnson's startling and highly suggestive comparison of Waller to Petrarch.

Cowley

1618–1667

Three months after Johnson completed his *Waller* he had finished the *Life of Cowley*, which he liked best of his *Lives*. In this, the proportion of biographical and critical matter is almost reversed. The life is slender, and the critical matter long and elaborate. Johnson uses Sprat's *Cowley* as his main source, and refers the reader to it, notwithstanding that it is "a funeral oration rather than a history . . . the character, not the life of Cowley." (I.1.) He supplements Sprat with a few facts from Antony à Wood, Dennis, and Downes.

The story that Cowley became a poet by finding, when a boy, a copy of Spenser's *Faerie Queene* lying in the window of his mother's room, Johnson uses to differentiate the "propensity for some certain science or employment, which is commonly called genius" from the true genius, which is "a mind of large general powers, accidentally determined to some particular direction." He follows this by remarking that Sir Joshua Reynolds, "the great painter of the present age, had the first fondness for his art excited by the perusal of Richardson's treatise." (I.2–3.) The implication is clear: Cowley had a natural bent toward poetry, but Reynolds was a man of great natural powers which *happened* to be focused on painting. (Reynolds' *Discourses* had been published just two years earlier.)

At any rate, at the age of ten Cowley had written *Pyramus and Thisbe*, and at twelve *Constantia and Philetus*, and both were *published* in his thirteenth year, giving Cowley a clear lead over the other two mentioned by Johnson who "lisped in numbers," (I.4), Milton and Pope. A pastoral comedy—"which requires no acquaintance with the living world" (I.5)—followed, and then a Latin comedy, neither popular nor learned, which he wrote at Cambridge as an undergraduate. As an adherent of the royal party, he was expelled from Cambridge at the beginning of the Civil War, and later found his way to Paris, where he was employed for several years in encoding and decoding the correspondence between the King and Queen. Meanwhile, his *Mistress* appeared. Because an earlier writer had stated that Cowley was not in love when he wrote the poem, Johnson attacks it as an exercise on the subject of love in the Petrarchian tradition, rather than a heart-felt effusion to a real woman. Thus Johnson evades the issue as to whether the poem is good or bad in itself.

Johnson passes quickly over Cowley's secret return to England as a spy in 1656, his arrest, and his release on bond. Meanwhile, he received an M.D., the chief result of which was a body of Latin poetry on botany that Johnson considers superior to Milton's Latin verse. But since the Restoration brought Cowley neither preferment nor success as a playwright, he retired to the country, from which he wrote complaining about his health, his tenants, his neighbors, and the neglect of his friends. Johnson prints the letter in full for "the consideration of all that may hereafter pant for solitude." (I.22.) Two years later Cowley was dead.

Johnson precedes his criticism of Cowley's poems by an extensive account of the metaphysical poets, a designation which he invented and which first appears here. (I.25.) Johnson did not define the term at this point, and neither his first definition in the *Dictionary*, "versed in metaphysics," nor his second, "in Shakespeare it means supernatural or preternatural," fits with any precision. He seems to have moved a little further from the second to translate it as "beyond or above the natural or the physical." His use of the expression is generally uncomplimentary. It will be recalled that a few months earlier he had written of Waller that his thoughts were "sometimes hyperbolical, and his images unnatural." (I.388.) Now "hyperbolical" and "unnatural" are key words in Johnson's general criticism of metaphysical poetry:

> If . . . that be considered as Wit, which is at once natural and new, that which, though not obvious, is, upon its first production, acknowledged to be just; if it be that, which he that never found it, wonders how he missed; to Wit of this kind the metaphysical poets have seldom risen. Their thoughts are often new, but seldom natural. . . .
>
> But Wit, abstracted from its effects upon the hearer, may be more rigorously and philosophically considered as a kind of *discordia concors;* a combination of dissimilar images, or discovery of occult resemblances in things apparently unlike. Of Wit, thus defined, they have more than enough. The most heterogeneous ideas are yoked by violence together; nature and art are ransacked for illustrations, comparisons, and allusions; their learning instructs, and their subtilty surprises; but the reader commonly thinks his improvement dearly bought, and, though he sometimes admires, is seldom pleased. (I.27–28.)

Johnson goes on to assert that the metaphysical poets failed to achieve the pathetic because they lacked engagement: they "wrote rather as beholders than partakers of human nature; as Beings looking upon good and evil, impassive and at leisure; as Epicurean deities making remarks on the actions of men, and the vicissitudes of life, without interest and without emotion. Their courtship was void of fondness, and their lamentation of sorrow." (I.28.)

Nor was sublimity within their reach, since that "is produced by aggregation, . . . Their attempts were always analytick. . . . What they wanted however of the sublime, they endeavoured to supply by hyperbole; their amplification had no limits; they left not only reason but fancy behind them; and produced combinations of confused magnificence, that not only could not be credited, but could not be imagined." (I.29–30.)

But Johnson, in fairness, will not go so far as complete condemnation: "Yet great labour, directed by great abilities, is never wholly lost: if they frequently threw away their wit upon false conceits, they likewise sometimes struck out unexpected truth: if their conceits were far-fetched, they were often worth the carriage." (I.30.)

He then moves towards Cowley, but since "critical remarks are not easily understood without examples" (I.32) he first gives forty-six quotations from Donne and Cowley, most of which are prefaced with short comments: "Of thoughts so far-fetched, as to be not only unexpected, but unnatural, all their books are full." (On Cowley's "To a lady, who made posies for rings," I.35, concerning making a posy for the equator.) "Of enormous and disgusting hyperboles, these may be examples [three from Cowley, including]:

> In tears I'll waste these eyes,
> By Love so vainly fed;
> So lust of old the Deluge punished." (I.40.)

"Their fictions were often violent and unnatural." (Cowley, "Of his Mistress bathing," I.41.)

Pointing to Donne's *Night*, Johnson remarks that "In forming descriptions," the metaphysical poets "looked out not for images, but for conceits." (I.50.) He clearly prefers a visual image, "yet where scholastick speculation can be properly admitted, their copiousness and acuteness may justly be admired." (I.51.) (The word "justly" may equally be admired in that sentence: we may with propriety admire, but admiration is not ravished from us.) And he quotes Cowley's "Against Hope" as an example. But his last general comment on the metaphysical poets is severe: "In all these examples it is apparent, that whatever is improper or vicious, is produced by a voluntary deviation from nature in pursuit of something new and strange; and that the writers fail to give delight, by their desire of exciting admiration." (I.53.)

Johnson then risks an absolute qualitative judgment: of all of the metaphysical poets, Cowley was "undoubtedly the best." (I.53.) Most modern critics would give that place to Donne. This introduces his comment on the *Miscellanies*, "written . . . with great variety of style and sentiment, from burlesque levity to awful grandeur," as "an assemblage of diversified excellence" such as "no other poet has hitherto afforded." (I.53.) He singles out for praise the poem to his Muse ("The Motto") and the "Ode on

Wit," the second "almost without a rival." (I.54.) In the elegy on Wotton, "the series of thoughts is easy and natural," which last word will recall how frequently Johnson has been condemning the forced and "unnatural" qualities of the metaphysical poets. But in the lines on the death of Hervey, Cowley suffers from the common fault of his group: there is "little passion." (I.55.)

On the other hand, the *Chronicle* brings out some of Johnson's most felicitous criticism. It is

> a composition unrivalled and alone: such gaiety of fancy, such facility of expression, such varied similitude, such a succession of images, and such a dance of words, it is vain to expect except from Cowley. His strength always appears in his agility; his volatility is not the flutter of a light, but the bound of an elastick mind. His levity never leaves his learning behind it; the moralist, the politician, and the critick, mingle their influence even in this airy frolick of genius. To such a performance Suckling could have brought the gaiety, but not the knowledge; Dryden could have supplied the knowledge, but not the gaiety. (I.56–57.)

One may pause momentarily to admire the grace and rhythmic variety of the first sentence of this paragraph. Johnson has moved far beyond the rather mechanical triads of some of his early prose. There is, moreover, not a single learned word in the passage.

Johnson likes Cowley's *Anacreontiques*—"those songs dedicated to festivity and gaiety, in which even the morality is voluptuous, and which teach nothing but the enjoyment of the present day. . . ." (I.59.) The moralist in the Great Cham is in one of his most relaxed and attractive moods. Even though Cowley's songs have lost Anacreon's simplicity, Johnson is satisfied: "Real mirth must be always natural, and nature is uniform. Men have been wise in very different modes; but they have always laughed the same way." (I.60.)

The Mistress, however, is another matter: "exuberance of wit" will not save praises "too far-sought, and too hyperbolical, either to express love, or to excite it. . . ." (I.61.) The type of wit described by Addison as "mixed" is, says Johnson, unnatural. The lines are such as might have been written "for hire by a philosophical rhymer who had only heard of another sex; . . . learned . . . trifling . . . ingenious . . . unnatural." (I.63–64.)

Johnson's handling of Cowley's Pindaric odes is perhaps more readily accepted by a modern reader. Cowley's purpose was "not to shew precisely what Pindar spoke, but his manner of speaking." (I.64.) This is strange enough, as if one should paraphrase Homer primarily to show the Homeric manner with less attention to his subject matter. But Johnson is willing to let his author be as experimental as he likes, provided that the experiment succeeds. It rarely approaches success. In the First Olympic Ode, the beginning is more elegant than Pindar, the ending less strong. In the Second, "pretty lines are not such as his *deep mouth* was used to pour." (I.65.) The First Nemaean Ode has "plays of words and fancy unsuitable to the original" (I.65), whereas, again in the Second Olympic, a mere hint in the original is inflated into eight lines of "rhyming prose." Johnson is indignant: "It is hard to conceive that a man of the first rank in learning and wit, when he was dealing out such minute morality in such feeble diction, could imagine, either waking or dreaming, that he imitated Pindar." (I.66.) Cowley's original Pindaric ode, "The Resurrection," begins with dignity but ends lamely, with a wild metaphor of the "Pindarick Pegasus" flinging both writer and reader to the ground.

Of these odes as a group, Johnson says that Pindar is "ill represented by such puny poetry; and all will determine that if this be the old Theban strain, it is not worthy of revival." (I.71.) He objects equally to the "uncertainty and looseness" of the prosody, where a line varying from two to twelve syllables replaces the regularity of the original. Though Pindar's lines have "very little harmony to a modern ear," we "have reason enough for supposing that the ancient audiences were delighted with the sound. The imitator ought therefore to have adopted what he found, and to have added what was wanting; to have preserved a constant return of the same numbers, and to have supplied smoothness of transition and continuity of thought." (I.72.) Finally, he is unwilling to dismiss Cowley's Pindaric Odes "with unabated censure; . . . many parts deserve at least that admiration which is due to great comprehension of knowledge, and great fertility of fancy." (I.74.)

Johnson now turns to Cowley's unfinished epic, *Davideis,* which "has crept through a century" with little regard. One reason is the sacred character of the subject. We are accustomed to "the nakedness and simplicity" of the Biblical narrative; thus "All amplification is frivolous and vain." (I.75–76.) The second reason for the failure of the poem is in Cowley's performance. "Whatever he writes is always polluted with some conceit" (I.80); and Cowley does not describe or present pictures to the mind, but "gives inferences instead of images, and shews not what may be supposed to have been seen, but what thoughts the sight might have suggested." (I.79.) By leaving the *Davideis* incomplete, Cowley deprived posterity of "more instruction than delight." (I.84.)

Johnson begins his summation thus: "In the general review of Cowley's poetry it will be found, that he wrote with abundant fertility, but negligent or unskilful selection; with much thought; but with little imagery; that he is never pathetick, and rarely sublime, but always either ingenious or learned, either acute or profound." (I.86.) Johnson censures Cowley's diction as "negligent," and expands on this with a statement of the reasons for using what has come to be known as poetic diction:

> He seems not to have known, or not to have considered, that words being arbitrary must owe their power to association, and have the influence, and that only, which custom has given them. Language is the dress of thought; and as the noblest mien, or most graceful action, would be degraded and obscured by a garb appropriated to the gross employments of rusticks or mechanicks, so the most heroick sentiments will lose their efficacy, and the most splendid ideas drop their magnificence, if they are conveyed by words used commonly upon low and trivial occasions, debased by vulgar mouths, and contaminated by inelegant applications. (I. 90–91.)

Just twenty-one years before Wordsworth's famous attack on poetic diction in the Preface to *Lyrical Ballads*, 1800, this passage gives the neo-classical position with precision. Johnson goes on to rebuke Cowley for careless versification, "dissonant and unpleasing" combinations of different measures, weak rimes, and excessive use of expletives such as "do." (For these last two, he had also censured Waller.)

Johnson's conclusion is rather more generous than the reader has been prepared for, and perhaps should be discounted a little in view of some harsh analysis earlier in the biography. Cowley brought to English poetry

> the enthusiasm of the greater ode, and the gaiety of the less; . . . he was equally qualified for spritely sallies, and for lofty flights; . . . he was among those who freed translation from servility, and, instead of following his author at a distance, walked by his side; and . . . if he left versification yet improvable, he left likewise from time to time such specimens of excellence as enabled succeeding poets to improve it. (I.100.)

Denham

1615–1668

The biographical part of Johnson's *Denham* is short and casual—birth in Dublin, education and dice at Oxford, the study of law and poetry, adherence to the Royal cause during the Civil War, the troubles of a second marriage—but Johnson does not mention a first.

As to his poetry, Johnson is pleased that in translating Book II of the *Aeneid*, Denham was "one of the first that understood the necessity of emancipating translation from the drudgery of counting lines and interpreting single words." (I.113.) Though the translation was "not pleasing," it "taught Dryden to please better." (I.113.) Like Waller and Cowley, he attempted religious poetry, and like them he failed.

On the other hand, *Cooper's Hill* is a work of a new species, "at least among us," *local poetry*, and therefore confers on Denham "the rank and dignity of an original author." (I.110.) Faults it has, but it has also lines which "must be numbered among those felicities which cannot be produced at will by wit and labour, but must arise unexpectedly in some hour propitious to poetry." (I.112.) These are:

> O could I flow like thee, and make thy stream
> My great example, as it is my theme!
> Though deep, yet clear; though gentle, yet not dull;
> Strong without rage, without o'er-flowing full. (I.111–12.)

Johnson glances briefly at what Pope called the "strength of Denham" (I.113), which he says consists in "weight" and conciseness, then moves on to a discussion of his prosody. He has already praised the music of the poem on the death of Cowley, the best of his shorter works, but now reverts to the youthful translation from Vergil in which "may be still found the old manner of continuing the sense ungracefully from verse to verse." (I.115.) Johnson quotes sixteen lines for example, lines which do not sound at all ungraceful to a modern ear accustomed to the run-on lines of Keats's *Endymion.* But before we condemn Johnson for rigidity he has already entered a demurrer: "From this kind of concatenated metre he afterwards refrained, and taught his followers the art of concluding their sense in couplets; which has perhaps been with rather too much constancy pursued." (I.116.)

Most of his riming is satisfactory, except when a word is "too feeble to sustain it." (I.117.) We have met this criticism earlier. Johnson's conclusion is highly complimentary:

> Most of these petty faults are in his first productions, when he was less skilful, or at least less dexterous in the use of words; and though they had been more frequent, they could only have lessened the grace, not the strength of his composition. He is one of the writers that improved our taste, and advanced our language, and whom we ought therefore to read with gratitude, though, having done much, he left much to do. (I.118.)

Milton

1608–1674

That Johnson, a monarchist and a member of the Church of England, should show lack of sympathy for some of Milton's views is not surprising. He is generally fair, however. After a straightforward account of the poet's ancestry and school-days, he glances at his early Latin compositions and finds him at fifteen "eminently skilled" (I.121), though less so than Cowley at the same age, whom he later so greatly excelled. Milton's rustication from Cambridge Johnson treats without any emotional involvement, but he observes that Milton, after taking his degrees, left the university without regret. He describes Milton's objection to amateur dramatics by students intending to become clergymen as merely peevish; furthermore, he suggests that Milton's unwillingness to subscribe to the tenets of the church did not arise from unbelief, but that "the thoughts of obedience, whether canonical or civil, raised his indignation." (I.127.)

After glancing at *Comus*, Johnson remarks that the mixture of short and long lines in *Lycidas* shows Milton's acquaintance with Tuscan poetry, a fact which I believe had not been noted before. Johnson then records the cordial reception accorded Milton and his poems in Florence, and this occasions the comment that the poet "had the usual concomitant of great abilities, a lofty and steady confidence in himself," though he was sparing in his praise of others. (I.130.) On his return to England Milton memorialized his friend Diodati in *Epitaphium Damonis*, "written with the common but childish imitation of pastoral life" (I.134), Johnson's unvarying attitude toward pastoral poetry.

In spite of Johnson's "veneration for Milton" he allows himself some merriment over the fact that Milton hastened home from Italy because of the imminence of the Civil War, and then spent the next three years teaching boys in a school which he set up in his house. Johnson describes this pejoratively as the action of a man "who hastens home, because his countrymen are contending for their liberty, and, when he reaches the scene of action, vapours away his patriotism in a private boarding-school." (I.135.) Although Johnson does not say so, he is surely reacting to Milton's own statement: "The sad news of civil war in England called me back; for I considered it base that, while my fellow-countrymen were fighting at home for liberty, I should be travelling at my ease for intellectual culture." (*Second Defense.*) Milton heard the news in December 1638, and took his own good time to return, in the following August.

In spite of Johnson's momentary amusement, he sees nothing disgraceful in Milton's teaching school at this time and is annoyed with some earlier biographers who tried to slur over those years as though they were disgraceful. He is not impressed with Milton's scheme of education in which some reading in the sciences was included, this in spite of Johnson's own long-standing interest in science. He prefers the usual emphasis on religious, moral, and historical knowledge: "Prudence and Justice are virtues, and excellencies,[2] of all times and of all places; we are perpetually moralists, but we are geometricians only by chance." (I.137.)

Milton's entry into political controversy began with *Of Prelatical Episcopacy*, which shows, says Johnson, "puritanical savageness of manners" (I.140), but this was followed by *The Reason of Church-government*, in which Milton promised to undertake something "of use and honour to his country." "From a promise like this," says Johnson, "at once fervid, pious, and rational, might be expected the *Paradise Lost*." (I.141.)

On the difficulties of Milton's first marriage, Johnson comments as might be expected: for a man convinced of his own merit, his wife's absence was intolerable; being inclined to divorce, he easily found arguments for it. On Milton's shift away from the Presbyterians, Johnson is even more severe: "He that changes his party by his humour, is not more virtuous than he that changes it by his interest; he loves himself rather than truth." (I.146.)

On the other hand, Johnson is thoroughly sympathetic with the problem raised in *Areopagitica*, licensing the press. He is afraid of "unbounded liberty," and equally of limiting it, and after a succinct discussion dismisses it as an unsolved problem. (I.147–48.) A far less important book, Milton's reply to Salmasius, was much read, says Johnson; "for paradox, recommended by spirit and elegance, easily gains attention; and he who told every man that he was equal to his King, could hardly want an audience." (I.155.) Johnson's comment on Milton's *Defensio secunda* is in much the same tone, and he shortly afterwards turns, with perhaps some relief, to the composition of *Paradise Lost*.

He mentions that Milton had first thought of King Arthur as a subject and had next thought of "an allegory, or mystery" (I.167), then of a tragedy. Of the two last, Johnson reproduced the cast and plot synopses at length from the Cambridge manuscript. Johnson is clearly glad to talk about purely literary matters:

> These are very imperfect rudiments of *Paradise Lost;* but it is pleasant to see great works in their seminal state, pregnant with latent possibilities of excellence; nor could there be any more

[2] excellencies: excellences, *1783, in error*

> delightful entertainment than to trace their gradual growth and expansion, and to observe how they are sometimes suddenly advanced by accidental hints, and sometimes slowly improved by steady meditation. (I.170.)

Johnson now comes to the events of the Restoration, and the uncertainty whether Milton would suffer for his part in the Commonwealth. Eventually he escaped with little harassment: "He was now poor and blind; and who would pursue with violence an illustrious enemy, depressed by fortune, and disarmed by nature?" (I.176.)

Johnson has some characteristic comments on Milton in retirement. On Milton's insistence that a friend read Latin to him with the Italian pronunciation inasmuch as this would be needed if foreigners were to understand him, Johnson objects that one can soon learn the continental pronunciation. (He had talked Latin in Paris in 1774, and had been understood.) And on Phillips' report that Milton could compose only in the autumn and winter months, Johnson remarks that such a notion was fanciful, but that the poet might still have been influenced by it.

Next Johnson examines the figures for the sale of the first edition of *Paradise Lost* between 1667 and 1669, and shows that 1300 copies were sold. By a shrewd comparison of the small reading public of that date with the far larger one of his own time, he is able to demonstrate that the sale was satisfactorily fast, especially when compared with the sale of the Shakespeare folios, perhaps 1000 copies in the first forty-one years. The use of such simple arithmetic is one of Johnson's favorite methods of demolishing windy surmise, as readers of Boswell know.

Over the last part of Milton's career, Johnson passes rather quickly. He is sympathetic not only with Milton's daughters in having to read aloud to their father in languages they did not understand, but with Milton in listening to incomprehending reading. He reports that "the licenser again fixed his claws" (I.198) on the *History of Britain*, which shows Johnson's opinion of licensing, and that Milton preferred *Paradise Regained* to *Paradise Lost*. A late polemical tract, *Of True Religion* "is modestly written" (I.201) and recommends "the diligent perusal of the Scriptures." (I.202.) So, in a tone of approval, Johnson ends his discussion of Milton's career.

The next section is a summary account of Milton's appearance, character, and opinions. Johnson touches briefly on Milton's physical traits ("eminently beautiful" [I.204]), his domestic habits (abstemious), his financial condition (adequate, but somewhat reduced after the Restoration), and his learning ("unquestionably great" [I.207]). Of English poets, he preferred Spenser, Shakespeare, and Cowley, in that order, and Johnson is surprised that Cowley ranks so high, since he differs so greatly from Milton. His theological opinions were at first Calvinistic, but he was of no church; his political opinions were those of a "surly republican." (I.210.) He was harsh in his domestic relations.

Johnson closes his biographical account by tracing Milton's descendants down to his granddaughter, for whose benefit in 1750 Johnson had arranged a performance of *Comus*, "and to this he who has now attempted to relate his Life, had the honour of contributing a Prologue." (I.215.)

Now Johnson turns to the poems. The early Latin poems are "lusciously elegant" (I.216), but essentially imitative, whereas the English poems of the same period are "original and unborrowed" (I.217), though marred by harshness and labored rimes and epithets. Johnson's condemnation of *Lycidas* is famous: "the diction is harsh, the rhymes uncertain, and the numbers unpleasing." (I.218.) He objects to Milton's use of the pastoral mode partly because it is fictional—"Where there is leisure for fiction there is little grief" (I.218)—partly because of the use of myth, which he considers a tired and worn-out convention, and last because of the mixture of the Christian religion with "these trifling fictions," which is "indecent." (I.220.)

L'Allegro and *Il Penseroso* are, on the contrary, quite to Johnson's taste: "every man that reads them, reads them with pleasure." (I.220.) In part his comment is psychological: he points out that, "among the successive variety of appearances, every disposition of mind takes hold on those by which it may be gratified." (I.221.) This he illustrates with some elaborateness: the cheerful man hears the morning lark, the pensive man, the evening nightingale. Each selects what feeds his mood, out of the possible sensations or imaginings at hand. Both are solitaries, both "delight in musick" (I.223); Johnson does not suggest that perhaps these shared qualities derive from Milton himself, though he is in some doubt that the characters are kept sufficiently distinct. All in all, "They are two noble efforts of imagination." (I.224.)

Comus Johnson considers the greatest of Milton's early poems, and one in which the "dawn" of *Paradise Lost* may be seen in its diction and mode of verse. (I.224.) As a drama, however, Johnson finds the action improbable and the speeches too long: "It is a drama in the epic style, inelegantly splendid, and tediously instructive." (I.227.) Johnson dislikes all of Milton's sonnets, with the possible exception of two, which are "not bad" (I.228), and he concludes his three sentences of comment with the astonishing remark that the sonnet has never succeeded in English. I shall not try to justify this lapse, but only remark that the sonnet reached its nadir in the eighteenth century, and at the moment when Johnson was writing, it was just struggling to a new birth.

Johnson turns with pleasure to *Paradise Lost*, which "with respect to design, may claim the first place, and with respect to performance the second, among the productions of the human mind." (I.228.) In this connection occurs Johnson's well-known definition of poetry, "the art of uniting pleasure with truth, by calling imagination to the help of reason." (I.228.) The epic, as the highest type, requires a great event as its basis, and, in the poet, the ability to distinguish characters, depict nature, make fiction real (that is, believable) in an extended vocabulary adjusted to "all the varieties of metrical modulation[3]." (I.229.) There must be an artful fable and great personages.

Johnson now measures the poem against his postulates, and finds that "this mighty poet" has generally succeeded. (I.232.) The event and the fable are unsurpassed. The characters of the evil angels are more diversified than those of the good: "The malignity of Satan foams in haughtiness and obstinacy." (I.233.) Adam's superiority to Eve is sustained throughout. As to the unity of the work, Johnson finds short digressions at the beginning of three books, "but superfluities so beautiful, who would take away?" (I.237.) He praises Milton's sentiments in a startling metaphor drawn from his interest in chemistry: "The heat of Milton's mind might be said to sublimate his learning, to throw off into his work the spirit of science, unmingled with its grosser parts." (I.239.)

[3] modulation: moderation, *1783, in error.*

The most serious fault of the poem, Johnson feels, is the "want of human interest." (I.249.) He is also unhappy with the allegory of Sin and Death, as moving uncertainly between the immaterial and the material, and he objects to the frequency of Milton's plays on words, as, it will be remembered, he objected to Shakespeare's puns. But his sense of proportion wins out in the end: "Such are the faults of that wonderful performance *Paradise Lost;* which he who can put in balance with its beauties must be considered not as nice but as dull, as less to be censured for want of candour, than pitied for want of sensibility." (I.255.)

Paradise Regained, Johnson thinks, has perhaps been "too much depreciated," and *Samson Agonistes* too much admired. (I.256.) There are beauties in the drama, but it has the fatal flaw of not engaging our interest. Part of this comes from the fact that Milton "knew human nature only in the gross, and had never studied the shades of character, nor the combinations of concurring, or the perplexity of contending passions." (I.257.)

A general discussion of Milton's qualities as a poet follows. His diction Johnson finds unique, sometimes too learned, sometimes harsh, but it has "copiousness and variety." (I.259.) In the discussion of blank verse which follows, one principal point emerges on the question of music: "The musick of the English heroick line strikes the ear so faintly that it is easily lost, unless all the syllables of every line co-operate together: this co-operation can be only obtained by the preservation of every verse unmingled with another, as a distinct system of sounds; and this distinctness is obtained and preserved by the artifice of rhyme." (I.260.) In the end, however, says Johnson, "I cannot prevail on myself to wish that Milton had been a rhymer; for I cannot wish his work to be other than it is. . . ." (I.261.) In the last sentence of the *Life*, Johnson adds emotion to rhetoric for his summation: "His great works were performed under discountenance, and in blindness, but difficulties vanished at his touch; he was born for whatever is arduous; and his work is not the greatest of heroick poems, only because it is not the first." (I.262.)

Butler

1612–1680

The biographical part of Johnson's *Butler* is relatively brief, and assembled from obvious sources. Johnson asserts that it is not possible to find further information, and that therefore "nothing remains but to compare and copy" these sources. (I.263.) This is his usual statement, and need not be taken very seriously. Indeed, in the critical section he says: "I am informed by Mr. Thyer of Manchester, the excellent editor of this author's reliques . . . [that he has] the common-place book, in which Butler reposited . . . such remarks, similitudes, allusions, assemblages, or inferences, as occasion prompted, or meditation produced." (I.281.) As was elsewhere the case, Johnson did not consult the book. It would be accurate to say that he had, in general, more than enough material to satisfy his publishers and saw no good reason to seek out still more.

Johnson closes the biographical notes with a typical sentence: "In this mist of obscurity passed the life of Butler, a man whose name can only perish with his language. The mode and place of his education are unknown; the events of his life are variously related; and all that can be told with certainty is, that he was poor." (I.272.)

The criticism begins with an equally typical sentence: "The poem of Hudibras is one of those compositions of which a nation may justly boast; as the images which it exhibits are domestick, the sentiments unborrowed and unexpected, and the strain of diction original and peculiar." (I.273.) Johnson hastens to point out that Butler is indebted to Cervantes for the original idea of the book, and then proceeds neatly to contrast the two heroes, showing that Cervantes "by matchless dexterity" made Don Quixote "ridiculous, but never contemptible," thereby holding the reader's sympathy throughout, whereas Butler gives up Hudibras "at once to laughter and contempt." (I.274.) Johnson states that one cannot judge the plot or action of the poem because it is unfinished, but that even if finished it would probably have been merely a series of events, leading nowhere in particular. But even this might be forgiven, if there had been enough action: "The scenes are too seldom changed, and the attention is tired with long conversation." There follows a passage which, I think, must reflect Johnson's own experiences in writing *Rasselas* twenty years earlier:

> It is indeed much more easy to form dialogues than to contrive adventures. Every position makes way for an argument, and every objection dictates an answer. . . . But whether it be that we comprehend but few of the possibilities of life, or that life itself affords little variety, every man who has tried knows how much labour it will cost to form such a combination of circumstances, as shall have at once the grace of novelty and credibility, and delight fancy without violence to reason. (I.277.)

Butler's wit pleases Johnson: "what poet has ever brought so many remote images so happily together?" (I.279); and he compares Butler's learning to Rabelais'. Moreover, Butler knew men as well as books: "He had watched with great diligence the operations of human nature, and traced the effects of opinion, humour, interest, and passion." (I.280.) (These last two sentences should be considered in view of what Johnson had written on the metaphysical poets, attacking their hyperbolical conceits and lack of imagery, and their disregard of human nature.)

The "perishable part" of *Hudibras* lies in its reliance upon "temporary and local" manners founded on opinions, "the progeny of error and perverseness," rather than "such manners as depend upon standing relations and general passions."(I.281–82.) (This is also, perhaps, why Johnson's *London* has suffered more from the lapse of time than *The Vanity of Human Wishes*.) One of the distinctions of Johnson's work is that he himself turns up everywhere in it, sometimes quite unexpectedly, always delightfully. Here he is discussing "the sour solemnity, the sullen superstition, the gloomy moroseness, and the stubborn scruples of the ancient Puritans" (I.282) attacked by Butler, and is reminded of a story:

> We have never been witnesses of animosities excited by the use of minced pies and plumb porridge; nor seen with what abhorrence those who could eat them at all other times of the year would shrink from them in December. An old Puritan, who was alive in my childhood, being at one of the feasts of the church invited by a neighbour to partake his cheer, told him,

> that, if he would treat him at an alehouse with beer, brewed for all times and seasons, he should accept his kindness, but would have none of his superstitious meats or drinks. (I.283–84.)

And in the next paragraph he reminds us that in the seventeenth century Gataker writing on *Lots* had to defend, against Puritan objections, throwing dice, card playing, or hiding a shilling for the reckoning. That the last phrase shows Johnson and Boswell throwing "heads or tails" to decide who pays for supper at the Mitre, I shall confidently affirm.

Johnson now turns to the diction of the poem ("grossly familiar") and its prosody ("purposely neglected"). (I.286.) Dryden had regretted that Butler did not use heroic couplets, but Johnson quite justly rejects this, contending that if the diction had been retained along with heroic verse, the result would have been "heterogeneous," and that if the diction had been changed, we would have a different poem. In his final remarks, Johnson predicts a rather uncertain future for the poem:

> Burlesque consists in a disproportion between the style and the sentiments, or between the adventitious sentiments and the fundamental subject. It therefore, like all bodies compounded of heterogeneous parts, contains in it a principle of corruption. All disproportion is unnatural; and from what is unnatural we can derive only the pleasure which novelty produces. (I.287.)

Rochester

1647–1680

After commenting on Rochester's immoral youth, edifying repentance, and early death, Johnson turns to his songs, which have "no particular character." (I.295.) But remembering *London* and *The Vanity of Human Wishes*, we are not surprised to find Johnson more interested in a similar poem by Rochester: "His imitation of Horace on Lucilius is not inelegant or unhappy. In the reign of Charles the Second began that adaptation, which has since been very frequent, of ancient poetry to present times; and perhaps few will be found where the parallelism is better preserved than in this. The versification is indeed sometimes careless, but it is sometimes vigorous and weighty." (I.295.) Johnson is still more interested in Rochester's poem *Nothing*, "the strongest effort of his Muse" (I.295), which Johnson compares very favorably with Jean Passerat's *Nihil*, emphasizing that Rochester balances with great skill the positive and negative senses of "nothing," as, "I need not fear thieves, I have *nothing;* and *nothing* is a very powerful protector" (I.296), the first *nothing* being negative, the second positive. It seems curious that Johnson should show such interest in "this barren topick . . . the boast of his fertility" (I.295); it is almost precisely the same kind of display of wit for the sake of wit, word-play for sheer sport, which Johnson found distasteful in the metaphysical poets.

Rochester's most famous poem, Johnson dismisses in a single sentence: "Of the satire against *Man*, Rochester can only claim what remains when all Boileau's part is taken away." (I.298.) Johnson is beginning to prepare a separate circle in hell for plagiarists.

Roscommon

1634?–1684

At the beginning of his *Life of Roscommon*, Johnson is much interested in the report that the boy, at school in Normandy, was supernaturally aware of his father's death in Ireland at the moment of the event. As with his investigation of the Cock Lane Ghost, reported by Boswell, and his interest in second sight in the Hebrides, Johnson asks, "Is reason or testimony to be rejected?" Citing Osborne on the appearance of sanctity, he suggests of such "impulses," "Do not wholly slight them, because they may be true: but do not easily trust them, because they may be false." (I.306.) After the Restoration, Roscommon formed a plan for a society to reform and fix the English language, ideas which Johnson had commented on in his Preface to the *Dictionary*. But Johnson has observed what had happened abroad: "The French Academy thought that they refined their language, and doubtless thought rightly; but the event has not shewn that they fixed it; for the French of the present time is very different from that of the last century." (I.309.) Forming an academy would be easy, Johnson thinks, but even in the unlikely event that the members agreed on anything, who would obey them? Nobody. "That our language is in perpetual danger of corruption cannot be denied; but what prevention can be found? The present manners of the nation would deride authority, and therefore nothing is left but that every writer should criticise himself." (I.310.)

Of Roscommon as a poet, Johnson says that "he is perhaps the only correct writer in verse before Addison" (I.313), and reminds us that "Pope has celebrated him as the only moral writer [i.e., poet] of King Charles's reign." (I.314.) As for the once famous *Essay on Translated Verse,* much over-praised by Dryden (when did Dryden under-praise an earl?), Johnson reduces it to these platitudes: "the author should be suitable to the translator's genius; . . . he should be such as may deserve a translation; . . . he who intends to translate him should endeavour to understand him; . . . perspicuity should be studied and . . . the style of the original should be copied in its elevation and depression." (I.315.) But Johnson does admire the "art" with which the rules are introduced, "and the decorations with which they are adorned." (I.316.) Roscommon's translation of Horace's *Art of Poetry* has been praised "not less . . . than it deserves. Blank verse, left merely to its numbers, has little operation either on the ear or mind: it can hardly support itself without bold figures and striking images." (I.317.) Precisely what Johnson means by the operation of meter "on the mind," I do not know. Apparently he means that he is not consciously aware of the five-beat structure of the blank verse line, since it is ordinarily not end-stopped, and therefore is deprived of the pleasure of recognition. At any rate, he finds the accuracy of the translation as unsatisfactory as the verse form. In conclusion, Johnson gives a clue to what he meant by correctness earlier in the biography: "His versification is smooth . . . and his rhymes are remarkably exact." (I.320.)

Otway

1651–1685

Johnson's *Otway* is short and unimportant. He has a brief speculation on whether different qualities are required for good actors and for good dramatists (probably), a reference to Otway as a boon companion to the "dissolute wits" of the Restoration, and an account of his early death. Inasmuch as Otway's plays, his only claim to fame, were not included in the poems for which Johnson was writing prefaces, he comments briefly on *The Orphan* and on *Venice Preserv'd*, both of which still held the stage after the lapse of a century. *The Orphan's* "whole power is upon the affections; for it is not written with much comprehension of thought, or elegance of expression. But if the heart is interested, many other beauties may be wanting, yet not be missed." (I.326.) *Venice Preserv'd* lacks morality in its design, and "despicable scenes of vile comedy" appear amidst the tragedy. Yet the images are stronger than in *The Orphan*, "and his language more energetick. . . . it is the work of a man not attentive to decency, nor zealous for virtue; but of one who conceived forcibly, and drew originally, by consulting nature in his own breast." (I.326–27.)

Over the poems, Johnson draws a veil: "part . . . I do not understand; and in that which is less obscure, I find little to commend. The language is often gross, and the numbers are harsh." (I.328.) With this, who shall say that Otway's poems are not due for revival?

Pomfret

1667–1703

It will be recalled that Pomfret was one of the four or five poets whom Johnson recommended for inclusion in the booksellers' project. His *Life of Pomfret* is nevertheless his shortest, consisting of six paragraphs, of which the last three may be quoted as an example of the lapidary's art:

> He published his poems in 1699; and has been always the favourite of that class of readers, who, without vanity or criticism, seek only their own amusement.
>
> His *Choice* exhibits a system of life adapted to common notions, and equal to common expectations; such a state as affords plenty and tranquillity, without exclusion of intellectual pleasures. Perhaps no composition in our language has been oftener perused than Pomfret's *Choice*.
>
> In his other poems there is an easy volubility; the pleasure of

smooth metre is afforded to the ear, and the mind is not oppressed with ponderous or entangled with intricate sentiment. He pleases many, and he who pleases many must have some species of merit. (I.414.)

Dorset

1638–1706

The wild life of the Earl of Dorset reached some sort of climax when he composed a once-famous song, *To all you ladies now at land* before a naval battle in which he fought—traditionally, he is supposed to have composed it the day before, but Johnson says that the Earl of Orrery told him that Dorset had been working on it for a week. After this, his two marriages must have been anticlimactic, but he was still the favorite of an indulgent public —and of Dryden, whose patron he was. Johnson reports that Dryden, "undertaking to produce authors of our own country superior to those of antiquity," told Dorset: "I would instance your Lordship in satire, and Shakspeare in tragedy." Johnson: "Would it be imagined that, of this rival to antiquity, all the satires were little personal invectives, and that his longest composition was a song of eleven stanzas?" But if Johnson is outraged at Dryden's sycophancy, he is just to Dorset, "whose performances are, what they pretend to be, the effusions of a man of wit; gay, vigorous, and airy." (I.420.)

Stepney

1663–1707

Johnson wonders why Stepney's youthful poems were admired, and decides that "One cannot always easily find the reason for which the world has sometimes conspired to squander praise." (I.423–24.) But he has already given the reason: Stepney went to Westminster School, then Trinity College, Cambridge, was very intimate with Lord Halifax, was introduced into public life by Lord Dorset, and was envoy to Brandenburg at twenty-nine. It is impossible that his poems should not have been admired. Johnson says that in his translations he is too far from the original, and that in his original poems "there is in the whole little either of the grace of wit, or the vigour of nature." (I.424.)

John Philips

1676–1708

In the biographical part of his *Life of Philips*, Johnson displays a typical healthy skepticism about receiving unlikely anecdotes concerning the famous: at Winchester, "as we are told by Dr. Sewel, . . . he was soon distinguished by the superiority of his exercises; and, what is less easily to be credited, so much endeared himself to his schoolfellows, by his civility and good-nature, that they, without murmur or ill-will, saw him indulged by the master with particular immunities." (I.425.)

Johnson is kind to Philips' poems: "*The Splendid Shilling* has the uncommon merit of an original design. . . . To degrade the sounding words and stately construction of Milton, by an application to the lowest and most trivial things, gratifies the mind with a momentary triumph over that grandeur which hitherto held its captives in admiration; the words and things are presented with a new appearance, and novelty is always grateful where it gives no pain." (I.431–32.) So Johnson distantly adumbrates Bergson on laughter. As for *Blenheim*, a serious poem not a parody, here the imitation of Milton is a blunder:

> He imitates Milton's numbers indeed, but imitates them very injudiciously. Deformity is easily copied; and whatever there is in Milton which the reader wishes away, all that is obsolete, peculiar, or licentious, is accumulated with great care by Philips. Milton's verse was harmonious, in proportion to the general state of our metre in Milton's age; and, if he had written after the improvements made by Dryden, it is reasonable to believe that he would have admitted a more pleasing modulation of numbers into his work; but Philips sits down with a resolution to make no more musick than he found; to want all that his master wanted, though he is very far from having what his master had. Those asperities, therefore, that are venerable in the *Paradise Lost*, are contemptible in the *Blenheim*. (I.433.)

Of Philips' last and "greatest" poem, *Cider*, Johnson says that it "continued long to be read, as an imitation of Virgil's *Georgic*, which needed not shun the presence of the original." (I.427.) But note that the remark is in the past tense. And it, too, alas, was in blank verse.

Walsh

1663–1708

William Walsh is better known for his encouragement of Pope than for his poems. Of his imitation of Horace, Johnson is able to say, "the first stanzas are happily turned; and in all his writings there are pleasing passages." The final sentence applies equally to many other versifiers: "He has however more elegance than vigour, and seldom rises higher than to be pretty." (I.454.)

Dryden

1631–1700

At the outset of the *Life of Dryden* Johnson complains that "His contemporaries . . . left his life unwritten; and nothing therefore can be known beyond what casual mention and uncertain tradition have supplied." (II.1.) He says much the same thing in his *Addison.* The notion of making a search for letters, diaries, or other records, seems never to have occurred to him. He therefore gives an account of Dryden's life which is largely a chronology of his published works, with scattered comments as those did or did not interest him. Two brief paragraphs deal with Dryden's boyhood, and then a school exercise on the death of Lord Hastings is discussed because of its conceits—smallpox pustules made rosebuds, then gems, and finally a constellation.

After Cambridge came Dryden's *Heroic Stanzas on the late Lord Protector*, competing with Waller and raising "great expectations." (II.4.) In the following year *Astraea Redux* celebrated the return of Charles II, and Johnson remarks that if Dryden changed, "he changed with the nation." (II.4.) In that poem Johnson defends the phrase "stillness first invades the ear" on the ground that, though "silence" is "mere privation" (II.5), there is ample precedent in English for using similar privatives ("darkness," "cold") as agents. To such minuteness of ridicule were Dryden's enemies eventually reduced.

Johnson then complains that settling the chronology of Dryden's publications is not easy, for first editions cannot be "easily found." (II.5.) The key word here is "easily." For the purposes of Johnson's Preface, a real search was scarcely required—and he was surely not being paid on the assumption that he would make one.

In 1663 Dryden began to write plays "compelled undoubtedly by necessity, for he appears never to have loved that exercise of his genius." (II.6.) His first piece, *The Wild Gallant*, was withdrawn and reworked, but yet remained defective, says Johnson. Then follows a curious remark: "I wish that there were no necessity of following the progress of his theatrical fame," but it must be done, "for the composition and fate of eight and twenty dramas include too much of a poetical life to be omitted." (II.7.) Johnson seems not to have stopped to think that what bores the author will bore the reader. But he plunges in. *The Rival Ladies*, he tells us, is prefaced by a defense of rimed drama. A collaboration with Sir Robert Howard, *The Indian Queen*, followed, also rimed. Then came *The Indian Emperor*, rimed again, but distinguished by the fact that playbills distributed at the door announced it as a sequel to *The Indian Queen*.

Johnson attributes Dryden's use of rime to the preference of the king and to the Earl of Orrery's example, and also, concomitantly, to the fact that his own skill in it would enable him to outdistance his rivals. Dryden's practical nature is thereby underlined, though Johnson does not make a particular point of it. He discontinued rime in tragedy only when, "by the prevalence of manifest propriety, he seems to have grown ashamed" of it. (II.8–9.) Just what Johnson means by "prevalence of manifest propriety" is not wholly clear, unless it is that most of us do not speak in rime. I hesitate to suggest that three big words led Johnson into a banality.

Next came Dryden's *Annus Mirabilis*, a poem in heroic quatrains, a stanza which he thought difficult. Johnson remarks that it was Dryden's habit "to recommend his works, by representation of the difficulties that he had encountered," without considering that "where there is no difficulty there is no praise." (II.10.) It seems more likely that Dryden knew that the reader would not think the stanza difficult unless he was told so.

In 1668 Dryden was made Poet Laureate, with annual stipends of a tierce of wine and one hundred pounds, "a revenue in those days not inadequate to the conveniencies of life" (II.11), an agreeable example of Johnson's long-time interest in the purchasing power of money in different periods of English history. Dryden's *Essay of Dramatick Poesie* now appeared, "an elegant and instructive dialogue" (II.11), and in the same year *Secret Love, or the Maiden Queen,* to which Dryden prefaced a discussion of whether a poet can judge well of his own work, concluding that "of the plan and disposition," and all that can be reduced to principle, he can, but that "where fancy predominates, self-love may easily deceive." Johnson objects that "what is good only because it pleases, cannot be pronounced good till it has been found to please." (II.12.) This may be true of drama; it is doubtfully true of any other form of writing.

Sir Martin Mar-all, Johnson notes, was charged "like most of the rest" with plagiarism (II.12); Johnson neither sustains the charge nor comments on it. But on the Dryden-Davenant alteration of *The Tempest,* he is sarcastic: "The effect produced by the conjunction of these two powerful minds was, that to Shakspeare's monster Caliban is added a sister-monster Sicorax; and a woman, who, in the original play, had never seen a man, is in this brought acquainted with a man that had never seen a woman." (II.13.)

In the Preface to *An Evening's Love, or the Mock Astrologer* Johnson finds Dryden's criticism of tragedy, comedy, and farce "judicious and profound," but he is unimpressed with Dryden's defense of the immorality of some of his comedies by instancing his predecessors. Johnson quotes without comment Dryden's defense of his plagiarism by Charles's alleged remark, "He only desired that they, who accuse me of thefts, would steal him plays like mine." (II.24.)

Tyrannic Love (1672) was conspicuous, says Johnson, "for many passages of strength and elegance, and many of empty noise and ridiculous turbulence." (II.24–25.) The next year, however, brought Settle's *Empress of Morocco* success on the stage, and Settle printed the play with engravings, the first so embellished. Dryden was enraged at this threat to his empire, and replied with a "malignant" pamphlet in which Settle is described as "an animal of a most deplored understanding, without conversation." (II.14.) Johnson quotes two pages more, much of which is concerned with tearing a single couplet to bits. Dryden ends: "Sure the poet writ these two lines aboard some smack in a storm, and, being sea-sick, spewed up a good lump of clotted nonsense at once." Johnson adds, "Here is perhaps a sufficient specimen" (II.16), with which the reader would gladly agree; but he is not yet let off: because the pamphlet is rare, Johnson quotes six pages more. "Such," he concludes, "was the criticism to which the genius of Dryden could be reduced, between rage and terrour"—a great mind leveled with the meanest because "Dryden and Settle had both placed their happiness in the claps of multitudes." (II.23.)

With evident relief Johnson turns to *The Conquest of Granada*, which shows "a theatrical meteor of incredible love and impossible valour." "Yet the scenes are, for the most part, delightful; they exhibit a kind of illustrious depravity, and majestick madness. . . ." (II.26.) So much for the supposed rigidity of Johnson's neoclassicism; he might almost be describing, with pleasure, a Gothic novel.

An account of the attack on Dryden by a minor writer named Martin Clifford may be omitted, except to say that it gave Johnson a chance to thank Dr. Percy, who unearthed it for him. Now Settle joined the attack, and after Johnson sarcastically refers to Dryden's "elegant animadversions" (II.29) already quoted, he feels that he owes Settle equal time. Fair play may be an interesting concept in blood sports, but giving Settle some seven pages of quotations does not make for conciseness in this part of Johnson's biography. He finally says, "Enough of Settle." (II.36.) The reader would have settled for nothing.

Marriage-a-la-Mode and *The Assignation* followed, the second with a "very elegant" (II.37) dedication, and then *Amboyna*, in which Dryden mixed verse and prose. *The State of Innocence and Fall of Man* used personages "such as cannot decently be exhibited on the stage," but even worse it was dedicated to the Duchess of York "in a strain of flattery which disgraces genius, and which it was wonderful that any man that knew the meaning of his own words, could use without self-detestation." (II.40–41.) In the preface to the play Dryden gives as his reason for printing it the fact that "many hundred copies" had been made without his consent. Johnson comments sharply that this is an obvious falsehood

—"but he that could bear to write the dedication felt no pain in writing the preface." (II.41.)

In *Aureng-Zebe* (1676) Johnson finds many passages "that may be read with pleasure," and dialogue "often domestick, and therefore susceptible of sentiments accommodated to familiar incidents." (II.42.) *All for Love* (1678), though marred with few faults of style or character, yet has one great one, "though rather moral than critical, that by admitting the romantick omnipotence of Love, he has recommended . . . that conduct which, through all ages, the good have censured as vicious, and the bad despised as foolish." (II.43.)

The Spanish Fryar (1681), a tragi-comedy "eminent for the happy coincidence . . . of the two plots," long remained popular, partly from its topical, anti-Catholic character, and partly "by the real power both of the serious and risible part." (II.38.) *The Duke of Guise*, on the other hand, deserves notice, Johnson says, only for its topical nature, an attack on the Covenanters.

Don Sebastian (1690), though having some "sallies of frantick dignity, and more noise than meaning," yet sometimes verges on real life, and "has some sentiments which leave a strong impression." Some scenes are inserted, "intended for comick . . . which I suppose that age did not much commend, and this would not endure." (II.44–45.)

King Arthur (1691) has in the dedication "a very elegant character of Charles, and a pleasing account of his latter life." (II.46.) In Dryden's last play, *Love Triumphant*, "The catastrophe, proceeding merely from a change of mind, is confessed by the author to be defective." (II.47.)

Johnson then comments on the lack of adequate financial reward in the theater of Dryden's day, when an author received only the third night's profits in addition to the proceeds from the dedication and copyright. And, though Dryden's dedications were written "with such elegance and luxuriance of praise, as neither haughtiness nor avarice could be imagined able to resist," yet "he seems to have made flattery too cheap." (II.48.) This is an amusing comment, in view of the fact that Johnson wrote more dedications than Dryden, and his highest known fee was five guineas.

Dryden's prefaces, Johnson remarks, often included criticism, "a kind of learning then almost new in the English language," and since he had "considered with great accuracy the principles of writing" (II.48), he was able to improve public judgment substantially.

Johnson now turns to Buckingham's *Rehearsal*, in which Dryden's heroic plays were ridiculed. In commenting on the number of collaborators employed, Johnson says, perhaps in defense of his own lack of detail here, "To adjust the minute events of literary history, is tedious and troublesome; it requires indeed no great force of understanding, but often depends upon enquiries which there is no opportunity of making, or is to be fetched from books and pamphlets not always at hand." (II.50–51.) Dryden was ridiculed as Bayes in the play, and Johnson suggests that Dryden's mannerisms of speech are used. But Johnson sensibly concludes that the ridicule did Dryden little mischief.

Now Johnson reverts to such non-dramatic works as he has omitted in surveying Dryden's career in the theater. To a collaborative translation of the *Epistles of Ovid* (1680), Dryden prefixed a discussion defending translators from "the shackles of verbal interpretation," i.e., word-for-word translation, which Johnson himself opposed, as such translation "must for ever debar it from elegance." (II.56.)

In 1681 *Absalom and Achitophel* appeared, and Johnson has a characteristic anecdote about its sale: "my father, an old bookseller, told me, he had not known it equalled but by Sacheverell's trial," to which Johnson adds: "There is no need to enquire why those verses were read, which, to all the attractions of wit, elegance, and harmony, added the cooperation of all the factious passions, and filled every mind with triumph or resentment." (II.57.) *The Medal* soon followed. Elkanah Settle, who had been attacked in the second part of *Absalom and Achitophel*, replied to both poems so successfully that "he left the palm doubtful." Nevertheless, Johnson comments, so complete was the revolution of fame, or "the prevalence of fashion," that no one, in a century, had even bothered to collect Settle's works. (II.59.)

Johnson sweeps aside a mass of material with one short sentence: "Of translated fragments, or occasional poems, to enumerate the titles, or settle the dates, would be tedious, with little use." (II.60.) Not for him "to run half over London, in order to fix a date correctly," as Boswell did a few years later when working on his *Life of Johnson*. (I.7.) And this unwillingness on Johnson's part led him into a grotesque error which could easily have been avoided. After the Revolution of 1688 Dryden lost his position as Laureate, inasmuch as he had embraced Roman Catholicism; he was succeeded by his enemy Shadwell: "Dryden . . . therefore celebrated the intruder's inauguration in a poem exquisitely satirical, called *Mac Flecknoe*. . . ." (II.69.) But *Mac Flecknoe* was published in 1682, seven years *before* Dryden lost his laureateship.

Johnson treats Dryden's conversion sympathetically, saying that such a change will be suspect when it seems to concur with interest, but concluding that "enquiries into the heart are not for man." (II.62.) He glances briefly at Dryden's translation of Maimbourg's *The History of the League* and of a *Life of St. Francis Xavier*, and then turns to *The Hind and the Panther*, Dryden's defense of the Catholic Church (the Hind). Johnson, a staunch member of the Church of England (the Panther), considered the poem a failure because of its theological position: "To reason in verse was, indeed, one of his powers; but subtilty and harmony united are still feeble, when opposed to truth." (II.65.)

In 1693 the translation of Juvenal and Persius by Dryden and others came out, with a dedication in which Dryden discussed his plans for an epic. A translation of DuFresnoy's *Art of Painting* followed, then Dryden's Vergil, and finally the *Fables*.

This brings Johnson to Dryden's death, on 1 May 1700. He here transcribes a lurid account of Dryden's funeral, the body shunted from one place to another, with splendid but unfulfilled promises of pompous burial, until decay set in. The story is now discredited, and Johnson says he "once intended to omit" it (II.80), as it was unconfirmed. Why he included it he does not say.

Now Johnson comes to Dryden's character, beginning with Congreve's high praise, which "adds our love of his manners to our admiration of his genius." (II.82.) To have excited such fondness in such a mind as Congreve's "is no small degree of praise." (II.83.) Yet Dryden was well aware of his own merit and ready enough to condemn his own faults, so that "we allow his claims, and love his frankness." (II.84.) He was reputed jealous, but one instance (inciting Creech to translate Horace so as to fail) admits of no proof. He was "described as magisterially presiding over the younger writers," but "he who excels has a right to teach."

(II.85.) He was said to be sluggish in conversation, and, by an enemy, accused of being lewd.

In his writings, however, he was licentious, and at this Johnson was grieved and indignant. But some consolation Dryden has given, "by living to repent, and to testify his repentance." (II.88.) Now Johnson returns to Dryden's "meanness and servility of hyperbolical adulation" in which, since Roman days, he has never been equalled, except in an address by Aphra Behn to Nell Gwyn. (II.88.)

In attempting to arrive at an estimate of Dryden's financial situation in his last years, Johnson has found at least one piece of evidence, the contract for the *Fables*, for 250 guineas, which "the late amiable Mr. Tonson" had shown him, and this he reproduces, with Dryden's receipt. (II.96–98.) Another letter, of which he has only heard, asks Tonson to bring money to a watchmaker who will not release a watch without cash. So much, remarks Johnson, was Dryden dependent on his bookseller. There was a report also that the Duchess of Ormond had made him a gift of £500 for the *Fables* and that "a musical society" paid £40 for *Alexander's Feast*. (II.100.)

Seeking anecdotes, Johnson had talked to two old men who had known Dryden and had learned only that at Will's Coffee-house literary disputes were appealed to him, and that his winter chair, by the fire, was moved in summer to the balcony—"and that he called the two places his winter and his summer seat." (II.101.)

Johnson begins his estimate of Dryden as a writer by calling him "the father of English criticism," the first "to determine upon principles the merit of composition." (II.103.) The *Essay of Dramatick Poesie* is early in Dryden's career, before he had established a reputation as a critic, and is therefore carefully wrought, with the result that "The account of Shakspeare may stand as a perpetual model of encomiastick criticism; exact without minuteness, and lofty without exaggeration." (II.105.) All subsequent critics of Shakespeare, says Johnson, have merely elaborated upon Dryden. Moreover, Dryden mingles "delight" with "instruction": Johnson is firmly in the tradition of Sidney's "teach and delight."

From another point of view, Johnson remarks that Dryden's criticism may be considered under two heads. When it is general, it may be relied upon, for it is based on "the nature of things, and the structure of the human mind." (II.108.) At other times it is occasional, when he is defending a particular position, or is merely lazy or capricious. Examples of this second type are his defense and abandonment of rime, and his owning the grossness of one of his plays but denying the relevance of the charge.

Dryden, says Johnson, was not learned in the formal sense, but full of knowledge accidentally acquired through conversation. Then comes a summary analysis of Dryden's prose style which is worthy of a place next to a similar passage on Addison. Dryden's prefaces

> have not the formality of a settled style, in which the first half of the sentence betrays the other. The clauses are never balanced, nor the periods modelled; every word seems to drop by chance, though it falls into its proper place. Nothing is cold or languid; the whole is airy, animated, and vigorous; what is little, is gay; what is great, is splendid. He may be thought to mention himself too frequently; but while he forces himself upon our esteem, we cannot refuse him to stand high in his own. Every thing is excused by the play of images and the spriteliness of expression. Though all is easy, nothing is feeble; though all seems careless, there is nothing harsh; and though, since his earlier works, more than a century has passed, they have nothing yet uncouth or obsolete. (II.114–15.)

Johnson now turns to Dryden's poetry, in which he refined and improved the language, the sentiments, and the versification of his predecessors. No poetical diction had existed as such, no language which excluded the grossness of domestic use or the specialization of a craft or profession. And Johnson's explanation of why such a diction is necessary to poetry is strikingly like Gray's demand for a lofty language a few years earlier. Johnson says: "From those sounds which we hear on small or on coarse occasions, we do not easily receive strong impressions, or delightful images; and words to which we are nearly strangers, whenever they occur, draw that attention on themselves which they should transmit to things." (II.117.)

As a sort of subdivision of his discussion of poetic diction Johnson comments on Dryden's requirements for a proper translation: it should follow the style of the original, whether "rugged magnificence," "hyperbolical ostentation," or "sententious affectation." (II.120.) Johnson was always interested in the problems of translation, and his occasional remarks deserve notice.

He now turns to "the sentiments," and his first concern is with metaphor. The reader will recall Johnson's dislike of metaphysical conceits, and Johnson now gives several examples of "forced conceits" from Dryden's early poems, such as that Charles "Could taste no sweets of youth's desired age" (*Astraea*), or that one is struck blind "with rays of prosperous fortune." (II.125.) Improper use of mythology—probably any use of mythology would have offended Johnson—and extravagant fictions and hyperboles are further examples of Dryden's early faults of sentiment. *To my Lord Chancellor* represents an apex of these: "after this he did not often bring upon his anvil such stubborn and unmalleable thoughts." (II.131.) In *Annus Mirabilis* "The general fault is, that he affords more sentiment than description, and does not so much impress scenes upon the fancy, as deduce consequences and make comparisons." (II.133.) Again there are lines "perhaps indecently hyperbolical" (II.134), and "the sublime [is] too often mingled with the ridiculous." (II.135.) It may be mentioned parenthetically that this last fault Dryden turns to a stunning virtue in his mock-heroic poem *Mac Flecknoe*.

Dryden now "addicted himself almost wholly to the stage" (II.141) in order to support himself, but since the plays were in verse and rimed, this work served to improve his diction and his versification. The results show in *Absalom and Achitophel:* "If it be considered as a poem political and controversial, it will be found to comprise all the excellences of which the subject is susceptible; acrimony of censure, elegance of praise, artful delineation of characters, variety and vigour of sentiment, happy turns of language, and pleasing harmony of numbers." (II.143.) It has some faults, largely inherent in its allegorical-historical structure, which does not permit the author enough freedom and allows too little imagery or description. All in all, nevertheless, it is a great poem.

Of Dryden's lyrics, Johnson particularly admires the ode on the death of Mrs. Killigrew, "undoubtedly the noblest ode that our language ever has produced" (II.147), a burst of praise which will convince few modern readers. Johnson is especially impressed with the first stanza, "a torrent of enthusiasm," though he admits that the rest of the poem does not hold up to the beginning. He thinks less of *A Song for St. Cecilia's Day*—the rimes are too far apart, "diapason" is too technical—but the first stanza is "vigorous and elegant" and the conclusion striking. *Alexander's Feast* is without a rival, superior as a whole to the ode on Mrs. Killigrew, though without the excellence of the first stanza of that poem. It too has faults. . . .

With *Religio Laici* Dryden attempted didactic poetry, and Johnson finds it a forceful and perspicuous example of "this middle kind of writing." (II.152.) After Dryden's conversion he explained his new position in a similar sort of poem, *The Hind and the Panther*, but Johnson is uneasy at the thought of theological discussion among beasts: it is "injudicious and incommodious." (II.152.) But much more important, Dryden has at last found the closed couplet too rigid and has broken the third and fourth couplets:

> Yet had she oft been chac'd with horns and hounds
> And Scythian shafts, and many winged wounds
> Aim'd at her heart; was often forc'd to fly,
> And doom'd to death, though fated not to die. (II.154.)

Johnson is struck with this new effect: "These lines are lofty, elegant, and musical, notwithstanding the interruption of the pause, of which the effect is rather increase of pleasure by variety, than offence by ruggedness." (In 1818 Keats was to reach for the same effect in *Endymion.*) This poem also has one feature the absence of which Johnson noted in *Absalom:* "an abundant multiplicity of images." (II.157.)

Johnson treats Dryden's translations at greater length than the modern reader will need. The Juvenal lacks grandeur; the Persius is uniformly mediocre; the Vergil, originally praised by his friends and attacked by one or two rivals (one attempted a translation which "when dragged into the world, did not live long enough to cry" [II.167]), was eventually found to have flaws.

But Johnson is finally tiring of what one might call the plus-and-minus school of criticism, and comes out in favor of Dryden's Vergil with a rousing affirmation:

> It is not by comparing line with line that the merit of great works is to be estimated, but by their general effects and ultimate result. It is easy to note a weak line, and write one more vigorous

> in its place; to find a happiness of expression in the original, and transplant it by force into the version: but what is given to the parts, may be subducted from the whole, and the reader may be weary, though the critick may commend. Works of imagination excel by their allurement and delight; by their power of attracting and detaining the attention. That book is good in vain, which the reader throws away. He only is the master, who keeps the mind in pleasing captivity; whose pages are perused with eagerness, and in hope of new pleasure are perused again; and whose conclusion is perceived with an eye of sorrow, such as the traveller casts upon departing day. (II.168–69.)

Johnson begins his summary of Dryden's literary character by declaring him dominated by "strong reason" rather than "quick sensibility" (II.173), a position to which few will object. Furthermore, his comedy arises from situation rather than "any original humour." He delighted in "wild and daring sallies of sentiment" (II.176) and could never "resist the temptation of a jest." (II.181.) (Johnson said the same thing of Shakespeare.) He is too fond of fashionable French words. Such "faults of affectation," however, are exceeded by his "faults of negligence; . . . he seldom struggled after supreme excellence." (II.182.) Johnson found in his poems no single correction after publication (though Dryden did revise his prose *Essay of Dramatick Poesie*). There follows an examination of Dryden's use of triplets and Alexandrines, on which Johnson is noncommittal, and his rimes, of which he generally approves.

We owe to Dryden, Johnson says, the refinement of our meter, our language, our sentiments. Finally, "What was said of Rome, adorned by Augustus, may be applied by an easy metaphor to English poetry embellished by Dryden, *lateritiam invenit, marmoream reliquit*, he found it brick, and he left it marble." (II.189.)

Smith

1672–1710

Readers of Boswell will not need to be reminded how often Johnson was roused to opposition by overpraise, as, when asked whether Derrick or Smart was the best poet, he replied, "Sir, there is no settling the point of precedency between a louse and a flea." (*Life*, IV.192.) In the *Lives of the Poets* it is easy to find many examples of the same sort of thing. One of the most notable occurs in the *Life of Smith*. Johnson reprints Oldisworth's very long "Character" of Smith on the grounds that it contains most of what is known of him. From a riot of unrestrained enthusiasm, two typical remarks may be quoted: "His condolance for the death of Mr. Philips is full of the noblest beauties, and hath done justice to the ashes of that second Milton, whose writings will last as long as the English language, generosity, and valour." (II.227–28.) "But as to *Phaedra*, she has certainly made a finer figure under Mr. Smith's conduct, upon the English stage, than either Rome or Athens; and if she excels the Greek and Latin *Phaedra*, I need not say she surpasses the French one, though embellished with whatever regular beauties and moving softness Racine himself could give her." (II.229–30.) Johnson withholds comment until the end, when he says, "Such is the declamation of Oldisworth, written while his admiration was yet fresh, and his kindness warm; and therefore such as, without any criminal purpose of deceiving, shews a strong desire to make the most of all favourable truth." (II.237.)

Johnson's praise, in the face of such provocation, is modest. He finds Smith's Latin ode on the death of Pocock "excellent" (II.238); of his lampoon on Dr. Aldrich, "I once heard a single line too gross to be repeated." (II.241.) He disagrees with Addison that the neglect of Smith's *Phaedra* is "disgraceful to the nation": "The authority of Addison is great; yet the voice of the people, when to please the people is the purpose, deserves regard. In this question, I cannot but think the people in the right." The mythology is false; the manners are so distant that one cannot sympathize with them. "What I cannot for a moment believe, I cannot for a moment behold with interest or anxiety." The diction "is too luxuriant and splendid for dialogue, and envelopes the thoughts rather than displays them. It is a scholar's play. . . ." (II.244–45.)

Johnson credits Walmesley, Registrar of the Ecclesiastical Court at Lichfield, with telling him many things about Smith, whom he had known, and ends the biography with three tributes now justly famous:

Of Gilbert Walmsley, thus presented to my mind, let me indulge myself in the remembrance. I knew him very early; he was one of the first friends that literature procured me, and I hope that at least my gratitude made me worthy of his notice.

He was of an advanced age, and I was only not a boy; yet he never received my notions with contempt. He was a Whig, with all the virulence and malevolence of his party; yet difference of opinion did not keep us apart. I honoured him, and he endured me.

He had mingled with the gay world, without exemption from its vices or its follies, but had never neglected the cultivation of his mind; his belief of Revelation was unshaken; his learning preserved his principles; he grew first regular, and then pious.

His studies had been so various, that I am not able to name a man of equal knowledge. His acquaintance with books was great; and what he did not immediately know, he could at least tell where to find. Such was his amplitude of learning, and such his copiousness of communication, that it may be doubted whether a day now passes in which I have not some advantage from his friendship.

At this man's table I enjoyed many chearful and instructive hours, with companions such as are not often found; with one who has lengthened, and one who has gladdened life; with Dr. James, whose skill in physick will be long remembered; and with David Garrick, whom I hoped to have gratified with this character of our common friend: but what are the hopes of man! I am disappointed by that stroke of death, which has eclipsed the gaiety of nations, and impoverished the publick stock of harmless pleasure. (II.252–53.)

Duke

1658–1711

Johnson's life of Richard Duke vies with that of Pomfret for brevity. The best that Johnson can bring himself to say of this friend of Otway is: "His poems are not below mediocrity; nor have I found much in them to be praised." (II.257.)

King

1663–1712

Johnson's brief *Life of King* is of interest chiefly as an unacknowledged abridgement of a biography by Johnson's friend John Nichols, as Nichols states in a note to his *Select Collection of Poems*, 1780 (III.3 n.). It contains no criticism, except a suggestion that King's verse was easy and his images familiar. I can venture no explanation for Johnson's silence as to his source, which is particularly curious inasmuch as Nichols, as one of the publishers of the *English Poets*, was regularly prodding Johnson to move ahead with his work.

Sprat

1636–1713

Johnson runs quickly through the *Life of Sprat*, the chief interest of which is his ecclesiastical career. Johnson's opinion of Sprat's poems is low: "There is in his few production no want of such conceits as he thought excellent; and of those our judgement may be settled by the first that appears in his praise of Cromwell, where he says that Cromwell's 'fame, like man, will grow white as it grows old.' " (II.276.)

Halifax

1661–1715

In the first paragraph of the *Life of Halifax* Johnson remarks that his account "may properly be proportioned not to his influence in the state, but to his rank among the writers of verse." (II.277.) It is accordingly brief. Although he was a patron of poets, and therefore praised by them, "Many a blandishment was practised upon Halifax, which he would never have known, had he had no other attractions than those of his poetry, of which a short time has withered the beauties." (II.284.)

Parnell

1679–1718

> The life of Dr. Parnell is a task which I should very willingly decline, since it has been lately written by Goldsmith, a man of such variety of powers, and such felicity of performance, that he always seemed to do best that which he was doing; a man who had the art of being minute without tediousness, and general without confusion; whose language was copious without exuberance, exact without constraint, and easy without weakness.
>
> What such an author has told, who would tell again? I have made an abstract from his larger narrative; and have this gratification from my attempt, that it gives me an opportunity of paying due tribute to the memory of Goldsmith. (II.285–86.)

To this graceful compliment to a man whose biography he was not going to write, Johnson adds another, on those poems by Parnell published by Pope: "Of these Goldsmith has given an opinion, and his criticism it is seldom safe to contradict" (II.289), but actually his agreement with Goldsmith is confined to praising three poems, "The Rise of Woman," "The Fairy Tale," and "Pervigilium Veneris." Whereas Goldsmith prefers "Night Piece on Death" to Gray's *Elegy*, in Johnson's opinion "Gray has the advantage in dignity, variety, and originality of sentiment." (II.290.) Moreover, Goldsmith has ignored the "Elegy to an Old Beauty," "perhaps the meanest," and the "Allegory on Man," the "happiest" of Parnell's poems. (II.290.)

In general, Johnson believes that Parnell lacked largeness or "fertility" of mind, as well as originality. Yet he has "easy sweetness" of diction; "in his verses there is *more happiness than pains;* he is spritely without effort, and always delights, though he never ravishes." (II.290–91.)

Johnson closes with a strange remark: these comments apply only to those poems published by Pope. "Of the large appendages which I find in the last edition, I can only say that I know not whence they came, nor have ever enquired whither they are going." (II.291.) This total lack of curiosity seems to imply that the world has had quite enough poems by Parnell already.

Garth

1661–1718

Johnson's *Life of Garth* is almost wholly devoted to *The Dispensary*, the one poem for which Dr. Garth was famous during his lifetime. The London College of Physicians in 1687 had decided to require its fellows and associates to give free treatment to the poor, but in a short time found that the high price of medicines frustrated this charity. They therefore proposed to compound the medicines in the laboratory of the College, and to dispense them at or below cost through the apothecaries. That group bitterly opposed the scheme, which was nevertheless put into effect. Garth's poem describes this quarrel, but by the time of Johnson's writing, the charity was dead, and the poem, too closely attached to a single event, was dying. Johnson comments on its "smooth and free versification," and its lack of many "eminently elegant" lines. (II.299.) The plan is not justly proportioned to the subject; the characters are not discriminated from one another. But the author was diligent, and, according to Pope, each corrected edition was an improvement over the preceding. That the poem "appears, however, to want something of poetical ardour" (II.300) is Johnson's last word. Who can disagree?

Rowe

1674–1718

The *Life of Rowe* is one of the few in which Johnson pays more than the scantest attention to the subject's father. In this case, John Rowe, a lawyer and an editor of law reports, had during the reign of James II remarked "how low his authors rated the prerogative." (II.302.) This must have required courage in the time of that headstrong upholder of the royal prerogative, and that is perhaps the reason Johnson gives the story. The son left law after the successful production of his first play, *The Ambitious Stepmother*, which was followed by *Tamerlane*, in which the hero represented William III and Bajazet Louis XIV. In it Rowe gave Louis "all that can raise horror and detestation; and whatever good was withheld from him, that it might not be thrown away, was bestowed upon King William." (II.303.) Such a black-and-white political drama soon lost its initial popularity.

The Fair Penitent, on the other hand, Johnson thought "one of the most pleasing tragedies on the stage, where it still keeps its turns of appearing, and probably will long keep them, for there is scarcely any work of any poet at once so interesting by the fable, and so delightful by the language. The story is domestick, and therefore easily received by the imagination, and assimilated to common life; the diction is exquisitely harmonious, and soft or spritely as occasion requires." (II.304.) And he found a chance to praise *Clarissa:*

> The character of Lothario seems to have been expanded by Richardson into Lovelace, but he has excelled his original in the moral effect of the fiction. Lothario, with gaiety which cannot be hated, and bravery which cannot be despised, retains too much of the spectator's kindness. It was in the power of Richardson alone to teach us at once esteem and detestation, to make virtuous resentment overpower all the benevolence which wit, elegance, and courage, naturally excite; and to lose at last the hero in the villain. (II.304–05.)

Johnson finds the fifth act below the others in its lack of action, and suggests that Calista's behavior shows not penitence but rage at being caught.

Ulysses, the next play, "is now generally neglected," the "common fate of mythological stories." Johnson now gives some reason for his regular objection to the use of ancient myths in eighteenth-century literature: "We have been too early acquainted with the poetical heroes, to expect any pleasure from their revival." (II.305.) I suspect that this means that readers learned to dislike them when they were in school. *The Royal Convert* is more promising, since it is laid in the dim mists of early British history. And here Johnson pays real tribute to the power of the imagination on the stage—a power which had been given considerable credit by Dryden, and was to be given still more by Coleridge: "when objects are imperfectly seen, they easily take forms from imagination." Johnson likes Rodogune, "a personage truly tragical, of high spirit, and violent passions, great with tempestuous dignity, and wicked with a soul that would have been heroic if it had been virtuous." (II.306.)

Rowe's only comedy, *The Biter*, amused Rowe greatly, but not the public. *Jane Shore*, however, "consisting chiefly of domestick scenes and private distress, lays hold upon the heart" (II.307–08), and consequently, says Johnson, still held the stage in his day. Although Rowe thought it written "in imitation of Shakspeare's style" (II.307), Johnson, more disinterestedly, insisted that it resembled Shakespeare in no respect whatever.

In Rowe's edition of Shakespeare, Johnson finds that "many passages are happily restored" (II.309), but is unimpressed with the Life or the Preface.

To a long eulogy by Rowe's biographer Welwood, Johnson added a complimentary remark by Pope, and then a bitter aside by Addison as reported by Pope. Johnson's comment on this shows his usual skepticism, a useful trait for a biographer: "This censure time has not left us the power of confirming or refuting; but observation daily shews, that much stress is not to be laid on hyperbolical accusations, and pointed sentences, which even he that utters them desires to be applauded rather than credited." (II.316.)

Of Rowe's non-dramatic poetry, only his translation of the *Pharsalia* impressed Johnson, and it impressed him highly:

> The version of Lucan is one of the greatest productions of English poetry; for there is perhaps none that so completely exhibits the genius and spirit of the original. Lucan is distinguished by a kind of dictatorial or philosophic dignity, rather, as Quintilian observes, declamatory than poetical; full of ambitious morality and pointed sentences, comprised in vigorous and animated lines. This character Rowe has very diligently and successfully preserved. . . . The *Pharsalia* of Rowe deserves more notice than it obtains, and as it is more read will be more esteemed. (II.319–20.)

Addison

1672–1719

Johnson's *Addison* is one of the longer lives, and is of more than routine interest. Johnson begins by saying, as he has done before, that omitting the names of schoolmasters of famous authors is "a kind of historical fraud." (II.321.) He therefore names Naish of Ambrosbury, Taylor of Salisbury, and Shaw of

Lichfield, "father of the late Dr. Peter Shaw." He thus gives pleasure to the relatives of those men, and salutes his own grammar school. This introduces an anecdote from Johnson's boyhood friend Andrew Corbet, who had it from his uncle. Toward the end of the seventeenth century, students in many schools indulged in a "savage" practice called "barring-out." As they grew restive with the approach of the summer vacation they "took possession of the school, of which they barred the doors, and bade their master defiance from the windows." (II.322.) Johnson finds it hard to believe that the master would do more than laugh, but he has forgotten that, by that season, the master's patience might be worn thin. At any rate, such a barring-out had occurred at Lichfield, with Addison as ringleader. That is all—the ending is missing. We are not told that the master was livid with rage and flogged the future Spectator to an inch of his life. It is useless that Johnson tells us that he inquired fruitlessly into the story; he should have invented an ending.

Addison continued his studies at Charterhouse, where he became intimate with Steele. Johnson judiciously observes that "Of this memorable friendship the greater praise must be given to Steele" (II.323), for Addison considered himself the superior genius, played jests upon Steele without danger of retort, and having lent Steele £100, got it back by an execution. In spite of such strains, the friendship survived. Addison went on to Oxford, where he "grew first eminent" in Latin compositions. With the subjects of his Latin poems, Johnson is not happy: "When the matter is low or scanty, a dead language, in which nothing is mean because nothing is familiar, affords great conveniences"; penury of thought is easily concealed. (II.326.) Johnson does not tell us that he, as a schoolboy, made a delightful translation of one of these poems, "The Battle of the Pygmies and Cranes."

Addison's first significant adult verse was a poem to Dryden, followed by a translation of part of Vergil's Fourth Georgic, which Dryden admired rather extravagantly. But Addison's power as a critic developed more slowly. His essays on the Georgics, Johnson calls "juvenile, superficial, and uninstructive." Moreover, in a poem on the principal English poets, he included "a very confident" character of Spenser, whom he had not read. (II.327.) Soon afterward, Congreve introduced him to Montague, and, says

Johnson, as "Addison was then learning the trade of a courtier [he] subjoined Montague as a poetical name to those of Cowley and of Dryden." (II.328.) He abandoned a plan to enter holy orders, wrote poems addressed to King William and Lord Somers, wrote another on the Peace of Ryswick, and though still without public employment was given a pension of £300 a year to travel. He was twenty-seven.

After a year in France he proceeded to Italy, "which he surveyed with the eyes of a poet." (II.329.) There he wrote his *Dialogues on Medals* and the first four acts of *Cato*, as well as his *Letter to Lord Halifax*, "the most elegant, if not the most sublime" of his poems. (II.330.) Of his *Travels*, published on his return, Johnson thought the part on "the minute republick of San Marino" the most amusing, but found in general that Addison's "elegance of language, and variegation of prose and verse" gained upon the reader. (II.330.)

Still no job. The Battle of Blenheim, however, prompted Godolphin, the Lord Treasurer, to complain that the victory had not been adequately celebrated in verse. Halifax retorted that there was no monetary encouragement for genius, and Lord Godolphin agreed that if a capable man could be found, he would be rewarded. Johnson now gives a capsule example of why Halifax was such a successful politician: he "then named Addison; but required that the Treasurer should apply to him in his own person." (II.332.) Godolphin did; Addison wrote *The Campaign* and thereafter immediately succeeded Locke as Commissioner of Appeals. Further advancement followed.

Then Addison, hoping to counteract the rage for Italian opera, wrote *Rosamond*, in English. It failed on the stage, and so he printed it, with a dedication to the Duchess of Marlborough, "a woman without skill, or pretensions to skill, in poetry . . . an instance of servile absurdity." (II.333.) The contrast between this servile dedication and the tactful way in which Halifax had handled Addison's *Campaign* is strongly implied.

In 1709 Lord Wharton, "a bad man," was appointed Lord Lieutenant of Ireland, and Addison went there as his secretary. Johnson is at some pains to justify Addison's working under such a man, insisting that a subordinate need not approve either the opinions or the conduct of his superior, so long as one is not "made the instrument of wickedness." (II.334.) Moreover, we are allowed to suppose that Addison accomplished some good and prevented some mischief.

While Addison was in Ireland, Steele began *The Tatler*, but within six weeks Addison had not only pierced his friend's anonymity but had contributed a paper. The collaboration continued, but by January 1711 the men had decided to issue a new paper, published daily instead of twice a week, "written with less levity" and "upon a more regular plan." *The Spectator* began to appear in about two months, and although Addison "had enough of the zeal of party" and Steele "at that time almost nothing else" (II.336), they soon managed to avoid party politics in favor of "subjects on which faction had produced no diversity of sentiments; such as literature, morality, and familiar life." There were occasional exceptions, such as when a preface to Dr. William Fleetwood's *Free Sermons*, "overflowing with Whiggish opinions," was reprinted in *The Spectator*, No. 384, "that it might be read by the Queen." (II.337.) Anne was presumably too wary to pick up a volume of sermons by a known Whig, but too devoted to *The Spectator* to miss anything in it.

Johnson comments that *The Spectator* continued the tradition of the courtesy books begun by della Casa and Castiglione in Italy and La Bruyère in France: "To teach the minuter decencies and inferior duties, to regulate the practice of daily conversation, to correct those depravities which are rather ridiculous than criminal, and remove those grievances which, if they produce no lasting calamities, impress hourly vexation. . . ." (II.337.) Johnson remarks that before Addison and Steele, England had "no masters of common life" except dramatists. (II.338.) (This is a most interesting exception, and I should think that a useful and amusing work on Restoration comedy might be written using such an hypothesis.) Johnson continues that England had lacked "an *arbiter elegantiarum*, a judge of propriety . . . who should survey the track of daily conversation, and free it from thorns and prickles, which teaze the passer, though they do not wound him." (II.338.) So close does Johnson come to Lord Chesterfield's insistence on the graces!

He then suggests that, "at a time when two parties, loud, restless, and violent, each with plausible declarations, and each perhaps without any distinct termination of its views, were agitating the nation," *The Tatler* and *The Spectator* "supplied cooler and more inoffensive reflections." (II.340.) (So much has Johnson's youthful Toryism moderated that, in old age, he now makes no distinction between the violence of Whig opinion and that of the Tories.)

Addison and Steele, however, did not merely carry on the tradition of the courtesy books: "they superadded literature and criticism, and sometimes towered far above their predecessors; and taught, with great justness of argument and dignity of language, the most important duties and sublime truths." (II.341.)

Cato was now ready for the stage, and Johnson comments that Addison used every precaution to secure a favorable hearing, from (perhaps) writing in *The Spectator* to prepare the audience for an ending in violation of poetic justice, through softening Pope's Prologue ("Britons, *arise*" to "Britons, *attend*"), to allowing Steele to pack the house. "The danger was soon over. . . . The Whigs applauded every line in which Liberty was mentioned, as a satire on the Tories; and the Tories echoed every clap, to shew that the satire was unfelt." (II.347–48.) Dennis attacked the play, but Addison was judicious enough not to reply to "a criticism, which, though sometimes intemperate, was often irrefragable." (II.352.)

Another essay-periodical followed, *The Guardian*, "with the same elegance, and the same variety" (II.352), as *The Spectator*, but Steele, its principal editor, soon dropped it in favor of *The Englishman*, which was primarily political.

As Johnson comes to the consideration of Addison's only comedy, *The Drummer*, he remarks that many of the essays "were written with powers truly comick, with nice discrimination of characters, and accurate observation of natural or accidental deviations from propriety" (II.353), and that such characters appear in the play. Nevertheless it failed. This "would raise wonder, did we not daily see the capricious distribution of theatrical praise." (II.354.)

Very different were the essays of *The Whig Examiner*, "in which is employed all the force of gay malevolence and humorous satire." (II.355.) Johnson takes the occasion to loose a blast at Swift, who had remarked "with exultation, that 'it is now down among the dead men.' He might well rejoice at the death of that which he could not have killed." (II.355.) Johnson, the erstwhile hard-shell Tory, continues: "Every reader of every party, since personal malice is past, and the papers which once inflamed the nation are read only as effusions of wit, must wish for more of the *Whig Examiners;* for on no occasion was the genius of Addison more vigorously exerted, and on none did the superiority of his powers more evidently appear." (II.355.)

Returning for a moment to biography, Johnson mentions that after the death of Queen Anne, Addison, as Secretary to the Regency, was required to notify Hanover that the throne was vacant. But he was paralyzed by "the greatness of the event" (II.357), and so hesitated over the choice of words that a clerk wrote the message instead. No such difficulty affected his next essay-periodical, *The Freeholder*, in which "his humour was singular and matchless. Bigotry itself must be delighted with the Tory-Fox-hunter." (II.358.) So comments Tory Dr. Johnson.

Addison's marriage to the Countess Dowager of Warwick, whom he had long courted, Johnson treats rather briefly. It was reported, without contradiction, to have "made no addition to his happiness; it neither found them nor made them equal." (II.360.) And though in the next year Addison was made Secretary of State, he found himself "unequal" to his duties, and resigned. (II.360.)

Among Addison's reported projects, Johnson says, was an English dictionary, and Johnson had been sent a collection of examples said to have been taken by Addison from Tillotson's works. (Both hedges in this sentence are typical of Johnson's skepticism in handling hearsay evidence.) But the collection "came too late to be of use. . . . I thought the passages too short." (II.362–63.) Johnson is recollecting the ample quotations—a whole sonnet for instance—with which he illustrated usage in his *Dictionary*.

Now at the end of Addison's life he found himself fighting Steele over a bill permanently fixing the number of peers, Addison pro, Steele con. Addison lost his good sense enough to write of "Little Dicky, whose trade it was to write pamphlets." (II.365.) Steele, for once, kept his head. Johnson comments sadly that "among the uncertainties of the human state, we are doomed to number the instability of friendship." (II.366.) Johnson notes that the controversy is not mentioned by Tickell, Addison's official biographer, probably because the heat of the controversy had not yet cooled. This brings him to some general comments about biography:

> The necessity of complying with times, and of sparing persons, is the great impediment of biography. History may be formed from permanent monuments and records; but Lives can only be written from personal knowledge, which is growing every day less, and in a short time is lost for ever. . . . The delicate features of the mind, the nice discriminations of character, and the minute peculiarities of conduct, are soon obliterated. . . . As the process of these narratives is now bringing me among my contemporaries, I begin to feel myself "walking upon ashes under which the fire is not extinguished," and coming to the time of which it will be proper rather to say "nothing that is false, than all that is true." (II.366–67.)

The reader will scarcely need to be reminded that Johnson knew that Boswell intended to write his life, and that Boswell had ample materials. It should nevertheless be clear that Johnson had no suspicion that Boswell would not spare persons and would indeed indulge in "unseasonable detection." (II.367.) On this point, see also Boswell's introduction to his *Life of Johnson.*

Johnson now repeats the story of Addison's calling in his wild stepson, the Earl of Warwick, to "see how a Christian can die." (II.368.) Then he comments on his character: he was not accused of any crime even by his political enemies; he was "timorous," although Steele said that he had "humour more exquisite and delightful than any other man ever possessed." (II.371.) Pope thought Addison's conversation "more charming than I have found in any other man," but found him stiff among strangers. (II.372.) This sounds like quite ordinary shyness.

Johnson is less than satisfactory in his account of the relationship between Addison and Pope:

> There is no reason to doubt that he suffered too much pain from the prevalence of Pope's poetical reputation; nor is it without strong reason suspected, that by some disingenuous acts he endeavoured to obstruct it; Pope was not the only man whom he insidiously injured, though the only man of whom he could be afraid. (II. 372.)

Johnson cites no evidence, and indeed he would have been hard put to find any. For once, his usual skepticism has wholly deserted him; he has accepted Pope's side of the story without question. The passage reads like a toned-down paraphrase of the Atticus portrait from the *Epistle to Arbuthnot*, published when Addison had been dead for thirteen years.

Addison's reported addiction to wine brings forth a little sermon on alcoholism:

> From the coffee-house he went again to a tavern, where he often sat late, and drank too much wine. In the bottle, discontent seeks for comfort, cowardice for courage, and bashfulness for confidence. . . . He that feels oppression from the presence of those to whom he knows himself superior, will desire to set loose his powers of conversation; and who, that ever asked succour from Bacchus, was able to preserve himself from being enslaved by his auxiliary? (II.375–76.)

Johnson is building on rather shaky ground here, and the passage may have more autobiographical than biographical significance.

Johnson concludes his "character" of Addison with a really splendid sentence:

> No greater felicity can genius attain than that of having purified intellectual pleasure, separated mirth from indecency, and wit from licentiousness; of having taught a succession of writers to bring elegance and gaiety to the aid of goodness; and, if I may use expressions yet more useful, of having "turned many to righteousness." (II.379.)

Johnson now comes to a consideration of Addison's poetry and finds little to praise: "it has not often those felicities of diction which give lustre to sentiments, or that vigour of sentiment that animates diction: there is little of ardour, vehemence, or transport; there is very rarely the awfulness of grandeur, and not very often the splendour of elegance. He thinks justly, but he thinks faintly." (II.380–81.) He passes over five poems in as many sentences, but finds that the *Letter from Italy* "has been always praised, but has never been praised beyond its merit." Nevertheless, Johnson's remark that the poem is "more correct" and "more elegant" than any other of his poems (though it has one broken metaphor) hardly inspires the reader to take Addison's poems down from the shelf. (II.382.)

Johnson has greater praise for *The Campaign*. After remarking that "War is a frequent subject of Poetry," he asks who has described it "with more justness and force," implying that few or none have done so. (II.383.) But he is not impressed with the originality of comparing Marlborough and an angel, though this brings out an interesting remark on similes: "A simile may be compared to lines converging at a point, and is more excellent as the lines approach from greater distance. . . ." (II.386.) Remembering Johnson's comments on the metaphysical poets, the reader will notice that though Johnson's distant objects converge, they do so without violence.

When Johnson turns to Addison's opera, *Rosamond*, he is much more pleased: it is "one of the first [i.e., best] of Addison's compositions," well chosen in subject, pleasing in fiction, and, in the praise of Marlborough, "the product of good-luck improved by genius." (II.387) If for "good-luck" we substitute "happiness" in Pope's sense ("For there's a happiness as well as care," *Essay on Criticism*, I.142), we see precisely what Johnson means. There follows a very brief technical analysis of exceptional interest. Having said that the versification is "easy and gay," Johnson continues, "There is doubtless some advantage in the shortness of the lines, which there is little temptation to load with expletive epithets." In other words, the form has imposed a healthy restraint on a tendency to give every noun an adjective. Finally, "The whole drama is airy and elegant; engaging in its process, and pleasing in its conclusion. If Addison had cultivated the lighter parts of poetry, he would probably have excelled." (II.387–88.)

This is more than Johnson can say of *Cato*, which has "forced its way" into the collection of poems "by the weight of its character" (reputation?), whereas plays by other authors were excluded. But this gives an opening for a shrewd remark on public opinion: "About things on which the public thinks long, it commonly attains to think right; and of *Cato* it has been not unjustly determined, that it is rather a poem in dialogue than a drama. . . ." (II.388.) We are not concerned with the action, nor with the characters, but with the sentiments and the expression of them. Having dismissed *Cato* as a play, Johnson now, incomprehensibly, quotes some twenty-three pages of Dennis' adverse criticism, which is concerned wholly with *Cato* as drama, principally condemning Addison's rigid observance of the unity of place, which results in considerable improbability, but also condemning the absence of poetic justice in the ending. On this last, Johnson has some comments:

> Whatever pleasure there may be in seeing crimes punished and virtue rewarded, yet, since wickedness often prospers in real life, the poet is certainly at liberty to give it prosperity on the stage. For if poetry has an imitation of reality, how are its laws broken by exhibiting the world in its true form? The stage may sometimes gratify our wishes; but, if it be truly the *mirror of life*, it ought to shew us sometimes what we are to expect. (II.393.)

The effect of the long series of quotations from Dennis—longer than all of Johnson's comments on Addison's poems put together—is to submerge Johnson's criticism entirely. This section could have benefited from a strong editorial blue-pencil. His concluding remarks are little more than a paraphrase of his opening ones, with the addition of one lame sentence: "He was however one of our earliest examples of correctness." (II.414.) His versification Johnson does not much admire: it is "too smooth" in *Cato*, and his rimes are "often dissonant." (II.415, 414.)

With apparent relief, Johnson then turns to Addison's criticism, less "scholastic" than Dryden's and therefore better suited to his purpose, which was "to infuse literary curiosity, by gentle and unsuspected conveyance, into the gay, the idle, and the wealthy" (II. 415–16) and to expand comprehension. In this double aim he has admirably succeeded, particularly in making Milton "an universal favourite" with readers of every class. Johnson is less pleased with Addison's "display of the beauties of *Chevy Chase*," for the simple reason that Johnson thinks that ballad "chill and lifeless." (II.417–18.) For Addison's *Remarks on Ovid*, however, and the essays on Wit and on the Pleasures of the Imagination Johnson has nothing but praise.

He ends with two famous paragraphs on Addison's prose, which must be quoted entire:

> His prose is the model of the middle style; on grave subjects not formal, on light occasions not groveling; pure without scrupulosity, and exact without apparent elaboration; always equable, and always easy, without glowing words or pointed sentences. Addison never deviates from his track to snatch a

grace; he seeks no ambitious ornaments, and tries no hazardous innovations. His page is always luminous, but never blazes in unexpected splendour.

It was apparently his principal endeavour to avoid all harshness and severity of diction; he is therefore sometimes verbose in his transitions and connections, and sometimes descends too much to the language of conversation; yet if his language had been less idiomatical, it might have lost somewhat of its genuine Anglicism. What he attempted, he performed; he is never feeble, and he did not wish to be energetick; he is never rapid, and he never stagnates. His sentences have neither studied amplitude, nor affected brevity: his periods, though not diligently rounded, are voluble and easy. Whoever wishes to attain an English style, familiar but not coarse, and elegant but not ostentatious, must give his days and nights to the volumes of Addison. (II.419–20.)

Hughes

1677–1720

The first poem by Hughes which Johnson mentions is Horace's "Integer Vitae," paraphrased "rather too diffusely." (II.421.) Perhaps Johnson had in mind his own schoolboy translation of the same poem, a fairly tight rendering. Six cantatas by Hughes "seem intended to oppose or exclude the Italian opera, an exotick and irrational entertainment." (II.422.) Thus Johnson aligns himself with the Addisonian opposition to the Italian opera, without committing himself on the quality of Hughes's productions. Translations from Fontenelle and Molière followed, with the result that he was "received as a wit among the wits." (II.424.) He contributed to *The Tatler*, *The Spectator*, and *The Guardian*, wrote an opera, *Calypso and Telemachus*, edited Spenser, and finally, at the close of his life, produced his one really popular work, *The Siege of Damascus*. Johnson remarks that the tragedy "still continues on the stage," and therefore "it is unnecessary to add a private voice to such continuance of approbation." (II. 426.) On "the character of his genius," Johnson quotes an exchange of letters between Swift and Pope. Swift: "He is too grave a poet for me; and I think among the *mediocrists*, in prose as well as verse." Pope: "what he wanted in genius, he made up as an honest man; but he was of the class you think him." (II.428.) By his silence, Johnson consents.

Sheffield

1648–1721

John Sheffield, Duke of Buckingham, was a warrior, statesman, and minor poet. An orphan at eleven, he quickly became dissatisfied with his tutor and decided to educate himself. Johnson is naturally impressed: "Such a purpose, formed at such an age, and successfully prosecuted, delights as it is strange, and instructs as it is real." (II.429.) He is less impressed with him as a poet: he "sometimes glimmers, but rarely shines, feebly laborious, and at best but pretty." (II.438.) It is a situation like that of Halifax—a peer who wrote verses was overrated by his contemporaries.

Prior

1664–1721

Prior first came into notice with his *The Country Mouse and the City Mouse* (with Charles Montague, later Lord Halifax). This satire on *The Hind and the Panther* was said to have caused Dryden "great pain" and tears. Johnson is skeptical as usual in assessing hearsay evidence: "Dryden had been more accustomed to hostilities, than that such enemies should break his quiet; and if we can suppose him vexed, it would be hard to deny him sense enough to conceal his uneasiness." (III.3–4.) Political preferment came not long afterward—secretary to the embassy at the Congress at the Hague, gentleman of the bed-chamber, secretary to the embassy at the Treaty of Ryswick, Under-Secretary of State, Commissioner of Trade. No wonder he considered King William a hero, and praised him as such in *Carmen Saeculare* (1700)—"one of his longest and most splendid compositions." (III.6.) Johnson is unexpectedly generous: "To Prior gratitude would dictate praise, which reason would not refuse." (III.7.) Among other things in the poem, Prior proposed a Society for Useful Arts, which should fix the English language, a notion later advocated by Swift and Tickell. Johnson has no comment.

Prior's poem on the Battle of Ramillies did call forth a Johnsonian comment: "Through the reigns of William and Anne no prosperous event passed undignified by poetry." Whereas in the Seven Years' War, the early stages of which Johnson had reported in *The Literary Magazine*, "no poet was heard amidst the general acclamation; the fame of our counsellors and heroes was intrusted to the Gazetteer." (III.9.) The contempt of that sentence is missed unless one remembers the mechanical dullness of that official paper.

In the negotiations for peace, Prior gained so much of the French king's confidence that Louis wrote to Anne, "I shall expect, with impatience, the return of Mr. Prior, whose conduct is very agreeable to me." (III.14.) But on the death of the Queen and the fall of the Tories he was imprisoned and impeached, though freed about two years later. On this treatment by Sir Robert Walpole, Johnson has a comment characteristic of his mature, not his youthful, attitude toward that statesman: "What made him so acrimonious does not appear: he was by nature no thirster for blood." (III.18.) The last years of Prior's life were occupied in publishing his poems and enjoying the society of his friends.

Of his character, Johnson remarks that "at a time when the rage of party detected all which it was any man's interest to hide," little was heard detrimental to Prior. (III.22.) Pope's opinion that Prior was fit only to make verses, is easily confuted by a mere reference to how many times he was recalled to perform the delicate negotiations for peace, with the trust of both Bolingbroke and Oxford. As to his private life: "His Chloe probably was sometimes ideal; but the woman with whom he cohabited was a despicable drab of the lowest species." (III.25.)

Johnson's estimate of Prior's poetry is relatively high: "He has tried all styles, from the grotesque to the solemn, and has not so failed in any as to incur derision or disgrace." His Tales are written with "great familiarity and great spriteliness." (III.27.) Johnson doubts whether any tale is original, but doesn't much care, since "the merit of such stories is the art of telling them."

(III.28.) The love-verses are less happy, since they have neither "gallantry nor tenderness," but only "the coldness of Cowley, without his wit." (III.28.) The occasional poems have begun to fade as their occasions recede into history, except for some "preserved by their inherent excellence," such as the burlesque of Boileau's *Ode on Namur*, which "has, in some parts, such airiness and levity as will always procure it readers." (III.29.) Johnson even suspects that he could praise or censure the *Carmen Saeculare* by caprice and not be detected, "for who can be supposed to have laboured through it?" (III.30.)

Alma, the only piece by Prior which Pope wished he himself had written, is less admired by Johnson. A professed imitation of *Hudibras*, it has one feature in common with Butler's poem: it has no plan. *Solomon* has only one major fault, tediousness, "the most fatal of all faults," as "novelty is the great source of pleasure." (III.33.) And Johnson decides that the tediousness of the poem results from the single point of view, "the continued tenour of the narration; in which Solomon relates the successive vicissitudes of his own mind, without the intervention of any other speaker, or the mention of any other agent, unless it be Abra." (III.34.) In other words, perhaps, the poem is far too long for a dramatic monologue, at least considering Prior's limited skill in that genre.

As Johnson moves to his conclusion his judgment becomes more severe: in general, Prior will be praised for "correctness and industry," rather than for "compass of comprehension, or activity of fancy." (III.35.) "Prior is never low, nor very often sublime. . . . He has many vigorous but few happy lines." (III.36–37.) And finally, "on higher occasions, and nobler subjects [than amorous verse], when habit was overpowered by the necessity of reflection, he wanted not wisdom as a statesman, nor elegance as a poet." (III.40.)

Congreve

1670–1729

Uncertain whether to believe Congreve, who said that he was born in England, or "everybody else," who said that he was born in Ireland, Johnson comments that "falsehoods of convenience or vanity, . . . are very lightly uttered, and once uttered are sullenly supported." (III.41–42.) Educated in Ireland, where his father was stationed, Congreve was then sent to London to study law at the Middle Temple, but like Steele's Templar in *The Spectator*, learned more drama than law. He wrote a novel, *Incognita: or, Love and Duty reconcil'd*, of which Johnson remarks, "I would rather praise it than read it." (III.43.) Johnson's comments on Congreve's precocity as a dramatist are somewhat undermined by the fact that he was unable to determine Congreve's correct age, and understates it by three years. Even for a writer of twenty-four, however, *The Old Batchelour* is remarkable. The Earl of Halifax became his patron, giving him two valuable government posts. Johnson shrewdly comments: "Congreve's conversation must surely have been at least equally pleasing with his writings." (III.45.) Johnson says further that comedy supposes an imitation of common life and manners, but that Congreve's play is one which might be made by a "mind vigorous and acute" (III.46), using characters from other plays and a dialogue consisting of constant reciprocation of conceits, or clash of wit, in which nothing flows necessarily from the occasion, or is dictated by nature. This analysis may well stand for all of Congreve's comedies, and Johnson adds little more, except by elegant variation: "his characters are commonly fictitious and artificial. . . . his personages are a kind of intellectual gladiators." (III.57.)

With Congreve's one tragedy, *The Mourning Bride*, Johnson is less pleased: "there is more bustle than sentiment" (III.48), but he quotes seventeen lines with very high praise: "if I were required to select from the whole mass of English poetry the most poetical paragraph, I know not what I could prefer. . . . He who reads those lines enjoys for a moment the powers of a poet; he feels what he remembers to have felt before, but he feels it with great increase of sensibility; he recognizes a familiar image, but meets it again amplified and expanded, embellished with beauty, and enlarged with majesty." (III.58–59.) Need I point out that these lines are in blank verse?

The rest of Congreve's poems Johnson quickly dismisses. That on the death of Queen Mary is "a despicable effusion of elegiac pastoral . . . in which all is unnatural, and yet nothing is new." (III.47.) His translation of Juvenal lacked "the massiness and vigour of the original" (III.63), an interesting note of two qualities in Juvenal which Johnson especially admired.

In discussing the controversy over the immorality of the stage, Johnson has an acute one-sentence vignette of Jeremy Collier: "He was formed for a controvertist; with sufficient learning; with diction vehement and pointed, though often vulgar and incorrect; with unconquerable pertinacity; with wit in the highest degree keen and sarcastick; and with all those powers exalted and invigorated by just confidence in his cause." (III.50.)

Finally, "Congreve has merit of the highest kind; he is an original writer, who borrowed neither the models of his plot, nor the manner of his dialogue." (III.57.)

Blackmore

c.1650–1729

Blackmore, after Westminster School, spent thirteen years at Oxford, where, Johnson suspects, he paid "very little attention to the business of the place" (III.65), inasmuch as classical proper names in his poems are "pronounced by chance." A shrewd deduction. But Blackmore acquired enough self-confidence, if not accuracy, so that he published four full-length epics, *Prince Arthur* and *King Arthur* in spite of the critics, and two others in spite of their silence. *Creation: a Philosophical Poem* was inserted in the *Poets* at Johnson's recommendation: he refers to Addison's praise in *Spectator* 339, and quotes Dennis', that the poem equals Lucretius in the beauty of its versification, and excels in its reasoning.

Johnson finds Blackmore's prose "languid, sluggish, and lifeless" (III.80), but *Creation* is successful in both ratiocination and description: "To reason in verse, is allowed to be difficult; but Blackmore not only reasons in verse, but very often reasons poetically; and finds the art of uniting ornament with strength, and ease with closeness. This is a skill which Pope might have condescended to learn from him, when he needed it so much in his Moral Essays." (III.94.) A modern critic will not easily be found to prefer Blackmore to Pope in any respect. Johnson ends with a long selection from *Prince Arthur*, the song of Mopas, a sop to the shades of Blackmore for omitting all four epics from the *Poets.*

Fenton

1683–1730

Johnson's *Fenton* is short: he had sought information from the poet's relatives in Staffordshire and had not got any. He remarks that Fenton's translations of Books I, IV, XIX, and XX for Pope's *Odyssey* have the merit of being indistinguishable from Pope's, and his tragedy *Mariamne* the merit of being rejected by Cibber and subsequently successful. On the versification of the play, Johnson has a curious comment: "*Mariamne* is written in lines of ten syllables, with few of those redundant terminations which the drama not only admits but requires, as more nearly approaching to real dialogue." (III.103.) This is a striking example of how Johnson's ear caught something wooden in the dialogue, and immediately found too little variation from the basic form. Of the rest of the poems, the "greatest fault" of one is its length, of another that it is "an occasional pastoral," of a third that it is an irregular ode (III.107), and therefore defective; in the *Paraphrase on Isaiah* he has "deserted his original," and so on, except that one poem is "no disagreeable specimen of epistolary poetry" (III.108), and that Pope thought the ode to Lord Gower excelled only by Dryden's *Cecilia.* With no more analysis, Johnson now concludes: "Fenton may be justly styled an excellent versifyer and a good poet." (III.108.) We are not convinced.

Gay

1685–1732

Johnson's *Gay* is also relatively slight but much more pointed. After Gay persuaded his master to discharge him as a silk-mercer's apprentice he found a place as secretary to the Duchess of Monmouth. In that post he composed his poem *Rural Sports,* dedicated to Pope, who admitted him to friendship, a further step up in the world. Next followed a comedy, *The Wife of Bath,* which failed, and then *The Shepherd's Week,* with images "drawn from real life, such as it appears among the rusticks in parts of England remote from London." (III.111.) Johnson notes that Pope had "incited" Gay to write the poems as part of the controversy over the alleged superiority of Ambrose Philips as a writer of pastorals. But he justly remarks that Gay's "became popular, and were read with delight, as just representations of rural manners" (III.112), and by those with no interest in the dispute.

A mock-tragedy, *The What d'ye call it*, brought the Prince and Princess of Wales to the theater, but *Three Hours after Marriage* was driven off the stage because the audience disliked some personal satire on Dr. Woodward the Fossilist. Gay had become known, however, as "a soft and civil companion" (III.114), and his many friends made the subscription edition of his poems a great financial success. This, and a present of a large block of South Sea stock, made him think himself rich, but he participated in the common disaster when the South Sea speculation collapsed. He returned to writing, produced a tragedy, *The Captives*, and then had *The Beggar's Opera* rejected by Cibber at Drury Lane. Rich accepted it for Covent Garden, and "as was ludicrously said," it made "Gay *rich*, and Rich *gay*." (III.118.) Johnson reports the conception and progress of the play from Spence's then unpublished *Anecdotes*, and, from the notes to Pope's *Dunciad*, the success of the play from London to Minorca. Johnson is equally unimpressed with Swift's claim that the tendency of the play is to place vice in the "most odious light" and another clergyman's censure that the play gave encouragement "not only to vice but to crimes." (III.121.) His saner comment is that the play was written "only to divert," and therefore unlikely to do much good or evil.

Johnson mentions Gay's other plays, without comment, and begins his formal criticism of the poems tepidly: "As a poet, he cannot be rated very high." (III.124.) But he at once credits Gay with the invention of a new species of composition, "though it be not of the highest kind," the ballad opera, which, already popular for half a century, "is likely to keep long possession of the stage." *Rural Sports* is neither very good nor very bad; *The Fan* is mythological, and the reader will recognize that word as pejorative in Johnson. Whether the fable is a distinct type, neither

Phaedrus nor Gay was very clear, but Gay's are nevertheless "told with liveliness; the versification is smooth, and the diction . . . is generally happy." (III.125–26.) *Trivia* is "spritely, various, and pleasant," though Johnson could have done without Vulcan and Cloacina. *Dione* is a pastoral—"A Pastoral of an hundred lines may be endured; but who will hear of sheep and goats, and myrtle bowers and purling rivulets, through five acts?" (III.127.)

Granville

1667–1735

When Granville was eighteen, he addressed three sets of verses to James II on his accession, the first of which, says Johnson, is profane (James II is compared to Christ). The others are unimportant. With the Revolution, Granville sided with the King, and Johnson prints a fine romantic letter to the boy's father, asking permission to join the royal forces. (This is the best and liveliest feature of the biography.) With the victory of William and Mary, Granville retired to write a series of plays, one of which, *Once a Lover and always a Lover* (*The She-Gallants*), Johnson had not seen, though he had heard that it was grossly indecent. Another, *Heroick Love*, is mythological, and "therefore" sank into neglect. (III.135.) The songs in *The British Enchanters* are lively, and that dramatic poem, Johnson thinks, is the best of his works, though his prologues and epilogues have a just claim to praise. On the whole he owes his reputation to his character, rather than to his writings.

Yalden

1670–1736

Yalden, a college-mate and friend of Addison, wrote a *Hymn to Darkness*, which Johnson thought his best performance, one stanza of which was "exquisitely beautiful" (III.149), though some others were marred with the combination of myth and religion. Another poem gave Johnson reason for a dictum with which the Romantic poets would have quarreled: "All wonder is the effect of novelty upon ignorance." (III.150.)

Tickell

1685–1740

Tickell was perhaps better known as the friend, eulogist, and editor of Addison than as a poet in his own right. Johnson found his praise of Addison's *Rosamond* "elegant" (III.152), but his *Prospect of Peace* "to be approved rather than admired." (III.153.) When Tickell's translation of the first book of the *Iliad* appeared simultaneously with the first part of Pope's translation, Addison declared Tickell's the superior. Pope was convinced that Addison had in fact made the translation to which Tickell put his name, and Johnson quotes from Spence's *Anecdotes* in support. Johnson merely notes that "the palm is now given universally to Pope" (III.157), though he himself prefers Tickell's opening lines, and he finds that Pope, in revisal, has "borrowed something" from Tickell. For the rest, the *Epistle to a Gentleman at Avignon* "stands high among party-poems" (III.158), perhaps a useful category worth reviving; the elegy on Addison is as sublime and elegant a funeral-poem as exists in English; and, finally, Tickell "cannot be refused a high place among the minor poets." (III.159.)

Hammond

1710–1742

The *Life of Hammond* is interesting only in that here Johnson declares that the work called Cibber's *Lives of the Poets,* the manuscript of which was in his possession, and which contained the life of Hammond, was in fact written by Robert Shiels, not Theophilus Cibber. Hammond's *Love Elegies,* which his friends admired, "have neither passion, nature, nor manners," "nothing but frigid pedantry" (III.164), and he has had the bad judgment to put them into pentameter quatrains, which ask for magnificence rather than sweetness.

Somervile

1675–1742

Somervile "writes very well for a gentleman." (III.168.) Now and then he is better than this, his serious pieces "sometimes elevated," and his trifles "sometimes elegant." And in his lines to Addison one couplet has "the most exquisite delicacy of praise." *The Chace*, however, is of no interest except to sportsmen, and *Hobbinol, or the Rural Games* is not helped by its vehicle: "If blank verse be not tumid and gorgeous, it is crippled prose." (III.170.)

Swift

1667–1745

Perhaps Johnson should not have written a life of Swift: basically he disliked him. He begins his account by a graceful compliment to Hawkesworth, for whose biography he had supplied much. He by-passes conflicting accounts of the place of Swift's birth, saying that the matter may be left "in the obscurity in which he delighted to involve it." (III.354.) Swift's economical traveling on foot and sleeping in the cheapest lodgings, Johnson is willing to attribute to a deep-seated passion, "the love of a shilling." (III.359.) He has been told that when Swift showed some poems to Dryden, the elder poet's unfavorable response caused Swift's "perpetual malevolence" to Dryden. (III.360.) He regards *A Tale of a Tub* as "certainly of dangerous example" (III.363), whatever Swift's motives. In "this wild work" some parts show "want of knowledge, or want of integrity" (III.364), and Johnson considers *The Battle of the Books* plagiarized.

Not all is so black. After an undistinguished college career, Swift set to work and educated himself. Moreover, his *Argument against Abolishing Christianity* is "a very happy and judicious irony" (III.365), and Johnson quotes a long paragraph reflecting his own views. And with Swift coming to London on behalf of the Irish clergy, there began "the busy and important part" of his life. (III.367.) In his *Examiner* papers, he excelled in argument, though Addison, in reply, excelled in wit.

A Proposal for Correcting, Improving and Ascertaining the English Tongue is "written without much knowledge of the general nature of language, and without any accurate enquiry into the history of other tongues." (III.369–70.) Johnson's experience in compiling his *Dictionary* had long since convinced him that no academy could ossify a living language. The success of *The Conduct of the Allies* Johnson attributes to "the mere weight of facts" (III.374) and to the receptive mood of the public. The *Journal to Stella* has "some odd attraction" (III.378), partly from the mention of the great men of the day.

On Swift's return to Dublin, as Dean, he had some difficulty with his Archbishop, which Johnson disposes of with succinctness and perhaps admiration: "it was soon discovered, that between prudence and integrity he was seldom in the wrong; and that, when he was right, his spirit did not easily yield to opposition." (III.381.) In 1716, Johnson reports, Swift married Stella, "as Dr. Madden told me, in the garden" (III.384); Johnson mentions, without comment, that they never cohabited. On the other hand, Swift's imbroglio with Vanessa aroused Johnson's sympathy, and he defends him: "Swift was then about forty-seven, at an age when vanity is strongly excited by the amorous attention of a young woman." Furthermore, "men are but men." (III.385–86.)

With the publication of the *Drapier Letters,* which forced the government to withdraw the new debased coinage, Swift reached a pinnacle of power in Ireland: "He was honoured by the populace, as the champion, patron, and instructor of Ireland; and gained such power as, considered both in its extent and duration, scarcely any man has ever enjoyed without greater wealth or higher station." (III.390.) Swift reached the peak of literary fame with *Gulliver's Travels,* "a production so new and strange, that it filled the reader with a mingled emotion of merriment and amazement." (III.392.) Everyone read it, but now that the initial excitement has cooled, judgment finds that the third part gives "the least pleasure" and the last the "most disgust." (III.393.)

The death of Stella brings Johnson to remark that by a private marriage, Swift had tried to have "all the pleasures of perfect friendship, without the uneasiness of conjugal restraint." (III.396.) The whole passage is marked by Johnson's warm sympathy for

Stella and his cool disdain of what he considered Swift's selfishness. Doubts as to the fact of the marriage Johnson dismisses, since it had been reported by the clergyman attending her last illness.

Swift's temper was not improved after Stella's death, but Johnson is fair to his writings of the period: "nothing fell from his pen in vain." (III.398.) Johnson now comes to a general account of Swift's work. In his London years the effect of his writing was such that he "dictated for a time the political opinions of the English nation" (III.406) and under George I "he delivered Ireland from plunder and oppression; and shewed that wit, confederated with truth, had such force as authority was unable to resist." (III.406.) Johnson's treatment of *A Tale of a Tub* is remarkable in that, though he detested much of the content, he admires its energy and its style: "It exhibits a vehemence and rapidity of mind, a copiousness of images, and vivacity of diction, such as he afterwards never possessed, or never exerted." (III.407.) As for the rest of Swift's prose, Johnson is particularly impressed by the diction: "His delight was in simplicity. . . . He studied purity" (III.407), and he was therefore able to convey his meaning clearly. Johnson, however, does not find that Swift used the passions. Evidently the suppressed fury of *A Modest Proposal* did not reach him.

Johnson is, however, disturbed by Swift's use of "disease, deformity, and filth," particularly in describing the Yahoos (III.419), and he has no suggestion why Swift used these, except that his mind was "tainted." That Swift used them for a satiric or philosophical purpose seems not to have occurred to him.

After quoting a long, laudatory character by Delany, Johnson turns very briefly to Swift's poems, commenting on their lightness, ease, and gaiety, the smoothness of the versification, and the exactness of the rime. Finally, he sums up with a measured and temperate statement: "It was said, in a Preface to one of the Irish editions, that Swift had never been known to take a single thought from any writer, ancient or modern. This is not literally true; but perhaps no writer can easily be found that has borrowed so little, or that in all his excellences and all his defects has so well maintained his claim to be considered as original." (III.424.)

Broome

1689–1745

Johnson's cousin Cornelius Ford, who had shared lodgings with Broome at Cambridge, thought the poet, as an undergraduate, "a mere versifyer." (III.426.) Later, Broome translated eight books of the *Odyssey* for Pope's version, and supplied all the notes, for which Pope gave less than due credit. (Johnson had sought out this information from Warburton and Langton.) In analysis, Johnson finds his lines "smooth and sonorous, and his diction . . . select and elegant." (III.430.) His rimes are sometimes inexact; his original work imitative. The modern reader will not need more comment.

Pope

1688–1744

Johnson's *Pope* is one of his major biographies, for several reasons. Most important, perhaps, is the fact that he admired Pope's poetry and was in harmony with most of Pope's aims in verse. Second, Pope was a near-contemporary: there was no great gap in time or ideas to be bridged. Third, Johnson had the advantage of information from friends of Pope, access to some of his working manuscripts, and, most important, the use of Joseph Spence's unpublished *Anecdotes*.

He is not uncritical of every aspect of Pope. Something of a snob, Pope was willing to have it known that his father was rich, but only through a Mrs. Racket was it discovered that the elder Pope had been a linen draper. As a boy of twelve, Pope asked to be taken to Will's Coffee House to see Dryden, and Johnson draws a shrewd deduction: a boy who wants to see an elderly poet must already "have felt the power of harmony, and the zeal of genius" (IV.6); but his first poem, an *Ode on Solitude*, is not remarkable. Nevertheless, two years later his lines *On Silence* show that he had "now formed his versification." (IV.7.) He was sixteen when he wrote his *Pastorals*, but they were not published for five years, during which time, Johnson suggests, they perhaps were polished. Wycherley encouraged the young man, as did Walsh, who suggested that, as no English poet had aimed at correctness, Pope should fill that void.

In 1709 he wrote the *Essay on Criticism*, "a work which displays such extent of comprehension, such nicety of distinction, such acquaintance with mankind, and such knowledge both of ancient and modern learning, as are not often attained by the maturest age and longest experience." (IV.14–15.) The poem was praised by Addison and attacked by Dennis, and Pope "made the proper use" of the attack (IV.18) by correcting his poem. Just the same, he felt Dennis' venom, and a life-long hostility began. About this time he wrote the *Verses To the Memory of an Unfortunate Lady*. Johnson failed to find the lady's name or much else, and so he accepted Owen Ruffhead's story that she was of high rank and fortune, under the care of a guardian who sent her abroad to recover from a love affair with a young man of "inferior condition." (IV.22.) She did not recover, but killed herself: "Poetry has not often been worse employed than in dignifying the amorous fury of a raving girl." (IV.24.) *The Rape of the Lock*, however, is wholly to Johnson's liking: "the most airy, the most ingenious, and the most delightful of all his compositions." (IV.24.) On this poem, Johnson's research had had some success: when in Paris he had talked to "Belinda's" niece, who considered the verses an insult to the Fermors. Excellent as the poem was in its original two-canto form, Pope decided to add the supernatural machinery in a five-canto version; the success demonstrated his "boundless fertility of invention." (IV.27.) Johnson's enthusiasm continues with *Eloisa to Abelard*, in which "he has excelled every composition of the same kind." (IV.28.) By "the same kind" Johnson appears to mean "that tender kind," a phrase which he has just used. But he is describing the poem from a reading not very recent, inasmuch as he mentions religious hope and resignation, which are not conspicuous in Eloisa.

In connection with the dispute over the superiority of Pope's *Pastorals* or Philips', Johnson is rather too ready to accept the view that Addison acted maliciously in printing a comparison in *The Guardian*. Seventy-eight years after the event, the motive was at least obscure. Johnson is here depending too heavily on his pro-Pope sources. At any rate, in the same year, 1713, Pope issued his proposals to publish a translation of the *Iliad* by subscription, a relatively new practice said to have begun with Dryden's *Vergil.* Johnson gives a detailed account of the origin, progress, and consummation of the work, and for this he had ample materials. Pope's profit was £5320, which he cautiously invested in annuities, so that he was never thereafter in financial straits. From the manuscript copy of the translation in the British Museum, Johnson printed several pages of variants along with the corresponding printed texts, showing Pope's progress from the "rudeness" of his first conceptions to the "elegance" of his last, leaving off only for fear of boring the common reader. (IV.55.)

After the first three books were finished, Lord Halifax asked Pope to read them to him, and not long thereafter Halifax made gestures towards securing the dedication. This Pope evaded, says Johnson, "because Pope was less eager of money than Halifax of praise." (IV.59.) This is a curious reason. I suspect that Johnson remembers his own imbroglio with Chesterfield over the *Dictionary*, and therefore sides with the sturdy author against the peer. It is at least equally possible that Pope had already decided to dedicate to Congreve. The publication of the first four books coincided with the appearance of a translation of Book I by Addison's protégé Tickell. Addison was reported to prefer Tickell's version, and before long Pope decided that Addison had in fact made the translation published under Tickell's name. Here again Johnson accepted Pope's account too uncritically, and described Addison's supposed act as "a crime." (IV.65.) Johnson was fully aware that Pope's mind was devious, but he was incapable of imagining how devious it was.

In 1717 Pope collected his works, prefixing a Preface of "great spriteliness and elegance," to which in later editions he added marginal variants of material originally omitted. Thus his "voracity of fame" enabled him to show both what he had printed and what suppressed. (IV.69.) His edition of Shakespeare, 1721, was attacked by Theobald, "a man of heavy diligence, with very slender powers" (IV.71), but in it Pope first showed how the text might be improved, and that early editions ought to be examined. His Preface "expanded with great skill" (IV.72) Dryden's character of Shakespeare.

Pope's *Odyssey* followed, of which Broome and Fenton translated half, with Broome furnishing all of the notes: "The public was carefully kept ignorant of the several shares; and an account was subjoined at the conclusion, which is now known not to be true." (IV.74.) The reader's attention might be drawn to the word "carefully" in the last sentence: when Johnson decided to damn someone, he could do it succinctly. An interesting by-product of Pope's *Odyssey* is that it introduced him to Spence, who criticized the translation. In him, Pope first found a man who "censured with respect, and praised with alacrity." (IV.76.) Friendship followed, and Spence was enabled to compile his invaluable *Anecdotes* of Pope.

In 1728 *The Dunciad* appeared, in which Pope tried to "sink into contempt" all his attackers, and "some others whom he thought unable to defend themselves." (IV.79.) Again Johnson points up in a few words the character of Pope's behavior. Theobald was the first hero, and was joined with others, whose names were in one edition indicated by the first and last letters, but in another given in full. Johnson suggests that if the victims had suffered in silence the poem would have sold slowly; but controversy gave it impetus. Dennis, Duckett, and Aaron Hill protested, and "Pope was reduced to sneak and shuffle, sometimes to deny, and sometimes to apologize; he first endeavours to wound, and is then afraid to own that he meant a blow." (IV.87.)

The story of the publication of Pope's letters follows—that the manuscript was offered to the piratical publisher Curll by a third, unknown, person, that Curll published, and that Pope was thus given a motive to publish a "correct" subscription edition. The belief that he had arranged to have the letters stolen was general. Johnson says that the letters made little stir, but that letters of a literary man were a decided novelty. He feels that the letters are on the whole "studied and artificial," and compares them with those of two of Pope's friends: "Pope may be said to write always with his reputation in his head; Swift perhaps like a man who remembered that he was writing to Pope; but Arbuthnot like one who lets thoughts drop from his pen as they rise into his mind." (IV.96.)

About *An Essay on Man*, Johnson has serious reservations: it was what Pope "persuaded himself to think a system of ethicks" (IV.97), and Johnson reports that Bolingbroke ridiculed Pope for adopting principles of which he did not see the consequences. Neither did the public, which admired the "splendid amplifications and sparkling sentences" (IV.101) of the poem. But the poem was attacked by the Abbé Crousaz (whose *Commentary* Johnson had translated) as leaning toward natural religion and against revelation. Warburton, who had not previously been Pope's friend, sprang to his defense, and Pope in gratitude put in motion the steps by which Warburton in time became the heir to his works, and a bishop.

In the *Epistle to Cobham* (*Characters of Men*) Pope introduced his theory of the ruling passion (each person is moved by a single, innate passion), which Johnson describes as "a kind of moral predestination," pernicious and false. (IV.113.) The theory does not fit well with orthodox Christianity, as Fielding showed in *Tom Jones*. Johnson also dislikes the imprecision with which Pope used the notion.

Johnson gives a brilliant sketch of Dr. Arbuthnot in introducing Pope's *Epistle* to him: "Arbuthnot was a man of great comprehension, skilful in his profession, versed in the sciences, acquainted with ancient literature, and able to animate his mass of knowledge by a bright and active imagination; a scholar with great brilliancy of wit; a wit, who, in the crowd of life, retained and discovered a noble ardour of religious zeal." (IV.117.) Johnson notes that Pope defends himself with dignity, but that in the unsent prose letter to Hervey, which originally accompanied the lines on Hervey, there is "nothing but tedious malignity." (IV.118.)

Johnson now considers the quarrel between Pope and Cibber, part of which consisted in Cibber's replacing Theobald as hero of *The Dunciad*. This "depraved" the poem, Johnson says, because the two heroes were of opposite nature: "by shewing that what he had said of one he was ready to say of another, he reduced himself to the insignificance of his own magpye, who from his cage calls cuckold at a venture." (IV.129.)

At Pope's death it was discovered that instead of printing only a few copies of *The Idea of a Patriot King*, as Bolingbroke had asked, he had ordered 1500. Bolingbroke was outraged, and no motive was easily suggested. Johnson says that Pope must have acted from "his general habit of secrecy and cunning; he caught an opportunity of a sly trick, and pleased himself with the thought of outwitting Bolingbroke." (IV.145.)

In commenting on Pope's character Johnson discusses his frugality, his pleasure in enumerating his friends among the nobility, and the unreliability of his letters in evaluating his personality, since they show an uninterrupted "effulgence of general benevolence." (IV.150.) Not that this is necessarily hypocritical: "The writer commonly believes himself." (IV.152.) Johnson has already called the letters "studied," and he now elaborates upon this. Pope's oft-repeated contempt of the world Johnson thinks a pose: "Swift's resentment was unreasonable, but it was sincere; Pope's was the mere mimickry of his friend." (IV.156.)

The two virtues which Johnson finds most prominent in Pope are liberality and friendship, and he cites as examples of the first, his lending Dodsley £100 to start up in business as a publisher, and paying half of a subscription of £40 a year to Savage. Johnson mentions Martha Blount and Bolingbroke as examples of the steadfastness of Pope's friendships. Johnson pays his respects to Pope's adherence to his religion, to his "great literary curiosity" (IV.160) as a young man, and to his study of the world around him as an older man. Among his intellectual qualities he had not only good sense but genius: "a mind active, ambitious, and adventurous, always investigating, always aspiring; . . . always imagining something greater than it knows, always endeavouring more than it can do." (IV.162.) To an excellent memory, he added diligence and unremitting attention to writing and correction of his work.

In sharp contrast to many, he wrote only what he wished: "His independence secured him from drudging at a task, and labouring upon a barren topick: he never exchanged praise for money, nor opened a shop of condolence or congratulation" (IV.165), and for the same reason he never hurried into print, but kept his work until it was ready. This introduces Johnson's justly famous comparison of Dryden and Pope, the climactic paragraph of which must be quoted in full:

> Of genius, that power which constitutes a poet; that quality without which judgement is cold and knowledge is inert; that energy which collects, combines, amplifies, and animates; the

> superiority must, with some hesitation, be allowed to Dryden. It is not to be inferred that of this poetical vigour Pope had only a little, because Dryden had more; for every other writer since Milton must give place to Pope; and even of Dryden it must be said, that if he has brighter paragraphs, he has not better poems. Dryden's performances were always hasty, either excited by some external occasion, or extorted by domestick necessity; he composed without consideration, and published without correction. What his mind could supply at call, or gather in one excursion, was all that he sought, and all that he gave. The dilatory caution of Pope enabled him to condense his sentiments, to multiply his images, and to accumulate all that study might produce, or chance might supply. If the flights of Dryden therefore are higher, Pope continues longer on the wing. If of Dryden's fire the blaze is brighter, of Pope's the heat is more regular and constant. Dryden often surpasses expectation, and Pope never falls below it. Dryden is read with frequent astonishment, and Pope with perpetual delight. (IV.170–71.)

Johnson now turns to a consideration of Pope's works, most of which he has already glanced at in the biographical section, and he again states that he will look less at "slight faults or petty beauties" than at "the general character and effect" of each work. (IV.172.) So far has Johnson attempted, at least, to advance beyond what I have called plus-and-minus criticism. The *Pastorals* show Pope to have reached early enough "power of language, and skill in metre, to exhibit a series of versification, which had in English poetry no precedent." (IV.173.) *Windsor-Forest* excels Pope's models in every respect. In the *Verses To the Memory of an Unfortunate Lady* the characterizations are unclear and the motivations inconsistent: the poem is a failure. The *Ode on St. Cecilia's Day* is second only to Dryden's *Alexander's Feast*, which excels because it is history, not fable, and therefore engages us more strongly. Both poems, however, lack "the essential constituent of metrical compositions, the stated recurrence of settled numbers." (IV.177.) Pope's poem carries a rather heavy freight of empty sounds, hyperbolical commonplaces, and mythology.

The *Essay on Criticism* establishes Pope's greatness as critic and poet; it excels in all that can "embellish or dignify didactick composition, selection of matter, novelty of arrangement, justness of precept, splendour of illustration, and propriety of digression."

(IV.179.) Johnson is particularly pleased with the comparison of a student's progress in learning with the journey of a traveler in the Alps, and he is led to discuss the difference between good similes and poor ones. (The reader will recall Johnson's discussion of conceits in his *Cowley*.) "A simile, to be perfect, must both illustrate and ennoble the subject." (IV.179.) This Pope's does; but a comparison of a ship race and a chariot race does neither, and comparing Apollo's pursuit of Daphne with a greyhound's chasing a hare degrades the gods.

Johnson moves next into a discussion of onomatopoeia, about which he is skeptical. He admits that there are a few imitative words in all languages—*thump*, *rattle*, *growl*, *hiss*, in English, for instance,—but only a few. And whereas the classical languages admitted duration (quantity), English does not. Motion, however, may be partly imitated, though he is suspicious that "the mind often governs the ear." (IV.182.) He then quotes the lines on Sisyphus from the *Essay:*

> With many a weary step, and many a groan,
> Up a high hill he heaves a huge round stone;
> The huge round stone, resulting with a bound,
> Thunders impetuous down, and smoaks along the ground.
>
> Who does not perceive the stone to move slowly upward, and roll violently back? But set the same numbers to another sense;
>
> While many a merry tale, and many a song,
> Chear'd the rough road, we wish'd the rough road long.
> The rough road then, returning in a round,
> Mock'd our impatient steps, for all was fairy ground.
>
> We have now surely lost much of the delay, and much of the rapidity. (IV. 182–83.)

Johnson has indeed imitated the metre with fair exactness, but he has omitted a feature very important to Pope's effect—all four aspirants in line two and the one in line three impede the flow of the line and give an effect of effort which is not the result of the subject matter. On the whole Johnson thinks that onomatopoeia, sought or achieved, is of slight value.

In examining *The Rape of the Lock* he attempts to uncover the sources of our pleasure in the poem, and finds that it excels in "the two most engaging powers of an author. New things are made familiar, and familiar things are made new." (IV.186.) (This sounds like the distribution of tasks between Wordsworth and Coleridge in *Lyrical Ballads.*) The new is the wholly-invented machinery of sylphs and gnomes, which the reader accepts into his acquaintance at once. The familiar is "the whole detail of a female-day" (IV.186), which is made striking instead of commonplace.

In returning to Pope's *Iliad*, Johnson is especially impressed with the music of the translation: it has "tuned the English tongue; for since its appearance no writer, however deficient in other powers, has wanted melody. Such a series of lines so elaborately corrected, and so sweetly modulated, took possession of the publick ear." (IV.191.) To the objection that Pope slights Homer's simplicity and grandeur, Johnson agrees, but insists that in an age of elegance some changes were necessary. Finally Johnson resorts to his "bow-wow" style:

> To a thousand cavils one answer is sufficient; the purpose of a writer is to be read, and the criticism which would destroy the power of pleasing must be blown aside. Pope wrote for his own age and his own nation: he knew that it was necessary to colour the images and point the sentiments of his author; he therefore made him graceful, but lost him some of his sublimity. (IV.194.)

As to *The Dunciad*, Johnson is willing to give it the praise of an original, though derived from *Mac Flecknoe*, since it is so "enlarged and diversified," and it is the best specimen yet of "personal satire ludicrously pompous." (IV.195.) He is not convinced that Pope's purpose was moral, but, surprisingly enough, he does not much care. In fact, he will go much further. Anyone who goes into print submits himself to public judgment, and "satirical criticism may be considered as useful when it rectifies error and improves judgement." (IV.197.) Fortunately for this noble stance, Johnson does not attempt to show that the poem does so.

The key to Johnson's rather cold attitude toward the *Essay on Man* may lie in his statement, "The subject is perhaps not very proper for poetry" (IV.198), i.e., vindicating the ways of God to man. Nevertheless, "Never were penury of knowledge and vulgarity of sentiment so happily disguised" by "the dazzling splendour of imagery, and the seductive powers of eloquence." (IV.199.) Philosophy, criticism, and judgment are overpowered by the pleasure the reader receives. Yet there are more faults, says Johnson, than in all Pope's other works. The deduction seems to me almost inevitable, that Johnson had been convinced by Crousaz' attack more than forty years earlier, and had not changed his mind since then. The *Characters of Men and Women* he praises highly and prefers Pope's *Characters of Women* to Boileau's *Satire on Women*, much as he admires Boileau.

After brief comments on the *Epistles* and the *Imitations of Horace*, the second written as "relaxations of his genius" (IV.203), Johnson lists what he calls "all the qualities that constitute genius" (IV.204), and illustrates them from Pope's work: invention (new events and scenes, *The Rape of the Lock*, and new embellishments of a known subject, the *Essay on Criticism*); imagination (a quality not defined which enables the writer "to convey to the reader, the various forms of nature, incidents of life, and energies of passion" [IV.204], *Eloisa*, *Windsor-Forest*, *Ethic Epistles*); and judgment, "which selects from life or nature what the present purpose requires." (IV.204.) To these Johnson adds music, "inarticulate poetry," according to Dryden; in "the melody" of Pope's meter, Johnson finds no serious flaw, and he rejects the criticism that his poetry is "too uniformly musical" as merely captious. (IV.205.)

Johnson closes with a charming and characteristic paragraph:

> After all this, it is surely superfluous to answer the question that has once been asked, Whether Pope was a poet? otherwise than by asking in return, If Pope be not a poet, where is poetry to be found? To circumscribe poetry by a definition will only shew the narrowness of the definer, though a definition which shall exclude Pope will not easily be made. Let us look round upon the present time, and back upon the past; let us enquire to whom the voice of mankind has decreed the wreath of poetry; let their productions be examined, and their claims stated, and the pretensions of Pope will be no more disputed. Had he given the world only his version, the name of poet must have been allowed him: if the writer of the *Iliad* were to class his successors, he would assign a very high place to his translator, without requiring any other evidence of Genius. (IV.208.)

Pitt

1699–1748

Pitt distinguished himself by a skillful and elegant translation of Vida's *Art of Poetry*, and later entered into competition with Dryden with a complete version of the *Aeneid.* In a burst of enthusiasm, Johnson calls these "the two best translations that perhaps were ever produced by one nation of the same author." But a chill wind of common sense destroys this airy edifice: we see "that Dryden's faults are forgotten in the hurry of delight, and that Pitt's beauties are neglected in the languor of a cold and listless perusal; that Pitt pleases the criticks, and Dryden the people; that Pitt is quoted, and Dryden read." (IV.243.)

Thomson

1700–1748

Thomson first comes alive in Johnson's short biography when, arriving in London, he walked through the streets "with the gaping curiosity of a new-comer" and had his letters of introduction stolen from him. (IV.248.) Fortunately the manuscript of *Winter* was not stolen, though the poem, "being of a new kind" (IV.250), was at first not easy to sell to a publisher or to the public. It caught on, however, and *Spring* and *Summer* raised great expectations for his tragedy *Sophonisba;* but the "splendid audience" was not much affected, and "rose as from a moral lecture." (IV.252.)

Not long afterward, the opposition to Walpole, in "clamours for liberty, of which no man felt the want, and with care for liberty, which was not in danger," aroused Thomson to write "a very long poem," *Liberty*. (IV.254.) It failed, says Johnson, from a repetition of the same images and examples "to prove a position which nobody denied." (IV.255.) Still later, Thomson had more success with his tragedy *Tancred and Sigismunda*, though Johnson finds it lacking in pathos, and having "declamation rather than dialogue." (IV.258.) Of Thomson's last work, *The Castle of Indolence*, Johnson has an appreciative characterization: "The first canto opens a scene of lazy luxury, that fills the imagination."

(IV.259.) Those somniferous Spenserian stanzas have perhaps never been better described.

In conclusion, Johnson gives Thomson very high praise: he is original, both in thought and in expression: "His numbers, his pauses, his diction, are of his own growth, without transcription, without imitation. He thinks in a peculiar train, and he thinks always as a man of genius; he looks round on Nature and on Life, with the eye which Nature bestows only on a poet; the eye that distinguishes, in every thing presented to its view, whatever there is on which imagination can delight to be detained, and with a mind that at once comprehends the vast, and attends to the minute." (IV.265–66.) (The reader whose attention has been perhaps too often called to Imlac's dictum on numbering the streaks of the tulip might well ponder Johnson's compliment on Thomson and the minute.) His blank verse is not Milton's, but his own. His diction is perhaps too florid, and his revisions of *The Seasons* may have "lost part of what Temple calls their *race;* a word which, applied to wines, in its primitive sense, means the flavour of the soil." (IV.268.) After this very striking *aperçu*, Johnson ends with a bow to the unimpeachable morality of Thomson's poems.

Watts

1674–1748

Johnson begins his *Watts* with recording that these poems were included at his recommendation. The early poems, although "deformed by the Pindarick folly" of the times (IV.271), still show remarkable promise in copiousness and splendor of diction. In his maturity, Watts improved on this by showing his brother Dissenters how to "court attention by the graces of language." (IV.276.) He also wrote "little poems of devotion" for children (IV.278), and Johnson is appreciative of the kind of man who can wrestle with Lockean psychology and at the same time look to the needs of four-year-olds. Moreover, he is talking out of his own experience: he has read "few books" with "greater pleasure" than Watts's *Improvement of the Mind*. (IV.280.) If we pause to think of the thousands of books which Johnson had read by his early seventies, when he wrote that sentence, the magnitude of his compliment can be appreciated. Part of the reason for his pleasure

—an artistic reason, not an evangelical one—follows at once: "The attention is caught by indirect instruction, and he that sat down only to reason is on a sudden compelled to pray." (IV.280–81.) He clearly appreciated the gracefulness and the subtlety of Watts's work.

Finally, Johnson praises Watts's exactness of judgment as a poet, his vigorous and active imagination, his ear, and, again, his diction, all displaying "his benevolence to man, and his reverence to God." (IV.284.)

Ambrose Philips

1675?–1749

Ambrose Philips has found a small place in a footnote to literary history for having written pastorals preferred by some of his contemporaries to those of Pope. Johnson's biographical sketch gives an opportunity for a brief history of the genre from Theocritus through Vergil to the revival of learning and Spenser. The reader will not now have to be told that Johnson dislikes the genre. One of Philips' plays, *The Briton*, has, however, a scene "truly poetical" and written "with great dramatick skill." (IV.296.) His periodical, *The Freethinker*, Johnson thinks unworthy of revival, but his poems of short lines, for which his opponents damned him as Namby Pamby, are his most pleasing, paying tribute in "smooth and spritely" numbers to persons ranging from a nursery babe to Sir Robert Walpole. (IV.299.)

West

1703–1756

Toward Gilbert West, Johnson is more friendly. He thinks his dissertations on Pindar should have been printed in the present edition; his character was such that he could be called "saint" as well as "poet" (IV.303); and Johnson has been interested enough in West's translation of Pindar to compare his first Olympic ode with the Greek, finding his expectation "surpassed, both by its elegance and its exactness." (IV.305.) One may be legitimately surprised that Johnson should have so closely examined the Greek: it is not wholly characteristic that he should have done so; and his examples leave no doubt of the fact. West, he thinks, has sometimes carried paraphrase too far, but shows not only "great labour" but "great abilities." (IV.306.) West's imitations of Spenser are successful, but do not, says Johnson, merit "the highest praise, the praise of genius": they lack "the noblest beauties of art . . . of which the effect is co-extended with rational nature, or at least with the whole circle of polished life." (IV.307.) Perhaps in the last words Johnson is thinking of Pope's *Rape of the Lock.*

Collins

1721–1759

Johnson had earlier written a character of Collins for a collection of his poems; this is now slightly expanded. They had known each other in London about 1744, when both were struggling writers. Collins had grandiose schemes, such as a history of the revival of learning, but Johnson, perhaps thinking of his own abortive edition of Politian, comments on the plight of a hack writer: "A man doubtful of his dinner, or trembling at a creditor, is not much disposed to abstracted meditation, or remote enquiries." (IV.310.) A publisher's advance for a projected translation of Aristotle's *Poetics* rescued Collins from a bailiff—Johnson saw the guineas "safe in his hand" (IV.311)—but a legacy from an uncle provided a permanent rescue, and neither book was written.

Collins was now able to indulge his bent: "fairies, genii, giants, and monsters" (IV.312), sometimes resulting in poetry of "sublimity and splendour." (IV.313.) Insanity intervened, and death came early: "Such was the fate of Collins, with whom I once delighted to converse, and whom I yet remember with tenderness." (IV.315.) Johnson's final comment on Collins' poetry is more severe than his earlier opinion just quoted: "his diction was often harsh, unskilfully laboured, and injudiciously selected. He affected the obsolete when it was not worthy of revival; and he puts his words out of the common order, seeming to think, with some later candidates for fame, that not to write prose is certainly to write poetry. His lines commonly are of slow motion, clogged and impeded with clusters of consonants." (IV.316–17.) Johnson mentions the "Ode on the Popular Superstitions of the Highlands" as having been seen by the Wartons, but since lost. (It was found and published a few years after Johnson's death.) His opinion of it might have been interesting; nevertheless, it is clear that Collins' lyrics, on which his fame principally rests, leave Johnson unmoved: he does not mention any of them.

Dyer

1700?–1758

Johnson's *Dyer* may be remembered for a single sentence: "*Grongar Hill* is the happiest of his productions: it is not indeed very accurately written; but the scenes which it displays are so pleasing, the images which they raise so welcome to the mind, and the reflections of the writer so consonant to the general sense or experience of mankind, that when it is once read, it will be read again." (IV.321.) The notion of "recognition" as part of our pleasure in literature had not previously been stated so surely or so clearly, and it is interesting to see Johnson adding one of his more common tests of a successful work: we return to it.

Shenstone

1714–1763

In *Shenstone*, Johnson remarks that the poet's concern with improving his garden and small estate was "an innocent amusement." (IV.327.) Although Johnson does not say so explicitly, I have the impression that he thinks of Shenstone's poems in much the same way: "His mind was not very comprehensive." (IV.329.) His elegies are "the effusion of a contemplative mind" on "domestick" topics, in "pure and simple" thoughts, wanting "variety." (IV.331.) But though such poems require smoothness, his diction is often harsh. Of lyrics other than elegies, Johnson comments that they are "light and airy," and "airy" is, as far as I know, always used by Johnson as a complimentary adjective. "Rural Elegance" has "poetical spirit." (IV.332.) But in the end Johnson finds that he prefers *The Schoolmistress*, Shenstone's Spenserian imitation, above all the rest of his poems, a judgment with which posterity has concurred: "The adoption of a particular style, in light and short compositions, contributes much to the increase of pleasure: we are entertained at once with two imitations, of nature in the sentiments, of the original author in the style, and between them the mind is kept in perpetual employment." (IV.335–36.)

Young

1683–1765

The rather long biographical part of the *Life of Young* was written for Johnson by Herbert Croft, Jr., and therefore requires no comment here. Johnson's criticism of the poems is very short. He finds that Young "has no uniformity of manner," that his verse is "sometimes smooth, and sometimes rugged," his style "sometimes diffusive, and sometimes concise." (IV.416.) *The Last Day*, "his first great performance," has an evenness and "propriety" (IV.416) that Young never achieved again: he is not a poet who learned from or built upon his early work. The subject, however, Johnson considers too awesome for poetry. *The Universal Passion* is "a very great performance" (IV.417), even though it consists of a series of epigrams. Johnson thinks Young's satire lies between Horace and Juvenal, having the "gaiety" of Horace and the "morality" of Juvenal; but he plays "only on the surface of life." (IV.418.)

Young's lyrics Johnson calls "turgid" failures; indeed, the modern reader would be hard-put to dredge up a single title. *Night Thoughts*, however, is "original," a term of very high praise in Johnson's critical vocabulary: moreover, it is "one of the few poems in which blank verse could not be changed for rhyme but with disadvantage." (IV.418.) Young's tragedies do not impress Johnson much; *Busiris* is "too remote from known life to raise either grief, terror, or indignation." (IV.420.) In the end, however, "He was a man of genius and a poet." (IV.422.)

Mallet

1705?–1765

David Malloch changed his name to Mallet after coming to London, to avoid being stigmatized as Scottish. This did not endear him to Johnson, whose pride in his own birthplace is well known. Of his early poems, *The Excursion* has many striking images and elegant paragraphs, but Johnson considers his *Verbal Criticism* only tolerable. *Eurydice*, his first tragedy, Johnson had not read, but had heard it called "a mean performance." (IV.426.) His *Life of Bacon* Johnson thinks elegant, but lacking in knowledge of science. In his long narrative poem *Amyntor and Theodora*, there are some qualities to praise—"But it is blank verse." (IV.430.) In conclusion, his works may have been kept alive in his lifetime by "personal influence" (IV.434), but, basically mediocre, they are now dead.

Akenside

1721–1770

The biographical part of Johnson's *Akenside* is marked by Johnson's antipathy to Akenside's "unnecessary and outrageous zeal for what he called and thought liberty" (IV.436), which Johnson is inclined to equate, in Akenside's case, with anarchy. But at any rate the young enthusiast produced, at age twenty-three, *The Pleasures of Imagination*, which shows "great felicity of genius, and uncommon amplitude of acquisitions." (IV.441.) The poem, however, is diffuse and verbose (are these aspects of "amplitude"?), and in the end the reader has "remarked little, and laid hold on nothing." (IV.443.) Johnson praises his blank verse as superior in its smooth flow and in its musical pauses, but he objects that "the full close does not recur with sufficient frequency." (IV.443.) This is a point worth the closest attention. Johnson elaborates on this by comparing the required stop of the heroic couplet with the absence of any such traditional requirement in blank verse, which may betray "luxuriant and active minds" into "exuberant" or "tiresome" loquaciousness (IV.443).

Akenside's other poems do not interest Johnson: the diction of the odes is sometimes "harsh and uncouth," they are "generally dull." (IV.446.)

Lyttelton

1709–1773

In the *Life of Lyttelton* Johnson is impressed principally with his subject's conversion from doubt to orthodox Christianity, and with the fact his *History of Henry the Second* had a nineteen-page list of errors. He gives a single paragraph to Lyttelton's poems, which "have nothing to be despised, and little to be admired." Nevertheless, one of his early poems shows a promise "which cultivation might have raised to excellence." (IV.484.)

Gray

1716–1771

Gray had been dead only ten years when Johnson published his life, and many of his surviving friends were outraged. The tone of the biographical part caused less offense than the criticism, but Gray is described as staying "sullenly" at Cambridge (IV.447), and the account of the quarrel between Gray and Walpole must have given pain merely by reviving old memories. Johnson traces the rise of Gray's reputation up to the death of Cibber, when he "had the honour of refusing the laurel" (IV.453), through his being rejected for and later appointed to the Professorship of Modern History at Cambridge. There he remained, "always designing lectures, but never reading them; uneasy at his neglect of duty, and appeasing his uneasiness with designs of reformation." (IV.454.) He wrote a "very curious and elegant" account of a journey to Scotland (IV.454), and an account of a later journey into Westmoreland and Cumberland makes Johnson wish that there had been more such journeys and such books.

He quotes from Mason the character of Gray written by Temple "to my friend Mr. Boswell" (IV.455), and adds, from reading some of Gray's letters, that "his mind had a large grasp" and that "he was a man likely to love much where he loved at all." (IV.458.)

His criticism of the poems is generally unsympathetic. In the ode on *Spring* "the language is too luxuriant" and the morality "too stale." (IV.460.) When he comes to the *Ode on the Death of a Favorite Cat*, Johnson suffers a total failure of sense of humor. The lines are a delicious self-parody, but Johnson discusses the poem as though it were just another ode. He thinks the question to the Thames in the *Eton College* ode "useless and puerile." (IV.461.) Yet he thinks that Gray has surpassed Horace's original in the *Hymn to Adversity. The Progress of Poesy* and *The Bard* he dislikes: in the first, he would like to know the meaning of the first stanza; he is contemptuous of the second stanza. He objects, on his usual ground, to "velvet-green": "An epithet or metaphor drawn from Nature ennobles Art; an epithet or metaphor drawn from Art degrades Nature." (IV.463.) The abrupt beginning of *The Bard* strikes him as being merely an abrupt beginning, and in the next stanzas are to be found "the puerilities of obsolete mythology" (IV.466), a remark which will surprise no one who has read so far in the *Lives*.

For the *Elegy*, however, Johnson has nothing but praise: "I rejoice to concur with the common reader; for by the common sense of readers uncorrupted with literary prejudices, after all the refinements of subtilty and the dogmatism of learning, must be finally decided all claim to poetical honours." (IV.469.) Johnson shrewdly comments that we recognize much in the poem as corresponding to our own experience—"images which find a mirrour in every mind," and that there are accordingly many responses, "sentiments to which every bosom returns an echo." This, remarkable as it is, is not all: Gray's art is so subtle that even when his ideas are wholly original he manages to convince the reader "that he has always felt them." This is an extraordinarily acute perception, and it is noteworthy as coming toward the end of the criticism of a poet with whom Johnson was not very sympathetic. He ends with high praise: "Had Gray written often thus, it had been vain to blame, and useless to praise him." (IV.469.)

So ends *The Lives of the Poets*, an astonishing work for a sick old man, running the gamut from routine treatment of a few poetasters in whom Johnson had no interest, through a shrewd, sometimes prejudiced, often original assessment of a large body of work.

The Lives of the Poets is Johnson's triumphant achievement. It could not have been written by any other man in the century, and perhaps could not have been written at any other time. Pope was too confined within the emerging but still very limited critical principles of his time. Moreover, there was not yet enough distance to make a valid judgement on the late years of the Restoration or the times of Queen Anne, when Defoe, Swift, Arbuthnot, Gay, and Pope were in a murky dispute for supremacy. By the last quarter of the eighteenth century some of the dust had begun to settle. Johnson could not, apparently, discern the massive but dimly outlined figure of Defoe. And he was torn between admiration for Swift's brilliance and concern for aspects of Swift which seemed psychopathic. But Dryden and Pope were luminaries who would give their names to the periods in which they flourished.

The Age of Johnson is a term which opens up into more and more lively ideas as we look closely not only at Johnson, but at such opposing luminaries as Gray, Walpole, and Cowper. Yet at every turn, when we think we have managed to corner Johnson and impound him as a neo-classicist or as an Augustan, he escapes us. He is not to be so enclosed. He has part of his mind always open to new things, and he has never made final or pedantic decisions which would encapsulate him in amber for a proper academic dissection. He continues to surprise us in freshness, in unorthodoxy, or even in perverse bull-headedness. After almost two hundred years his *Milton* and his *Gray* can arouse anger. What eighteenth-century critic would not have wished for an immortality linked with such poets? Such a rhetorical question is soon answered.

But what other critic had a James Boswell who was convinced that his mentor was wrong about some of the emotional forms of poetry and some of the pressing ideas of the day? For better or for worse, Johnson and Boswell had been reacting to the ideas of each other since they had met in 1763. Johnson had thought Boswell should settle down, should write on Corsica from a personal point of view, and so on. Boswell's ideas on the American colonies, on slavery, on feudalism were generally opposed to Johnson's.

When they were opposed, which happened often, there were sparks, and often injured feelings. Johnson, as a father-figure, was stronger and more venerable, Boswell more resilient. As people, they were, if not necessary to each other, extraordinarily stimulating. Johnson at seventy-five was still alive to what was happening in the world of literature. Boswell was partly responsible.

JAMES BOSWELL

I

Early Career: *Journals*

James Boswell was born in Edinburgh, on 29 October 1740, of an old upper-middle-class Scottish family, a heritage of which he was always proud, and one to which he referred what he called his "feudal" attitudes. He was sent to a private school before he was six; from the age of eight to thirteen he was educated by tutors, and then attended the University of Edinburgh till he was eighteen. In the summer of 1759 he studied a little law and showed some interest in the stage, particularly in one of the actresses at Edinburgh. As a result, his father sent him off to the University of Glasgow. There he attended lectures in moral philosophy given by Adam Smith, who, not long before, had written a short review of Johnson's *Dictionary*, but who had not yet published the work which established his great fame, *The Wealth of Nations*.

Boswell's father, an eminent lawyer, was a judge in the Court of Sessions at Edinburgh, the highest Scottish court, and bore the courtesy title, from his judgeship, of Lord Auchinleck, after the family estate in Ayrshire. His father rather naturally wanted his oldest son—the others were less promising—to follow him in a legal career, where a wide Scottish acquaintance, both social and professional, was already at hand. Young Boswell, equally naturally, found it necessary to assert himself against his father in order to establish some identity of his own. He decided that his father was a conservative, which was largely true, though in many ways Boswell was even more conservative. (For example, he was romantically inclined toward what he thought were feudal ideals, and many years later tried to restrict the inheritance of his estate to his male heirs, which was far too conservative for his father's taste.)

Accordingly, Boswell revolted in such ways as were available and seemed interesting. Originally a Presbyterian, he was for a time a Methodist. He was briefly converted to Catholicism, but soon returned to his own church. More seriously, he decided that a career in the Footguards interested him more than did the Scottish bar. The Guards were quartered in London, and after only one visit Boswell was sure that London was the center of Great Britain, not Edinburgh. He therefore mounted a major campaign to get a commission, using his friends and his family's friends to obtain that prize.

Much of this is spread out in his *London Journal, 1762–63,* which was sent in the form of journal letters to his friend John Johnston in Scotland. These were not, then, private entries for himself alone; he was confident enough to share them with somebody else. The entries show more and more about Boswell. He makes it clear that the reasons for his choice of a career in the Guards were not merely romantic—a colorful uniform, frequent balls—but practical. The Seven Years' War was still on and other military units might be called into action, but not the Guards. They were attached to the King's person, and would probably not be sent into battle. A commission in this regiment was, unfortunately, not forthcoming, and when Boswell was offered one in another regiment he explained precisely, honestly, and with a total lack of tact, just why it would not do. His influential friends were outraged.

Boswell had been in London briefly before. But in the winter of 1762–63 he began his first long visit. He had reached some sort of accommodation with his father. In London he fell in love with, or at least was infatuated with, a charming actress, Louisa, just twenty-four, who seemed to promise years of happiness. Boswell's journal gives his careful plans for this conquest, not all of which succeeded. She was beautiful, and she did not immediately capitulate. He called on her; three days later he declared his love; after another three days she needed a small loan to meet a debt, and accepted both the two guineas and a warm embrace. Boswell's excitement increases and the reader is by this time thoroughly caught up in the chase. Two days thereafter, however, Boswell's tenseness prevented his making love.

By this time, willy-nilly, his story begins to take on unintentional overtones of the comic. A few days later, on the day after Christmas, Louisa wanted to wait for a week. On New Year's Day, she proposed a meeting for the following day, and on the second Boswell was torpid, until her landlady was at hand. A further delay; then she promised to spend a whole night with him. Still another postponement, but after nearly a month from the beginning of this siege, they spent a night together at an inn on Fleet Street.

It was wholly delightful, and Boswell was as pleased with his sexual athleticism as with the economical prudence which he had used, the whole expense of the evening being eighteen shillings. Up to that moment. For it was not long before Boswell discovered that he had a venereal infection, which he attributed to Louisa. His reaction against her was as violent as his love had been. It did not occur to him, nor would his doctor necessarily have guessed this, that his illness might have been a flare-up of an infection he had had two years earlier. Instead, he reacted with quite understandable and characteristic male outrage.

He had thought he was Louisa's first love; he demanded, in a violent letter, the return of his two guineas; she returned them without comment; and the reader is by turns astonished that Boswell should be willing to write himself down an ass, and filled with admiration that he should be able to do so. It is precisely this quality, his ability and his need to record the event without lying even to himself, which makes Boswell's journal unparalleled in his century. Later on, in his published works, he will arrange his materials with much greater skill, but the basic ability to see what happened and to record it underlies everything else.

There were soon compensations for the blow to his pride in the Louisa affair. He had met John Wilkes, the wild, brilliant young Whig, friend of the satirist Churchill and co-editor with Churchill of *The North Briton*, the opposition journal. And he was soon to meet Johnson, author of *The Rambler*, compiler of the *Dictionary*. On Monday, 16 May 1763, he did so in the bookshop of their mutual friend Tom Davies. The meeting got off to a poor start because of Boswell's nervousness, and took a serious turn for the worse when Johnson rebuked Boswell for defending Garrick against a charge of selfishness. Nevertheless, it ended on a friendly note. Boswell recorded his first impression of Johnson's gross size (Boswell was very short) and unattractive appearance, as well as a few fragments of their conversation. That there are only fragments of conversation here does not adequately prepare us for the fact that, many years later, Boswell was able to use this short passage for the basis of the great scene in his *Life of Johnson*, where he builds up a lively and even dramatic episode from these raw hints. I shall look at it more closely in discussing his *Johnson.*

From the diary, however, no one would guess that Boswell, in his twenty-third year, had reached a turning point in his career. In the next four days, Johnson is not mentioned, but rather the girls Boswell had sexual intercourse with, and whether he used a contraceptive or not, and why.

Within a week after first meeting Johnson, however, Boswell felt drawn to pay him a call, and their intimacy quickened. By the end of July, Johnson had agreed to accompany Boswell to Harwich to see him off for Holland, where he was to proceed with his legal studies, and the last entry in the *London Journal* records the night before they set out. Johnson was a childless widower, fifty-three years old, with energies and affection to spare. Boswell needed parental affection a little less demanding than Lord Auchinleck's, as well as the assurance of the Rambler that the legal profession was a happy choice for a young man, and particularly for this young man. Since their first meeting they had talked at length about these things as well as books to read—almost "the choice of life" which concerned Rasselas.

As the first volume of Boswell's journals, as published, comes to a close, the reader is aware that he has been reading a type of diary quite new to English literature. We may therefore stop for a minute to look at some of its characteristics. First, there is nothing which Boswell is unwilling to set down. This characteristic does not come solely or even primarily from a lack of inhibition. Chatterton and Wilkes use four-letter words more commonly than Boswell does; in fact, he rarely if ever uses them. But he is not prevented by pride from setting down occurrences in which he might be thought to come off second best. Much more important, he has a keen sense of the dramatic, which, though not always conscious, seems to operate with remarkable consistency.

For instance, in the Louisa story just given, the reader is drawn into caring whether Boswell will succeed. A few months later we are led to hope that Boswell will survive Johnson's initial rebuff. It would be wrong, I think, to suggest that Boswell always wrote his journal with an audience in mind. Yet he did write the *London Journal* for himself and one intimate friend, John Johnston, and the impression is inescapable that he turned from a few rough notes to a full journal in the Hebrides with the idea that he would show it to his fellow-traveler, Johnson.

Boswell in Holland is less exciting than Boswell in London. His full journal for this year of legal study was lost in transit to England, but his rough notes and letters survive in sufficient numbers to provide us with the facts and something of the emotional and intellectual tone of his life during that period. The notes, however, are an inadequate artistic substitute for the fully-written journal and make us recognize with how great skill Boswell has elsewhere expanded such raw materials. He tried to settle down to study. There were no such companions as Wilkes to make life exciting. His Dutch relatives were respectable. He enjoyed the company of Zelide (Belle de Zuylen), talked to her of love and religion, and sought to show her that no female deist could be a proper wife for a Scottish laird. He also talked to her father. The reader is not sure which one is the blue-stocking. After a chill, damp ten months in Holland, he left Zelide and Holland forever and began his grand tour of Europe.

With the beginning of the tour, in June 1764, Boswell's full journal is again available. In Germany he goes from one princely court to another, prepared with letters of introduction, and finds himself able to join in the local court life without much trouble. It was not particularly stimulating. He did see Chesterfield's son, the recipient of the famous letters, and thought him a dull young man. Posterity has agreed.

Switzerland, however, was another matter. Voltaire was at Ferney, just across the border in France, and Rousseau was near Lausanne. They were prizes worth capturing. Boswell had by no means made lion-hunting a profession. He had met the Duke of York, brother of George III, but the Duke does not play a prominent part in the diaries. He tried to meet Frederick the Great, without success, and his failure had not crushed him. But he had long been determined to meet the two greatest writers on the continent, and he laid his plans with care.

His approach to Rousseau was not by means of the usual letter of introduction, but by a letter, in French, about himself, which he summarizes in his diary: ". . . I informed him that an ancient Scots gentleman of twenty-four was come hither with the hopes of seeing him. I assured him that I deserved his regard, that I was ready to stand the test of his penetration. Towards the end of my letter I showed him that I had a heart and a soul. I have here given no idea of my letter. It can neither be abridged nor transposed, for it is really a masterpiece. I shall ever preserve it as a proof that my soul can be sublime." (*Grand Tour*, I.212.) This approach succeeded; Boswell sent his letter by a maid from his hotel, and told her not to wait for an immediate answer, which might be an impulsive "no," but to return after an interval, in which Rousseau would have a chance to think the matter over. The elaborate calculation worked, and Rousseau allowed Boswell to pay him a short visit that same day. A few days later Boswell sent Rousseau a lengthy and elaborate autobiographical sketch on which he spent great pains, as existing rough drafts show. It is not only a fairly just account of what Boswell at twenty-four thought had occurred in his life up to that point, and therefore of tremendous interest in his development as a man and as a writer, but it is also quite clearly slanted to engage Rousseau's attention. The philosopher's *Emile or a New System of Education* had been translated into English two years earlier, soon after its first appearance in French, and it was in great vogue. A sentence in Boswell's opening paragraph sounds like a direct reference to the book: "You will see in me an extraordinary example of the effects of a bad education." (Pottle, *James Boswell*, p. 1.) A few lines later he mentions his hereditary melancholy, a "temperament of tender hearts" which requires "a very careful education." He refers to his delicate health as a child, his exploiting this ill health to avoid school, and expresses shock at such depravity: "In a state of Nature, a child should feel miserable in illness and joyful in health." (Pottle, p. 2) There is a good deal on his mother's evangelical piety, which probably predisposed him for his brief attraction to Methodism; then some candid remarks about his tutors, whom he greatly preferred to his school. He gives his opinion of his father with equal frankness and it perhaps shows more charity than his father would have shown him at that moment. (Lord Auchinleck had forbidden Boswell to go beyond Germany to Italy, and Boswell was doing just that.)

He writes about his adolescence with some directness and with less melodrama than was customary with Shelley and Byron in a later generation of Romantics, discussing his first extended love affair and referring with suspicious curtness and brevity to his affair with Louisa. Ending rather abruptly, he appeals to Rousseau for help: "My mind is weak but my soul is strong. Kindle that soul, and the sacred fire shall never be extinguished." (Pottle, p. 6.) Who could resist this? Certainly not Rousseau, whose relations with his Swiss neighbors were just then reaching the breaking point. An acquaintance which began with some chillness on his part ripened quickly. Boswell's journal gives a most vivid account of their conversations, which, however, like the autobiographical sketch, are in French, so that in the translation available we are at one remove from the words themselves.

Boswell had made a list of the subjects he wanted to have Rousseau discuss. The over-familiarity of the Scots, which Boswell found at variances with his own social position and his notions of feudal grandeur, was one. Concubinage was another. He suggested that he would like to have thirty women, and, if rich, sire children by them all and marry them off, with dowries, to willing peasants of the neighborhood. (At this point, Thérèse Le Vasseur, Rousseau's mistress, left the room.) Rousseau raised objections to this roseate, feudal picture: jealousy will cause trouble. Boswell suggested that a harem might be the answer, and Rousseau interposed that harem life is slavery, and Boswell then adverted to the Patriarchs of the Old Testament, whose example he would like to follow. All of this has a curious dream-like character, wholly without reference to the actual social situation in which Boswell would be living at Edinburgh, or Auchinleck, or London. And with a nice reversal of roles, it was the romantic novelist Rousseau, whose five illegitimate children by Thérèse had been packed off to an orphanage, who kept bringing in the harsh light of common sense.

A question of rather more immediate importance was Boswell's uneasy relationship with his father. Rousseau shrewdly suggested that they engage in some sport together such as shooting, but unfortunately Lord Auchinleck was wholly uninterested in such frivolities. On the last day of Boswell's visit to Môtiers Rousseau entertained him at dinner, and they explored many subjects, including Dr. Johnson, Corsica, Voltaire, and religion. As the unusually long visit drew to a close, Boswell spoke of his powers as a mimic, a talent rightly thought to be dangerous. As they embraced and said farewell, hoping to meet again, Boswell used a sentiment he had prepared in advance, as his notes show: his wish to be bound to the philosopher by a thread, even as fine as a hair. Rousseau responded in kind, and Boswell quoted appropriately from *Emile*, to the effect that one must live till his last hour. His host agreed. Adieu. It is very much like a dance. It is easy to hear the music in the background.

The six interviews with Rousseau had been a great success, and Boswell's recording of them in his journal is brilliant. The aging, ill philosopher comes through these pages in a most engaging manner. Boswell is constantly lively; Thérèse in the background, occasionally in the foreground, is a thoroughly real person.

Less than ten days later, on Christmas Eve, 1764, Boswell was at Ferney, Voltaire's chateau a few miles from Geneva. In this instance he had no hesitation in using the letter of introduction he carried. There was no question here that he would be admitted. Voltaire was not a solitary like Rousseau, but a rich old man who lived in splendor, surrounded by servants and guests. After a little while Voltaire saw him, gave him a few witticisms which he could use in his journal—and dinner was announced. This meant the end of the interview, and Boswell had to leave almost at once, since the gates of Geneva, where he had lodgings, closed at 5 p.m. But even the short talk with Voltaire had been something of an achievement: Boswell had got him to speak English.

With so much accomplished, next day Boswell set the Ferney campaign in motion, a variant on the siege of Rousseau. He had to get Voltaire long enough to himself so that the important questions, like religion, could be canvassed, and he therefore had to be a house guest at the chateau. Voltaire's hostess was his niece, Mme. Denis, and to her Boswell directed his request, in English, being fairly certain that Voltaire would see it: He had seen some bright rays shine from the illustrious man, but surely Voltaire was in full blaze only in the evening; might not a bed for one night be found for this Scot, even if only made up of two chairs in the bedroom of Mme. Denis' maid?

Voltaire himself replied, in English, pretending to be his niece: Boswell would be welcome and would not have to sleep on two chairs. Two days later Boswell was there, sitting beside the "infidel," who was playing chess, and he again got him to speak English, sometimes on trifling matters, sometimes, with enthusiasm, on the British constitution. Inevitably the subject of religion came up, and it is impossible to believe that Boswell did not originate it. Then did Voltaire "rage," and they continued to dispute while the rest of the company went to supper. The scene now became as melodramatic as any bad opera. As the argument rose in intensity, Voltaire trembled, cried out that he was sick, and let himself "gently" fall into a chair. (The modifier is superbly suggestive—the fall was fake, and Boswell recognized it.) Voltaire recovered, and Boswell pressed his case, sure that the greatest writer in Europe could not be all bad. He solemnly demanded a confession of Voltaire's true belief, and got it: Voltaire venerated and loved God and was resigned to his will. Boswell extracted other articles of faith, was moved, was sorry, then suddenly had his doubts and twice pressed Voltaire to declare his sincerity. Voltaire did so. As Boswell describes the interview in a letter to Temple, he inevitably thinks of it in theatrical terms, and is reminded of Voltaire's own tragedies. There was an hour and a half of this, but Boswell's description, with great art, goes no further.

He stayed two more days, and there were other conversations. In the last one Boswell again brought up religion, in connection with the article on "soul" in Voltaire's *Philosophical Dictionary*, trying unsuccessfully to make his host come out with a flat affirmation for immortality, which Voltaire would not do. He was willing to declare himself a monotheist, and if Boswell insisted on public worship would have four grand services a year, with music. . . . Yes, Boswell might write to him, and in English. He would answer. And he did.

Having left, Boswell recorded the conversation and also set down a piece of self-analysis. It is mostly congratulatory, but not without truth. He finds that there is a pliancy in him by which he can adjust himself to the "tone" of a man, so that that man can behave as freely as with another self. This is mostly the case, as the reader comes increasingly to see, and it is accomplished without toadyism or the loss of Boswell's own very decided individuality.

A day or two later, he heard for the first time the story of Rousseau's sending away his children, which shocked him so much that he never quite recovered his former attitude toward that mentor. But he was now on his way to Italy, with his father's permission to stay four months, and he entered into this new phase of his Grand Tour with enthusiasm.

In his Italian journal, Boswell customarily recorded the conversation in the language in which it took place, French or Italian, and it is so given in the Malahide Papers. In *Boswell on the Grand Tour*, such passages are translated. It is not easy to give a literary judgment of a diary in three languages, especially as Boswell's French and Italian are of a free and easy sort, but that in itself may suggest a sort of judgment: Boswell made himself at home in both languages quickly, and there was no substantial barrier between him and his acquaintances.

His first main stop was Turin, where he found his friend Wilkes, who had fled England for a while to avoid being sentenced for treason on a contrived charge. He also found the Italian ladies attractive, and fell in love at once. The love affair was unsatisfactory, but the opera was good, and as he left the city, he had the great luck of witnessing a hanging, after which he went to church in "great devotion." (*Grand Tour*, II.43.) There is again something decidedly theatrical about this, and Boswell even speaks of "three successive scenes: . . . love . . . horror . . . devotion."

At Milan he saw some of the sights and went to the opera, where he wished he had some gingerbread or liquorice to give to the boys who were carrying the ladies' trains during such times as they were not scratching their heads or blowing their noses. It is typical that he comments on the people, on stage and off, but not the music; he does not even name the opera.

Then on to Piacenza and Parma, where, at the end of January, his fully written journal breaks off. The memoranda which follow for the next eight months are mostly the raw materials for a journal he did not have time to write up. He went to Rome, where he saw the antiquities, including a statue of Cicero which "resembles him a great deal." (II.65.) He saw Michelangelo's "Moses," but thought the beard too long. In May he wrote to Rousseau, having now determined to visit Corsica, and asked him for a letter of introduction, which he sent. In the middle of June, he joined the party of Lord Mountstuart, son of the Earl of Bute and a dissipated young man near Boswell's age, and they moved north through Ferrara to Padua and Venice.

There Boswell saw Baretti, who showed him some letters from Dr. Johnson. A few days later, writing to Wilkes, Boswell is still thinking about Johnson: "Could my feeble mind preserve but a faint impression of Johnson, it would be a glory to myself and a benefit to mankind." (II.106.) This is apparently the first indication that Boswell was thinking, however vaguely, of writing a life of Johnson. He was only twenty-four.

After a fortnight in Venice, the party visited Vicenza, Verona, Brescia, and came again to Milan, whence Mountstuart was called home. Boswell continued his tour: Parma, Florence, and finally Siena, where he formed a passionate attachment to an Italian lady, Girolama Piccolomini, who fell deeply in love with him. At the end of September he left Siena and his love, stopped briefly at Lucca and Pisa, and reached Leghorn, where he made arrangements for the short voyage to Corsica.

On 11 October 1765 he sailed for the island. Because of a dead calm the ship did not dock until the evening of the twelfth. A single leaf of Boswell's fully written journal survives for the eleventh, showing him seasick and plagued with mosquitoes and "other vermin," but recovering enough to eat and to join in some music with his flute. (II.147.) He tried to read up on the Corsican question, but was unable to concentrate. In the evening when everyone knelt to say the Ave Maria, he was much affected. It is a lively and typical entry.

For the tour of Corsica itself, only a few pages of notes survive, but how Boswell utilized his materials can be shown by part of a paragraph from his published *Account* dealing with the day just described: "The first day was the most tedious. However, there were two or three Corsicans aboard, and one of them played on the *cetra*, which amused me a good deal. At sunset all the people in the ship sung the Ave Maria with great devotion and some melody. It was pleasing to enter into the spirit of their religion, and hear them offering up their evening orisons." (II.159.) He has reduced his own part to little more than that of an inactive spectator and condensed the whole to about a quarter of its original length.

After describing his first day on the island, he abandons a day-by-day account, in order, he says, to give a freer and more continuous description of what he saw or heard. It also, as the Yale editors observed, enabled him to give the impression that he had spent much longer than a week with General Paoli.

Boswell describes some episodes with great vivacity. In one, he is taken to see three prisoners, a man accused of killing his wife, a wife who had hired a servant to strangle a woman she was jealous of, and the servant who had done so.

> The murderer of his wife had a stupid, hardened appearance, and told me he did it at the instigation of the devil. The servant was a poor despicable wretch. He had at first accused his mistress but was afterwards prevailed with to deny his accusation, upon which he was put to the torture by having lighted matches held between his fingers. This made him return to what he had formerly said, so as to be a strong evidence against his mistress. His hands were so miserably scorched that he was a piteous object. I asked him why he had committed such a crime; he said, "Because I was without understanding." The lady seemed of a bold and resolute spirit. She spoke to me with great firmness and denied her guilt, saying with a contemptuous smile as she pointed to her servant, "They can force that creature to say what they please." (II.167.)

In another incident, Boswell has applied for a Corsican passport at the house of the Chancellor, who read him some of the minutes of the legislative body while the document was being prepared. "When the passport was finished and ready to have the seal put to it, I was much pleased with a beautiful, simple incident. The Chancellor desired a little boy who was playing in the room by us to run to his mother and bring the great seal of the kingdom. I thought myself sitting in the house of a Cincinnatus." (II.168.)

In both episodes, Boswell is at or near the center, and it is his reaction which brings the scene to life for the reader. Unfortunately, the same thing cannot be said for the central part of the book, that devoted to conversations with General Paoli. For the most part one does not "see" Paoli, or hear the proper tones of his voice. It is possible that Boswell was too much in awe of him, but it may be that he had not yet perfected a method of transferring his rough notes into a printed account. The extraordinarily vivid conversations with Rousseau and Voltaire were written up, apparently, soon after they occurred. The conversations with Paoli, on the other hand, appear never to have been expanded till he was preparing the book for publication, a year and a half later. Then it was too late to give more than isolated statements, which lack flesh and reality. It is conceivable that Boswell intended to write up his full journal immediately after leaving Paoli, but before leaving Corsica. If so, he was partly disabled by an attack of malaria, which left him weak and enervated.

Boswell's approach to Paoli was characteristically direct: he had come from Rome, the ruins of a once free people, to see the rise of another nation of free men. Paoli was polite, but apparently held Boswell off for a while, thinking him a spy, as he told Fanny Burney later. He did notice Boswell taking notes when he had looked away for a moment, and this may have induced him to be cautious. He spoke French to Boswell, but at dinner, where most of those present were Corsicans, he naturally spoke Italian. Boswell asked him if he spoke English (an inevitable question) and he did, tolerably well: he had learned it at Naples from some Irish gentlemen, but was out of practice.

It becomes clear at this point that Boswell was groping toward the method he perfected many years later in his *Tour of the Hebrides* and his *Johnson*: he was attempting to give his hero the center of the stage. Paoli speaks in direct discourse: "could I render this people happy, I would be content to be forgotten"; whereas Boswell is indirect: "I asked him how . . . I asked him if . . . ," with the result that the focus is on Paoli, not Boswell. (II.174.) But it is not enough. There is little or no give and take, and too many of Paoli's utterances are isolated; they do not cumulatively build up to any peak of emotion or interest, as Boswell is later able to do with conversations in the books for which he is properly famous.

The picture of Boswell, on the contrary, emerges clearly, particularly when he is not with Paoli—no doubt for the good reason that he is more relaxed when he is not in a posture of worship. He had a Corsican costume made, "in which I walked about with an air of true satisfaction." He became "a great favourite" with the peasants and soldiers, who asked him "a thousand questions" about his country. They easily persuaded him to play his flute, and after one or two Italian airs he gave them some old Scots tunes, "Gilderoy," "The Lass of Patie's Mill," and "Corn rigs are bonny." (One is inevitably reminded of George Primrose in *The Vicar of Wakefield* playing his flute for the French peasants to dance by.) No wonder the Corsicans were charmed. Finally he sang "Hearts of oak are our ships, Hearts of oak are our men," and when he translated it for his audience they were delighted: "Cuore di quercia," they cried, "bravo Inglese." (II.185.) This is far better than any scene in which Paoli appears.

As the visit came to a close, Boswell asked Paoli if there was any way to show his respect and attachment. Paoli replied, "Remember that I am your friend, and write to me." Boswell responded with the hope that Paoli would write not only as a general but as a philosopher and a man of letters. "He took me by the hand and said, 'As a friend.'" Boswell's reaction was typically emotional:

> I dare not transcribe from my private notes the feelings which I had at this interview. I should perhaps appear too enthusiastic. I took leave of Paoli with regret and agitation, not without some hopes of seeing him again. From having known intimately so exalted a character, my sentiments of human nature were raised; while by a sort of contagion I felt an honest ardour to distinguish myself, and be useful as far as my situation and abilities would allow; and I was, for the rest of my life, set free from a slavish timidity in the presence of great men, for where shall I find a man greater than Paoli? (II.200–01.)

The ninety-mile ride to Corte in the center of the island was rough, the weather was bad, and Boswell was coming down with malaria, but the trip was merry. Part of the way he was accompanied by a "great swarthy priest . . . a very Hercules," who "would burst out with comical songs about the devil, and the

Genoese, and I don't know what all." (II.201.) And one night on the way, four Corsican guards performed a local dance: "It was truly savage. They thumped with their heels, sprung upon their toes, brandished their arms, wheeled and leaped with the most violent gesticulations. It gave me the idea of an admirable war-dance." (II.202.) The picture of Boswell in his surroundings has come to life again.

He wrote to Paoli from Bastia and had a fine reply from him in December, which he permitted Boswell to use in his book, along with Boswell's translation. The last two sentences put the reader in the right frame of mind for the conclusion to Boswell's second volume: "Wherever I am, your friendship will be present to my mind, and I shall be desirous to continue a correspondence with you. Meanwhile, believe me to be your most affectionate friend, Pascal Paoli." (II.216.) In the published book, the end is a compliment to Paoli from the elder Pitt: "He is one of those men who are no longer to be found but in the *Lives* of Plutarch."

By December Boswell was in Genoa, where he found, to his great satisfaction, that his movements in Corsica had been closely observed and reported by Genoese spies. He now resumed a more fully written journal, and we follow him across the Italian Riviera into France, arguing with his Swiss servant Jacob, who thought him stingy, and beating his dog with senseless ferocity. At some later date Boswell apparently had twinges of conscience about the dog, for he crossed out the passages describing those beatings. The Yale editors have managed to read them.

After savoring the French Riviera, Boswell turned north. At Lyons he heard that Rousseau had been hounded from Switzerland when his abandonment of his children became known, and was now about to leave Paris for England to visit David Hume. Boswell wrote enthusiastically to Rousseau, expressing the hope that he and Johnson might meet—and left off writing his full journal, no doubt because of his hurrying to Paris. Not long after his arrival, he saw a newspaper notice of his mother's death, and a day later a letter from his father confirmed the news.

Rousseau's mistress, Thérèse, was now to follow him to England, and Boswell decided to escort her. She gave him some comfort in his distress, and, in turn, he seduced her. Unfortunately, although he wrote up these interesting events in some detail, the journal was destroyed in recent years before the papers came to this country. Modern readers have therefore been deprived of an episode which seems to have had the rich comic overtones of the Louisa affair in London. For according to Col. Isham, who saw the manuscript, the middle-aged Thérèse tried to teach young Boswell how to make love.

In February 1766, Boswell was in London seeing Rousseau and asking Johnson's advice on writing a book on Corsica. But it seems fairly clear that he had already decided on such a book. He went to Edinburgh, was admitted to the bar, and defended his first client, John Reid, a sheep-stealer. But his main occupation, interrupted now and again by his search for a wife, seems to have been as a publicist for the Corsican cause. For almost a year there are no journal entries, but in 1767 they are resumed. In October of that year he completed his first important book. Even more worthy of note, it is his first typical work.

II

Corsica; Tour of the Hebrides

THE SUCCESSFUL writings of Boswell's literary career are very much of a piece: they are those in which his interest in people is dominant—himself, Johnson, Voltaire, Rousseau, and many others. The form may be diary or biography; it is rarely if ever anything else. In his *Life of Johnson*, the diary forms the firm basis of the *Life*.

Not that Boswell did not try many other forms. When he was twenty-six, he published *Dorando*, a short allegorized narrative of the Douglas affair, supporting the claims of Archibald Douglas to the family name and estate. The thin little story is a flat failure: Boswell shows no interest in the person, but only in the romantic character of the story—a young man of obscure birth on the Continent coming to Scotland and finally making the courts accept his improbable account. Someone else might have made it a novel, but Boswell's genius did not lie in that area.

Boswell had been a diarist for many years, beginning in his teens and continuing, with few long interruptions, till his death. (The longest interruption, about two years, occurred just after his happy marriage.) Boswell is always at the center of his journal, but often shares the center with one or more people. An event is important as it happens to *him*: it is his "search for identity." And he had not been writing many years before he tried to capture that most evanescent of human experiences, conversation. No earlier diarist in England had tried such a thing—can anyone recall a single conversation in Pepys?—and no subsequent diarist has so greatly succeeded.

The first significant book culled from Boswell's diary is his *Account of Corsica* (1768), based on his visit three years earlier. The materials this time were right: a wild, little-known island struggling for freedom, Boswell's own involvement, considerable publicity in British newspapers about the revolution and the later careers of the Paolis, and above all Boswell's diary on which to base his book. Johnson urged that Boswell in writing it pay less attention to gazetteer or statistical information than to the personal, and, as far as he was able, Boswell did.

The book begins with a gracious dedication to Paoli which sounds like Johnson, not Boswell:

> Dedications are for most part the offerings of interested servility, or the effusions of partial zeal; enumerating the virtues of men in whom no virtues can be found, or predicting greatness to those who afterwards pass their days in unambitious indolence, and die leaving no memorial of their existence but a dedication, in which all their merit is confessedly future, and which time has turned into a silent reproach.
>
> He who has any experience of mankind, will be cautious to whom he dedicates. Publickly to bestow praise on merit of which the publick is not sensible, or to raise flattering expectations which are never fulfilled, must sink the character of an authour, and make him appear a cringing parasite, or a fond enthusiast. (*Account of Corsica*, pp. v-vi.)

Johnson probably wrote this, as he wrote dozens of similar dedications for his friends. Then there follows an extended preface, in which Boswell states that he has been induced to publish by "the ardour of publick curiosity" since his return, and by Paoli's encouragement. (p. ix.) He gives his printed sources, hits at Smollett for erring as to Paoli's age, and thanks a number of people for help, from the nineteen-year-old Thomas Day (later author of *Sandford and Merton*), to his Scottish friends Monboddo and Hailes. He pays his respects to Johnson and the *Dictionary*, and at last speaks of his own hope of fame: "He who publishes a book, affecting not to be an authour, and professing an indifference for literary fame, may possibly impose upon many people such an idea of his consequence as he wishes may be received. For my part, I should be proud to be known as an authour; and I have an ardent ambition for literary fame. . . ." (p. xix-xx.) There is something disarming in this, and, moreover, it is an accurate prediction for the future: the Dedication is, symbolically, dated on Boswell's twenty-seventh birthday.

The Introduction proper begins with an essay on liberty which is not particularly remarkable, and then describes Boswell's plan to give a description of the island and its history, to which he will "subjoin" his journal with its anecdotes and memoirs of Paoli.

Actually, the *Account* seriously overbalances the journal; it is twice as long, and it contains, as Dr. Johnson suspected it would, little firsthand material. Moreover, eighteen pages of Appendix, in Italian, intervene before the journal begins. It was artistically an error in proportion which Boswell did not make again. On the other hand, the reader of 1768 was no doubt more interested in Corsica than in Boswell.

The book was a spectacular success, and the journal, at least, is still readable after two centuries, especially as we see the young Boswell, just turned twenty-five, throwing himself into the Corsican cause and reporting it with infectious enthusiasm and disarming naïveté.

For a fledgling author, the success must have been heady: three printings in London, three in Ireland, and translations into Dutch, German, Italian, and French. But Boswell, perhaps sensibly, did not try at once to produce some sort of sequel. Instead, he devoted himself to his professional law career, treating literature with his left hand only. He contributed papers on legal, literary, and other matters to *The London Chronicle* with some frequency (nine in six months of 1770), but none of these are of great importance, except to show his constant wish to see his words in print. He had already become a partner in *The London Magazine*, and wrote for it three essays on acting and an occasional paper on the law. He also agreed, a little later, to do a series of essays called "The Hypochondriack." These were delayed, perhaps from failure of inspiration at the moment.

Biography, moreover, kept tugging at his mind. After Gray's death in 1771, Boswell had published a "Sketch" of the poet, which included a "character" by Temple. In the same month, he noted in his diary his "constant plan" to write a life of Johnson; he mentioned this to Johnson, who made no objection and even agreed that "all the little circumstances of his life" which Boswell wanted would "come out by degrees" (31 March 1772). Two weeks later, after talking to the widow of a minor poet, he regretted that he did not know her well enough to ask her "minute particulars" concerning her late husband (*Journal*, 13 April 1772). He added immediately: "I have really a genius for particular history, for biography." Boswell's insistence on particulars or "little circumstances" is noteworthy as part of his method, even this early in his career. He was thirty-one.

Boswell and Johnson had discussed a trip to Scotland and perhaps to the Hebrides in 1772; in the autumn of 1773 it was accomplished. Fortunately for Boswell's literary career—and for us—he was ready. He was fully accustomed to keeping a diary. It was his practice to jot down brief notes before going to bed, often in a sort of speed-writing with vowels or syllables omitted and with occasional symbols for words. This helped fix the events of the day or evening in mind and more especially the topics of conversation, with a brief word or two to indicate the point of view of the speakers. Next morning, or as soon as he had time, before the notes began to lose their power of recall, Boswell filled them out into as complete a record as he could. Needless to say, neither the evening's notes nor the day's expansion was always done, but the task was accomplished so often that Boswell's journal has no rival in fullness.

Part of his success arises from the fact that he was no passive spectator of the events or listener-in on the conversations. He had discovered early that Johnson often needed to be prodded into talk; he would not exert himself to engage in small talk. Thus, when James Beattie was going to London and hoped to meet Johnson, Boswell was explicit: "lead him to tell. . . . Bring him upon something worthy of his abilities as soon as you can. . . ." And Boswell's own practice was to do this. Over and over he is the one to introduce the subject: "I mentioned Foote's taking him off." (*Journal*, 21 March 1772.) This was certain to produce a reaction, because Johnson had let it be known that he would beat the mimic if he was made the object of ridicule. Again, on 10 April, "I started the question if duelling was lawful." This was an especially good gambit, because it produced a difference between Johnson and Goldsmith, who was also present. Moreover, Boswell displayed the tenacity of a terrier when Johnson was unwilling to discuss a subject. Twice Johnson avoided Boswell's wish to find out his opinions on purgatory. The third time Johnson, "in excellent good humour," obliged. (*Journal*, 28 March

1772.) Boswell's keen interest in all three topics can be demonstrated. This, with the fact that he introduced the discussion, was of the greatest assistance to his memory in getting the conversation down in writing later on.

In spite of the fact that the journey through the Hebrides had been long anticipated, Boswell did not begin to keep a full journal for several days after he and Johnson left Edinburgh. This suggests that he had at first no plan to write a book about the tour, as Johnson did not at first either. Indeed, they were both familiar with Martin Martin's *Description of the Western Islands* (1703) and with Pennant's recent *Tour in Scotland*. There might not, at the outset, have seemed reason for two more books on the subject. But Boswell had made rough notes of conversations before the pair left the capital, and Johnson decided on a book before they reached the Hebrides.

Johnson's *Journey to the Western Islands* (1775) may, indeed, have partly determined Boswell to publish his own book. Johnson had let him see the manuscript, and when the book appeared, there were some things in it with which Boswell disagreed. He meditated publishing a "Supplement" to the *Journey*, or "Remarks" on it, a project which Johnson did not encourage. Johnson did read Boswell's manuscript diary of the tour, however, and within a few weeks of Johnson's death Boswell had resolved to publish it. Characteristically, he advertised it in his *Letter to the People of Scotland:* "This Journal, which was read and liked by Dr. Johnson, will faithfully and minutely exhibit what he said was the pleasantest part of his life: and, while it gives the remarks which Mr. Boswell himself was able to make, during a very curious journey, it will convey a specimen of that conversation, in which Wisdom and Wit were equally conspicuous."

When it came to making a book out of the diary, Boswell experienced some trouble. Fortunately, Edmond Malone, lawyer, Shakespearean editor, and friend of both Johnson and Boswell, was willing to look over his shoulder and advise him, as he was later to do with the *Life of Johnson.* Most of the manuscript of *The Journal of a Tour to the Hebrides with Samuel Johnson, LL.D.* has survived among the Boswell Papers at Yale and has been published, so that it is possible to see in detail what changes Boswell made. Briefly, he added a good deal of introductory matter, changed the emphasis of the diary slightly so that Johnson moves a little more into the center of the picture, omitted some details which merely clutter the narrative, such as dinner menus (at Malone's insistence), and added some comments on Johnson's book and other afterthoughts.

The *Tour* is dedicated to Malone, who, says Boswell in a sort of blurb, can vouch for the accuracy of the book, as Johnson's friends can judge the fidelity of the conversations reported. Here Boswell is staking out the claims on which he will base the importance of his *Life of Johnson*. The book itself begins with a parade of names, which Boswell is artist enough to weave into a narrative instead of a mere list of recommendations: Voltaire was willing that Boswell should go to the Hebrides so long as he did not insist that Voltaire go along; Mrs. Thrale was willing to give the expedition her encouragement—"I'll give thee a wind." (*Tour*, p. 168.) William Robertson, the historian, urged that Johnson come, and Beattie added his good offices in person in London. It was arranged that Robert Chambers, Johnson's protégé and Blackstone's successor at Oxford, should conduct him to Newcastle, and another friend conduct him to Edinburgh.

There follows a fairly elaborate character sketch of Johnson, with side references to Lord Pembroke and Adam Smith, a short comment on Johnson's prejudice against Scotland, and an implied comparison with himself: "I am, I flatter myself, completely a citizen of the world." (p. 172.)

Once Boswell turns to Johnson's arrival in Edinburgh the narrative begins, and takes on directness, color, and even order. At the inn, a waiter put a lump of sugar into Johnson's lemonade "with his greasy fingers" (p. 173) and Johnson indignantly threw it out the window. As the two men walked to Boswell's house the "effluvia" of the open sewers assailed them, and Johnson grumbled, "I smell you in the dark!" (p. 173.) And the conversations begin: on a trial by duel, on a lawyer's duty to a client who is in the wrong, on emigration. These are not long, perhaps owing to Boswell's not having extended notes, but they are partly cast in direct discourse, and have some liveliness. Hume was mentioned, but Johnson was "much too rough," whereupon Boswell suppressed the remark (and says so), which will drive a modern reader to the edition of the manuscript: "B. 'But why attack his heart?' J. 'Why, Sir, because his head has corrupted it. Or perhaps it has perverted his head. I know not indeed whether he has first been a blockhead and that has made him a rogue, or first been a rogue and that has made him a blockhead.'" (*Tour*, ed. Pottle and Bennett, p. 17n.)

The great men of Edinburgh came to meet Johnson, who performed as hoped for: he agreed that Burke had knowledge and imagery, but denied that he had wit, and insisted that he used only conceits, which Johnson considered "low." (His opinion of Shakespeare's puns is notorious.)

Burke was very much alive when this was published, but his reaction is not recorded. Here, almost at the beginning of his book, Boswell is printing derogatory remarks about living persons. It was essential to his purpose in drawing a picture of the whole Johnson, but it had its dangers. Boswell was twice challenged to duel as a result of such frankness.

As the travelers are described leaving Edinburgh, Boswell inserts a self-portrait:

> . . . a gentleman of ancient blood, the pride of which was his predominant passion. He was then in his thirty-third year, and had been about four years happily married. His inclination was to be a soldier; but his father, a respectable Judge, had pressed him into the profession of the law. He had travelled a good deal, and seen many varieties of human life. He had thought more than any body supposed, and had a pretty good stock of general learning and knowledge. He had all Dr. Johnson's principles, with some degree of relaxation. He had rather too little, than too much prudence; and, his imagination being lively, he often said things of which the effect was very different from the intention. (p. 192.)

And two paragraphs later, as if to show how far he could relax his principles, he mentions that Johnson left in a drawer in Edinburgh "a pretty full and curious Diary of his Life. . . . I wish female curiosity had been strong enough to have had it all transcribed, which might easily have been done. . . ." (p. 192.) But his wife had not even glanced at it.

They traveled north to St. Andrews, where Boswell resumed writing his full diary, which, he says, Johnson read from this point. At Montrose Boswell decided to do a bit of stage-managing to make the Great Bear perform. He knew that Johnson and Lord Monboddo did not like each other. Johnson was contemptuous of

Monboddo's search for men with tails and ridiculed his hope that orangutans could be taught to speak. But although Monboddo's belief in the connection between man and the higher apes was not worked out with much precision, he held it passionately, and that meant a possibility of fireworks. Boswell therefore asked Monboddo to invite them to stop, which he did.

The meeting began badly, with Monboddo maintaining that our ancestors were better men than we, which Johnson denied, adding that we are as strong, "and a great deal wiser." (p. 208.) Monboddo let that pass, to Boswell's surprise, and the disputants managed to find it possible to disagree on whether Vergil was a practical farmer. They expressed enthusiasm over Homer, and particularly with regard to Homer's reflection of the manners of the age: "Monboddo. 'The history of manners is the most valuable. I never set a high value on any other history.' Johnson. 'Nor I, and therefore I esteem biography, as giving us what comes near to ourselves, what we can turn to use.' " (p. 209.) From this point, the two elderly gentlemen did well and much later parted better friends than they had been before. Boswell's management produced a good scene for his book, and one which ended in amity. It is strikingly like the famous one in the *Life of Johnson*, where Boswell arranged to have Wilkes seated next to Johnson at dinner.

At Aberdeen, next day, Johnson was surprised to find the great-grandson of Waller the poet studying there instead of at one of the great English schools. On reflection, however, he decided that a dull boy or an idle one might be neglected at a large school, whereas at a small one "constant attention is paid to them, and they are watched. So that the question of publick or private education is not properly a general one; but whether one or the other is best for *my son*." (p. 213.) This is a typical Johnsonian examination of the problems of educating children, handled with his usual absence of dogmatism in that area. Boswell, moreover, reports it directly and without comment, which may suggest that he agreed.

Still at Aberdeen; although entertained at dinner with some of the notable academic men of the city, Boswell was disappointed at the dearth of conversation and thought the professors afraid to speak. When the Ossianic controversy was introduced, Johnson spoke "calmly"—the word is important, and shows that Boswell was keenly aware of the difference between Johnson attacking and Johnson thinking aloud—"If the poems were really translated, they were certainly first written down. Let Mr. Macpherson deposite the manuscript in one of the colleges at Aberdeen, where there are people who can judge; and, if the professors certify the authenticity, then there will be an end of the controversy." (p. 219.) But the calmness of this statement produced no sport; Boswell was bored and Johnson irritated with too much kindness. Later, alone at their inn, they agreed that there had been no good *talk* at Aberdeen.

A few days later they were entertained by a country gentleman whose life, Boswell decided, was no better than that in a jail. Johnson agreed that such men "had not enough to keep their minds in motion." (p. 228.) To some degree this was rationalization, as a reader will hardly need to be told. Both men had chosen urban society, almost as a vocation, years earlier. Not long after, Johnson refused to walk through a country estate; he had seen such before, and had come to Scotland to see new things, "wild objects,—mountains,—waterfalls,—peculiar manners." (p. 230.) These things might stretch his mind.

Occasionally Boswell shows an odd lack of self-consciousness in transferring diary-material to his book. A clergyman remarked in a sermon that some men, acting as companions to those of "distinguished talents, . . . tried to deck themselves with their merit. . . ." (p. 241.) Surely a commonplace. But Boswell not only applies it to himself and Johnson, but draws the reader's attention to something which the average person would have suppressed. The line between self-advertisement and naïveté may be narrow, but here, I think, the reader is likely to be sympathetic.

Boswell retains even the absurd from his journal. At one rough inn he and Johnson debated briefly whether they would be disturbed by bedbugs more if they wore their clothes to bed or stripped. They decided to strip, and after prayers Johnson fell asleep at once. Not so Boswell: "I fancied myself bit by innumerable vermin under the clothes; and that a spider was travelling from the *wainscot* towards my mouth." (p. 248.) At last he slept, unbitten.

Boswell always had trouble omitting the irrelevant and inessential (this is not padding, but a real unwillingness to leave out anything which interests him, however remote the possibility of interesting the reader); so he prints a long epitaph on a MacDonald whom he once knew and two letters from the young man to his mother. The only connection with the tour is that Johnson said that the epitaph should have been in Latin.

Confined by bad weather in Skye, Boswell decided again that rural life is not for him: he looked forward to teatime not merely from hunger but "from the cravings of vacuity of mind." (p. 262.) Later, the party visited a great cave on the island of Raasay, which was below Boswell's expectations. He remarks of it, "I find a great difficulty in describing visible objects" (p. 272), but, in truth, he was not really interested in topography. One need only compare Gray's reaction to the Alps, for example, to show what a vast difference in temperament is here. Thomas Pennant or Gilpin, even nearer contemporaries of Boswell, show a fascination with the picturesque, a new mode of seeing, but this is quite foreign to Boswell.

A few days later the travelers were entertained by Flora Macdonald, and Johnson slept in the same bed where Bonnie Prince Charlie had been concealed from his pursuers after the failure of the rebellion of 1745. Dr. Johnson and the rescuer of the Prince had some conversation about her role in the rescue. Boswell, however, is not satisfied with reporting this, but introduces a thirteen-page digression in which he gives a fairly full story of the event. It is interesting in itself, but an error in judgment, since it stops the tour dead in its tracks for too long a time. The eighteenth century reader, however, was much less put off by digression than we are: the long story by the Old Man of the Hill in *Tom Jones* is one of many such.

Boswell a few days later brought up the subject of Burke, and Johnson, again denying that Burke had a good sense of humor, praised his eloquence, particularly his "copiousness, and fertility of allusion," though he lacked "the highest elegance." (p. 301.) Boswell is rather freer in talking of Burke in the *Tour* than in the *Life of Johnson.* By the time he wrote the later book, there had been some estrangement between the two men, though at one period Boswell had hoped that Burke might help him in politics.

An unexpected hardship which Johnson and Boswell found in one house in the Hebrides was lack of privacy: "the good people had no notion that a man could have any occasion but for a mere sleeping-place; so, during the day, the bed-chambers were common to all the house. Servants eat in Dr. Johnson's; and mine was a kind of general rendezvous of all under the roof, children and dogs not excepted." (p. 337.)

One of the best set scenes in the *Tour* is the storm off the isle of Col. The Hebrides are notorious for bad weather, and Johnson and Boswell had been having plenty, but this storm was the worst. Johnson in his *Journey* characteristically treated it in four sentences, of which two are: "I was sea-sick and lay down. Mr. Boswell kept the deck." Boswell, on the other hand, gives an elaborate account, not so much descriptive of the storm itself as of its effect on him. They had set sail from Skye in a small ship, and for "many hours" Boswell enjoyed the motion. Johnson grew sick and went below. "I kept above, that I might have fresh air, and . . . exulted in being a stout seaman, while Dr. Johnson was quite in a state of annihilation. But I was soon humbled; for after imagining that I could go with ease to America or the East-Indies, I became very sick, but kept above board, though it rained hard." (p. 347.)

The storm worsened; it was dark; there was doubt that they could make any nearby harbor safely. They decided to run for Col before the wind, and Boswell was temporarily relieved:

> But my relief was but of short duration; for I soon heard that our sails were very bad, and were in danger of being torn in pieces, in which case we should be driven upon the rocky shore of Col. It was very dark, and there was a heavy and incessant rain. The sparks of the burning peat flew so much about, that I dreaded the vessel might take fire. Then, as Col was a sportsman, and had powder on board, I figured that we might be blown up. Simpson and he appeared a little frightened, which made me more so; and the perpetual talking, or rather shouting, which was carried on in Erse, alarmed me still more. A man is always suspicious of what is saying in an unknown tongue; and, if fear be his passion at the time, he grows more afraid. (pp. 348–49.)

Boswell tried to quiet his mind by thinking that the Deity might intervene to save them (and mentions one author opposed to the idea and another favoring it). Finally he asked young Col, who was conducting the party, what he could do to help. "He, with a happy readiness, put into my hand a rope, which was fixed to the top of one of the masts, and told me to hold it till he bade me pull." Boswell later realized that Col was just giving him something to occupy himself and keep him out of the way. It worked: "Thus did I stand firm to my post, while the wind and rain beat upon me, always expecting a call to pull my rope." (p. 349.) When they reached harbor and cast anchor, they went below and found Johnson on one of the bunks: "He was lying in philosophick tranquillity, with a greyhound of Col's at his back, keeping him warm." (p. 350.) It is a good story, superbly told.

Neither of the travelers was favorably impressed with really primitive life. On Col they saw a small, very smoky hut occupied by a man and his family, with one bed for all. Johnson was sarcastic that philosophers should have equated this simplicity with happiness. "Boswell. 'The philosophers, when they placed happiness in a cottage, supposed cleanliness and no smoke.' Johnson. 'Sir, they did not think about either.' " (p. 357.)

As Boswell moves on toward the last part of his book, there is some evidence of lack of revision. On 14 October, for example, he runs through the day's events and then writes up a conversation of that morning which he had neglected to put in its proper place. In one way, this adds a degree of realism, since the reader is kept aware of the framework of a diary. The same thing happens on the next day, when Boswell recalls a number of pieces of conversation from recent weeks.

A few days later, coasting alongside the island of Mull, Boswell shows Johnson in a mood of ruminant satisfaction: "If this be not *roving among the Hebrides*, nothing is." (p. 384.) And Boswell was led to imagine how the present adventures would appear when recollected in tranquillity: "I have often experienced, that scenes through which a man has passed, improve by lying in the memory: they grow mellow." (p. 384.) He speculates that this may come from comparing the past with the "listless" present, but is curious as to why evil aspects grow dimmer while "pleasing scenes improve by time." (p. 385.) He reaches no conclusion.

On occasion Boswell was quite ready to drive Johnson to rudeness just to see the fireworks. One morning their hostess, Lady Lochbuy, a very old woman, proposed before Johnson came down that

> he should have some cold sheep's-head for breakfast. Sir Allan seemed displeased at his sister's vulgarity, and wondered how such a thought should come into her head. From a mischievous love of sport, I took the lady's part; and very gravely said, "I think it is but fair to give him an offer of it. If he does not choose it, he may let it alone."—"I think so," said the lady, looking at her brother with an air of victory. Sir Allan, finding the matter desperate, strutted about the room, and took snuff. When Dr. Johnson came in, she called to him, "Do you choose any cold sheep's-head, sir?"—"No, MADAM" said he, with a tone of surprise and anger.—"It is here, sir," said she, supposing he had refused it to save the trouble of bringing it in. They thus went on at cross purposes, till he confirmed his refusal in a manner not to be misunderstood; while I sat quietly by, and enjoyed my success. (p. 391.)

That day they left the islands, none too soon one might think, and at Oban found a paragraph in a Glasgow newspaper about their being detained on Skye by the bad weather. Boswell quotes it with approval: "Such a philosopher, detained on an almost barren island, resembles a whale left upon the strand. The latter will be welcome to every body, on account of his oil, his bone, &c. and the other will charm his companions, and the rude inhabitants, with his superior knowledge and wisdom, calm resignation, and unbounded benevolence." (p. 392.)

Once on the mainland of Scotland, Boswell soon desisted from keeping a full journal, and although the travelers continued to visit families of prominence, there is less conversation reported. While they were being entertained by Boswell's father at Auchinleck, however, an unnamed gentleman asked the sort of direct question which always irritated Johnson because a favorable reply is always expected: how did he like the Highlands? He answered, " 'How, sir, can you ask me what obliges me to speak unfavourably of a country where I have been hospitably entertained? Who *can* like the Highlands?—I like the inhabitants very well.'—The gentleman asked no more questions." (p. 416.)

A week later they were back in Edinburgh, and the *Tour* comes rather quickly to a close, ending with some letters from friends praising Johnson's book or commenting on it and a few paragraphs in which Boswell justifies his use of conversation in the book. This may seem to be an unusual way to end until one raises the question, what way would be better?

And here I might pause to point out the virtually complete absence of models for such a book as Boswell wrote. No major English diaries had been published as yet; both Pepys's and Evelyn's were still forty years in the future. Some travel diaries had indeed seen the light, but it may be doubted that they would have been of much use as models, and their authenticity was usually highly suspect. Very high credit must be given Boswell as an originator of a form, and also for daring to print many remarks which were certain to cause resentment when read. The same spirit of innovation and daring brought the *Life of Johnson* to a successful conclusion six years later.

III

Life of Johnson

For the *Life of Johnson,* Boswell did have models, though it is questionable how useful most of them were. Johnson had recommended Izaak Walton's *Lives* to him, and in the summer of 1774 he read all five. But excellent as these are, they are short and hardly comparable in any way with the two big quartos Boswell published in 1791. Nor are Johnson's own *Lives of the Poets* really of the same type. Johnson felt no especial urge to include letters to or from his subjects, and used these in a quite random fashion, as they happened to be at hand. In this respect Johnson is wholly in the tradition of biography as it existed in England till 1774. In that year William Mason used Gray's letters as a major part of his biography of the poet, principally, it would seem, because Gray's career was so uneventful that some padding was required to give it bulk. As is well known, Mason handled the letters quite unscrupulously, cutting, pasting together, and suppressing at will in order to present the image he wished, whatever the facts.

Except for Boswell, Mason's innovation made no great impact on biographical method in the last quarter of the century. Boswell, however, was impressed, decided to follow Mason, and acknowledges his example (*Life*, I.29). Fortunately, Boswell had been saving Johnson's letters for years, and those of dozens of other people. Fortunately also, and even more important, he had his own journal to use as a basis for the conversations which made his biography a wholly new kind of work in English literature. Such things as so-and-so's "table talk" had been reported in print before, and we have Ben Jonson's "Conversations" with Drummond of Hawthornden, but these are in no way comparable with the long and elaborate conversations which Boswell now had ready to use in his biography.

Boswell's Dedication to Sir Joshua Reynolds accomplishes two purposes. First, it launches the book under very distinguished auspices. Reynolds had known Johnson much longer than Boswell had, and intimately; his approbation, therefore, would ensure "credit and success." (*Life*, I.2.) He had, Boswell reminds the reader, already commended the "authentick and lively manner" in which Johnson's conversation appeared in the *Tour*. Secondly, Boswell explains why he is somewhat more reserved in this book than he had been in the *Tour:* his candor had been misinterpreted by some fools as being "simply unconscious of the pointed effect of [Johnson's] satire." (*Life*, I.3.) How serious Boswell is in this second point is perhaps not wholly clear, but the fact is certain that he suppressed his own name in many cases, and those of other persons as well. (Fortunately for the curious modern reader, a high percentage of the unnamed speakers can now be identified, thanks to the preservation of Boswell's diaries.)

In the Advertisement which follows, Boswell stakes out his claim to authenticity by remarking, "I have sometimes been obliged to run half over London in order to fix a date correctly." (*Life*, I.7.) This regard for fact gives a firmness to his chronology which is very reassuring to the reader, particularly if we compare Boswell's narrative with Hawkins' *Johnson* or Mrs. Piozzi's *Anecdotes*. Valuable as these other accounts are, they leave the reader hanging in mid-air much of the time, in puzzlement as to *when* some event took place. Boswell goes on to thank Malone for having listened to him read his whole manuscript and for having read half of the proofs. This again is some reassurance to the reader, for Malone's pre-eminence as a Shakespearean scholar was becoming known. He closes with a letter from Johnson's old friend Dr. Adams praising the *Tour*, and an expression of his own satisfaction in providing so much of the wit and wisdom of Dr. Johnson "for the instruction and entertainment of mankind."

Boswell begins his book with the wish that Johnson had written it, with which few readers will agree, since Johnson did not write about himself with much ease or pleasure. After listing his own qualifications for writing about Johnson, Boswell charges Hawkins' life with inaccuracy, padding, and a "dark uncharitable cast" (*Life*, I.28); he acknowledges Mason's *Gray* as a model, and then expresses his confidence that his book is a truly unique achievement: Johnson "will be seen in this work more completely than any man who has ever yet lived." (*Life*, I.30.) This is a bold boast indeed; it would be a bolder critic who attempted to dispute it. The introduction closes with some extended quotations from *The Rambler*, No. 60, on the writing of biography, and a bow in the direction of the man who takes down the pithy sayings of others.

On the whole, Boswell's introductory section is brief, considering the very long book ahead, and considering also the rather revolutionary change in biographical writing which he is offering.

The structure of the *Life* is chronological. Boswell begins with a short sketch of Johnson's father, a Jacobite and high-churchman, subject to the same melancholia later shown by his son. Johnson's mother, says Boswell, was a woman of "distinguished understanding" (I.38), an assertion for which, I believe, no evidence exists. On the other hand, Boswell prints a statement from Johnson's schoolmate Hector that Mrs. Johnson was not vain of her son but valued him properly. This is entirely credible. It should be remembered that Boswell never met Johnson's mother, and that all the reports of Johnson's childhood date from some fifty years afterwards, when Johnson was himself old and famous. It is no wonder, therefore, that some of the reports are doting. One sample will do. At age three Johnson was brought to the cathedral to see the famous Dr. Sacheverell, and a friend asked Mr. Johnson why he brought a child out in such a crowd. Mr. Johnson replied that he believed the boy had caught the popular zeal for the clergyman and would not stay home. One may hope that Michael Johnson was joking. At any rate the story is reported by the friend's granddaughter, and bears the usual marks of a tale handed down in a family—the myth has obscured whatever actuality was there.

Stories of Johnson's early ability to memorize and to versify are both more credible and better authenticated. It does not strain belief that Johnson should have been able to memorize a prayer of three or four lines *after he had learned to read.*

Boswell next touches upon Johnson's poor vision (he was blind in one eye), but gives striking evidence from the Highlands tour and from a journey into Derbyshire that Johnson did very well with his one good eye in seeing the mountain country. This can be checked against Johnson's own accounts, especially in his diaries, and is reliable. Boswell characteristically adds a note of human interest to his discussion of Johnson's powers of vision: he was "nicely and minutely critical" of female dress. (I.41.)

With hardly a change of movement Boswell brings the sick child to London to be touched for the king's evil by Queen Anne, the last monarch to try the royal power to cure scrofula. There is a small picture here, borrowed, with proper credit, from Mrs. Piozzi: Johnson remembered "a lady in diamonds, and a long black hood." (I.43.) The royal touch was ineffective, but Johnson was soon put to school with Dame Oliver, where he learned to read. She in turn asked young Sam (aged six or eight) to get a black-letter Bible from his father's bookshop for her to read; and many years later, when he was about to leave, belatedly, for Oxford, she brought him some gingerbread. Boswell has treated the reading, the Bible, and the gingerbread in almost as few words as I have used here—but a pause for analysis is in order. It seems to me quite unusual that a small boy in Johnson's circumstances should be taught to read in school rather than at home. His remark about Dame Oliver being able to read a black-letter Bible, then going into obsolescence, looks like a small tribute, and the story of the gingerbread is a real triumph: Lichfield in 1728 was not a village in which the departure of a young man for the university would have been a red-letter day; it was a city. But Dame Oliver, whose pupil Johnson had been fourteen or fifteen years before, had been warned that a coming-of-age, in effect, was at hand, and she was there with her gingerbread. It will not do to condescend to these happenings. Johnson remembered them with affection and gratitude in his old age, and he was right to do so and to tell Boswell of them. Every piece of encouragement was important to him. Boswell shrewdly recognized that this anecdote was not just local color.

After Johnson left the dame's school, his next schoolmasters commanded more respect than love. Tom Brown dedicated a spelling-book to the universe, without discernible effect on Johnson. Hunter beat him, and he learned Latin, but did not, thereby, learn to love Hunter, who was not only severe but "wrong-headedly severe." (I.44.) Nevertheless, he thought beatings preferable to proddings to rivalry, which would "make brothers and sisters hate each other." (I.46.) Boswell goes on to comment on Johnson's physical torpor while he was growing up—that huge body, even by twentieth-century measurements—and his tenacious memory. Finally, in this extraordinarily brief survey of Johnson's parentage and early youth, about ten pages to cover fifteen years, we are given a new motif—Johnson learns to escape from the humdrum world through reading the romances of chivalry. It is not possible to name a title with certainty here, though later he read *Felixmarte de Hircania* and *Amadis of Gaul*. If we knew what romances were in Michael Johnson's shop, we might be fairly safe in guessing that Johnson read them.

But these romances did not release him from school. For a while he lived out of town with an uncle, and then was both a pupil and assistant at Stourbridge, where he wrote many schoolboy poems unusual enough to be preserved by both the schoolmaster and his friends. Boswell gives lengthy samples of these, which are a tribute to the foresight of Johnson's early schoolmaster, as well as to Boswell's diligence in ferreting them out.

Johnson returned to Lichfield to be a clerk in his father's bookstore, instead of going to the university, for which no money was available. Gibbon was able to enter Oxford at fifteen, but Johnson had to wait till he was nineteen, and his scanty funds lasted only thirteen months. (Boswell, in a rare mistake, says three years.)

At Oxford, Johnson not only found himself in a nest of singing birds, all of whom knew Latin, but he found a surrogate father, his tutor Jorden: "Whenever (said he) a young man becomes Jorden's pupil, he becomes his son." (I.61.) No relationship could have impressed Boswell more: he had taken Johnson as such a father. Jorden, in whatever capacity, persuaded Johnson to translate Pope's *Messiah* into Latin, and it was Johnson's first publication, in an Oxford anthology.

About this time Johnson began to be seriously troubled with melancholia, which, indeed, remained with him for the rest of his life. In time he learned "how to manage it" (I.64), as he said. At this time also, he told Boswell, his early religious doubts received some satisfaction from reading William Law's *Serious Call*. His diaries, however, show that some religious doubts remained, or recurred, to plague him almost until his death. Boswell suppresses this bit of information in order to present Johnson as a sage and mentor having the stability which Boswell lacked. That Boswell actually suppressed it, rather than merely being ignorant of it, is certain, since he possessed and used the diaries referred to.

Boswell reports that while at Oxford, Johnson read solidly in Greek, particularly Homer and Euripides, and added to the broad foundation of general reading which probably began when the stock in his father's bookshop aroused his curiosity. Boswell comments at this point that "Dr. Adam Smith, than whom few were better judges on this subject, once observed to me that 'Johnson knew more books than any man alive.'" (I.71.)

By quizzing Johnson, and by searching out his early friends, Boswell is able to give a few illuminating glimpses into Johnson's months at Oxford. One is Johnson talking to himself, overheard by one of the masters: "Well, I have a mind to see what is done in other places of learning. I'll go and visit the Universities abroad. I'll go to France and Italy. I'll go to Padua.—And I'll mind my business. For an *Athenian* blockhead is the worst of all blockheads." (I.73.) Another is his own comment to Boswell: "Ah, Sir, I was mad and violent. It was bitterness which they mistook for frolick. I was miserably poor. . . ." (I.73–74.) A third is someone's well-meaning attempt to help him by leaving a pair of new shoes at his door: he indignantly threw them away.

Back at home in Lichfield, Johnson's social education was begun, or perhaps was continued, by some of the "best families" (I.80), who interested themselves in this awkward, brilliant young man. The chief among these people was Gilbert Walmesley, a lay officer of the ecclesiastical court. He was a gentleman and a Whig, and at his dinner table, Johnson wrote later, he enjoyed "cheerful and instructive hours" with Robert James, later a well-known physician, and David Garrick. (I.81.) Johnson paid tribute to all three in the biography of Edmund Smith in the *Lives of the Poets*, from which Boswell extracted these comments. Boswell mentions many others, particularly the Aston sisters (Johnson's wife was jealous of one of them) and Hill Boothby, to whom Johnson may have proposed after the death of his wife.

He was at loose ends. His father died, and two and a half years after leaving Oxford he found a job as a teacher in a school in Leicestershire. It was not nearby, but he went on foot. Here is

Boswell giving the important and lively detail; no further discussion of Johnson's poverty is needed. The overbearing patron of the school, however, was even more intolerable than poverty, and Johnson left after a few months. An extended visit to his schoolmate Hector in Birmingham had really important results—he produced his first book, and he found a wife. I give these two events in Boswell's order, which is, in fact, chronological, though it may as easily be conceived as climactic. As usual, Boswell gives extraordinary life to both events by careful choice of detail. Johnson met a local publisher, wrote some essays, now lost, for his newspaper, and suggested that a translation of Father Lobo's *Voyage to Abyssinia* might be worth doing. An agreement was reached, and Johnson began, but soon slowed down to a stop. Here Boswell brings life to the narrative. Johnson was persuaded that the printer and his family were suffering from the lack of this piecework, and so Johnson lay in bed and *dictated* his translation to his patient surgeon-schoolmate Hector. Not only does Boswell give a vivid picture, but a pattern is established: Johnson always procrastinated and always produced.

Johnson's marriage is given equally lively treatment. The widowed Elizabeth Porter had grown children, but on the morning of the wedding she acted like a coquette. Johnson told Boswell,

> "Sir, she had read the old romances, and had got into her head the fantastical notion that a woman of spirit should use her lover like a dog. So, Sir, at first she told me that I rode too fast, and she could not keep up with me; and, when I rode a little slower, she passed me, and complained that I lagged behind. I was not to be made the slave of caprice; and I resolved to begin as I meant to end. I therefore pushed on briskly, till I was fairly out of her sight. The road lay between two hedges, so I was sure she could not miss it; and I contrived that she should soon come up with me. When she did, I observed her to be in tears." (I.96.)

A few months later the pair set up, with the bride's money, a boarding school for boys at Edial near Lichfield. David Garrick, his brother George, and one other boy were the only pupils, and the school soon failed. Once more, however, Boswell gives us a brilliant picture, from Garrick: Johnson's "oddities of manner, and uncouth gesticulations, could not but be the subject of merriment to them; and, in particular, the young rogues used to listen at the door of his bed-chamber, and peep through the key-hole, that they might turn into ridicule his tumultuous and aukward fondness for Mrs. Johnson. . . ." (I.98.) Garrick is also responsible for the description of Mrs. Johnson given by Boswell, "very fat, with a bosom of more than ordinary protuberance, with swelled cheeks, of a florid red, produced by thick painting, and increased by the liberal use of cordials; flaring and fantastick in her dress, and affected both in her speech and her general behaviour." (I.99.) Fortunately, a portrait of Mrs. Johnson as a beautiful young woman survives in the collection of Mrs. Donald F. Hyde to balance Garrick's lively caricature.

After the failure of his academy, Johnson left his wife in Lichfield and went to London with Garrick, both seeking fame and fortune. Garrick said that they "rode and tied" (I.101 n.), one riding to a milepost, tying the horse there, and walking the next mile, and so on. Boswell, believing the story to be an embellishment of the facts, reduced it to a footnote, no doubt regretfully, as this part of the narrative needs whatever enlivening it can get.

For Johnson's early years in Lichfield, Boswell could get reports from Johnson's friends still living there and especially from Lucy Porter, Johnson's stepdaughter, who lived with Johnson's mother in Lichfield till the old lady's death and finally died there herself. For the period between 1737, when Johnson came to London, and 1763, when Boswell met him, the situation was totally different. There were almost no *women* alive who had known Johnson intimately in London during this period. His wife was long since dead, and during their long years of poverty she had not ordinarily entertained friends in their lodgings. So the domestic picture of Johnson during these years is very obscure. To be sure, Johnson had founded the Ivy Lane Club for social life outside of his home, and even from its earlier years there were some survivors. The chief of these was Hawkins, who had written the official and rival life of Johnson and was not, therefore, a good source of information for Boswell. Of other men who knew Johnson well, Savage was dead and Dr. Bathurst, and Reynolds did not know Johnson before the fifties. Two of the inmates of Johnson's household, Mrs. Desmoulins and Miss

Williams, had known him for years, but for one reason or another they were not particularly good sources of information. Boswell was forced therefore to rely to a heavy degree upon publishers and on the history of Johnson's literary work, fleshing out this material as frequently as possible with his letters, which are usually lively.

Johnson's occasional reminiscences helped. On first coming to London he dined habitually at a nearby tavern with a strange group of men. "Several of them had travelled," he told Boswell. "They expected to meet every day; but did not know one another's names." They appear to have been men who had come down in the world (they had traveled) but were preserving their anonymity in hope of a comeback. "It used to cost the rest a shilling, for they drank wine; but I had a cut of meat for sixpence, and bread for a penny, and gave the waiter a penny; so that I was quite well served, nay, better than the rest, for they gave the waiter nothing." (I.103.) The use of wine by the others is very remarkable. A poor man's drink was beer, or gin if he wanted quick results. But for these men to have drunk either would have constituted an admission of social defeat. Johnson was saving what little money he had. Here again Boswell has seized upon a most revealing picture.

After a few months without employment, Johnson returned to Lichfield, finished a draft of his tragedy *Irene*, took his wife to London, and finally established a relationship with Cave, the publisher of the *Gentleman's Magazine*. He wrote a good deal for the magazine and soon became, effectively, its editor. There isn't much life in Boswell's account here, because the quotations from Johnson's works do not at all involve the reader. The printing of *London*, however, is another matter. It was a major poem and Johnson's first success. Its anonymity led some readers to attribute it to Pope, who was sure that the real author would soon be unearthed. He was, but fortune did not follow. Pope attempted to get Johnson a schoolmastership, and he himself inquired about a legal career, but nothing came of either effort, and he settled into translating and writing for the *Gentleman's Magazine*.

The letters which Boswell prints of this period are all concerned with publishing; only one of them ends on a note of human interest: "impransus"—supperless. (I.137.) One episode almost comes to life. It is displaced by about fourteen years because Boswell wants to link it to his account of Johnson's nervous gesticulations. Hogarth, visiting Samuel Richardson's house, finds a man there, to whom he is not introduced, shaking his head, rolling about, and violently inveighing against the brutality of George II in executing Archibald Cameron in 1753 for his part in the Rebellion of '45. The materials for a Boswellian portrait are there—two men already famous and another soon to be, with the publication of the *Dictionary*. But the story is thirdhand, Hogarth to Reynolds to Boswell, and, still worse, is told without dialogue and in the third person. Boswell could have given the story the dramatic quality it demands had it occurred ten years later when he might have been present. He could not even embellish it much, for Sir Joshua was still alive.

One story, in 1742, is tantalizing. Johnson had been making up the Harleian *Catalogue* for the bookseller Osborne. Gossip had it that during an argument Johnson had knocked Osborne down "in his shop, with a folio." Two more engaging details could hardly have been thought of: to knock someone down with a folio would be equivalent to using a sledge hammer; and in his own shop it would be violation of his castle. Johnson denied the second part and ignored the first: "I beat him. . . . [but] it was in my own chamber." (I.154.) We are told less than we need. Boswell picked up more skill as he went along.

The next major event treated by Boswell is the publication of the *Life of Savage*. This gets off to a good start with a picture of Reynolds beginning to read the book standing and leaning against a chimney piece and unable to put the book down till he finished it, when he found his arm benumbed. Boswell then examines with some care Savage's claim that he was the illegitimate son of Lady Macclesfield, which, despite Johnson's belief, Boswell rejects as, at best, unproved. This is worth noting because it is the first of several instances where Boswell takes issue with Johnson. It may hurt him to disagree with the master, but nevertheless he does. It is this independence of spirit which makes him much more than a mere reporter in the conversations he prints later.

The next two years Boswell passes over quickly with the mere mention of Johnson's publications. In 1747, however, the *Plan of a Dictionary* appeared, and in short order Boswell gives samples of direct speech which come across vividly. One occurs in the shop of Dodsley, the publisher who suggested the *Dictionary*: "Johnson seemed at first to catch at the proposition, but, after a pause, said, in his abrupt decisive manner, 'I believe I shall not undertake it.'" (I.182.) The next comes from his old friend Dr. Taylor, who thought that the *Plan* was probably helped by the fact that several people had read it before publication. Johnson: "No, Sir; it would have come out with more bloom, if it had not been seen before by any body." (I.185.) The third involves Dr. Adams, later Master of Pembroke College at Oxford: "ADAMS. This is a great work, Sir. . . . But, Sir, how can you do this in three years? JOHNSON. Sir, I have no doubt that I can do it in three years. ADAMS. But the French Academy, which consists of forty members, took forty years to compile their Dictionary. JOHNSON. Sir, thus it is. This is the proportion. Let me see; forty times forty is sixteen hundred. As three to sixteen hundred, so is the proportion of an Englishman to a Frenchman." (I.186.) The noteworthy feature of all these episodes is that they took place when Boswell was seven or eight years old. Dodsley was dead, and his story was therefore thirdhand. Yet all three are given "live" and in Boswell's mature manner. The one involving Adams is, I think, the first dialogue in the *Life* longer than a line or two. And almost all of the words must be original with Boswell: there was no diary to rely on. Yet every one sounds like Johnson. It is a great feat; in the twenty-five years since he had met Johnson, Boswell had learned to think himself back into the even more distant past and to produce, imaginatively, the very tone and voice of his subject.

In 1749 Johnson's second major poem was published, and Boswell prints a very revealing comment on it by Garrick: "When Johnson lived much with the Herveys, and saw a good deal of what was passing in life, he wrote his 'London,' which is lively and easy. When he became more retired, he gave us his 'Vanity of Human Wishes,' which is as hard as Greek. Had he gone on to imitate another satire, it would have been as hard as Hebrew." (I.194.) Again Boswell is using secondhand material (from Langton), and this time we can hear Garrick entertaining guests at his dinner table. It is, of course, not serious criticism, and Boswell does not mistake it as such; it is much better—the raw materials of biography brought to life by an artist. Garrick was accused by some of his friends of performing even at home, and this is an excellent example of his manner.

When Garrick finally brought Johnson's *Irene* to the stage, there were inevitable conflicts between the actor and the author. Taylor intervened. "Sir," said Johnson to him, "the fellow wants me to make Mahomet run mad, that he may have an opportunity of tossing his hands and kicking his heels." (I.196.) Adams told Boswell about the first performance. When Mrs. Pritchard as the heroine was about to be garroted on stage, "The audience cried out '*Murder! Murder!*' She several times attempted to speak; but in vain. At last she was obliged to go off the stage alive." (I.197.) Twice more Boswell has brought the reader into direct contact with the events.

The pleasant visits to the greenroom of the theater did not last indefinitely. When Garrick told Johnson he hoped he would come back often, Johnson said: "No, David, . . . I will never come back. For the white bubbies and the silk stockings of your actresses excite my genitals." (*Boswell Papers from Malahide Castle*, I.128.) But this direct statement seemed to need fig leaves, and in the *Life* Boswell has given it decent covering: "I'll come no more behind your scenes, David, for the silk stockings and white bosoms of your actresses excite my amorous propensities." (I.201.)

In treating *The Rambler*, Boswell is less successful, perhaps because the material is less tractable. He testifies to Johnson's seriousness of purpose by printing a short prayer on his undertaking the project; he remarks on the scantiness of the help Johnson received; and he then moves to one of Johnson's methods of composition, the use of very short jottings from which, often at the last minute, he developed the final essay. Boswell prints the complete notes for two essays, but he does nothing with them. They remain raw materials, and unless the reader is willing to pull Johnson's works off the shelf and compare the notes with the finished product, they are of little interest. They are dead.

Of the comments on *The Rambler*, the most interesting comes from Johnson's wife: "I thought very well of you before; but I did not imagine you could have written any thing equal to this." (I.210.) The words are simple, as Johnson recalled them many years after Tetty's death, but they tend to reverberate in the heart. They are her only known comments on his work. She died a few days after *The Rambler* was concluded.

Boswell says that Johnson's "most ardent" love for his wife was "unimpaired" until his death. (I.236.) To keep this statement from any sort of challenge, he suppressed clear and unequivocal entries in Johnson's diaries, which he copied but did not print, which show that after a year of mourning Johnson decided to seek a second wife. Boswell's motive for this curious action may be the same as the motive behind his smoothing out Johnson's religious doubts and scruples: he had decided to present a certain image and feared that the whole truth might make that image less credible. Behind this may be something more complex: Boswell's own uncertainties about religion were as notorious as his innumerable infidelities to his wife; therefore, for his own security in his feeling for his surrogate father he had to do some arranging of evidence.

Boswell now turns to some of Johnson's friends, particularly Sir Joshua Reynolds, whom he met about this time. Part of the attractiveness of the biography lies in its portrayal of the circle of these friends, most of whom were strong personalities and none of whom could properly be described as a sycophant. One has only to think of the slavish admirers of Richardson, for instance, sitting in the garden listening to the master read *Clarissa* aloud, to realize the difference in the Johnsonian group. For the latter did not provide an audience but rather the play of opposing minds, or even combat. It was exciting, and something of the excitement reaches us after two centuries.

It is significant that Reynolds attracted Johnson because he was unusual and that Boswell caught this point easily. Two ladies "were regretting the death of a friend, to whom they owed great obligations; upon which Reynolds observed, 'You have, however, the comfort of being relieved from a burthen of gratitude.'" (I.246.) The ladies were shocked, but Johnson knew that he had found an original mind, and a lifelong friendship began.

Not long afterwards, he met two young men of a very different sort, Bennet Langton, who had not yet gone up to Oxford, and Topham Beauclerk, his fellow-student. Like typical undergraduates, they were prowling about London one night and decided to wake up their middle-aged friend. At 3 a.m. he came to the door in his shirt and quickly agreed to join them. They went to Covent Garden Market, where the produce was just being unloaded; after a drink they hired a boat for a row on the Thames. Langton, of an old Lincolnshire family, was relatively staid; Beauclerk, wilder, was corespondent later in a celebrated divorce case. It was his wife whom Johnson later refused to dignify with any other name than "whore." Johnson's genius for friendship shows in the diversity of these young men. In another decade, Boswell was added to the number.

As the *Dictionary* approached completion Chesterfield was moved to write two essays in a periodical praising the work. Johnson decided that this interest was too belated to be genuine and that seven years of uninterrupted neglect could not be so casually passed over. And so he wrote his celebrated letter—"Is not a Patron, my Lord, one who looks with unconcern on a man struggling for life in the water, and, when he has reached ground, encumbers him with help?" (I.262.) It is one of the high points of the biography, and Boswell had not only the copy which Johnson had dictated to him from memory, but also the one dictated to Baretti, apparently near the time the original was written, and corrected in Johnson's hand. His eagerness to have both copies for comparison is characteristic, and the reader is as pleased as Boswell to know that the variations are trifling. In order to protect himself from piracy, Boswell had a few copies printed off a few weeks before the *Life* was published. This he did also with another prize, the conversation between George III and Johnson. Both were entered in the Stationers' Register, thus giving him the protection of copyright. He had a reporter's keen sense of what a rival would covet most.

When Boswell tries to appraise the *Dictionary*, he sensibly takes up the Preface first as a manageable unit. Here he is fortunate to have available a wry comment by Johnson himself: "There are two things which I am confident I can do very well: one is an introduction to any literary work, stating what it is to contain, and how it should be executed in the most perfect manner; the other is a conclusion, shewing from various causes why the execution has not been equal to what the authour promised to himself and to the publick." (I.292.) This makes a nice contrast with the somber tone of the Preface, from which Boswell quotes, and turns the reader from literary criticism, which is not Boswell's forte, to the biographical, which is. He also records Johnson's reply to the lady who asked how he happened to give the wrong definition of *pastern:* "Ignorance, Madam, pure ignorance." (I.293.) In discussing some of the idiosyncratic definitions, Boswell points out one characteristic which is easily missed, Johnson's playfulness, and gives a good example, "*Lexicographer,* a writer of dictionaries, a *harmless drudge.*" (I.296.)

One of Boswell's virtues is his insatiable curiosity, which led him into a never-ending search for biographical materials. It is connected, however, with a difficulty which plagued his writings: he hated to leave anything out, and his judgment as to relevance was poor. The reader may recall his query to Malone while preparing the *Tour to the Hebrides,* "Shall the dinner *Stet?*" In commenting on a variety of book reviews by Johnson, Boswell devotes two sentences to the execution of Admiral Byng. Boswell had transcribed an epitaph on Byng from the family vault and prints it here, where it has no place whatever. It occupies several more lines than his mention of Johnson and Byng. In his diary everything has relevance because it happened to Boswell, who is the central figure; but this is not so in the *Life.*

Some of the pages dealing with Johnson's life in the years just following the *Dictionary* are arid because Boswell has little to work on. The letters, however, give the tones of Johnson's voice now and again. He writes to Langton: "I am not much richer than when you left me; and, what is worse, my omission of an answer to your first letter, will prove that I am not much wiser." (I.324.) It is remarkable how often he mentions himself, knowing, perhaps, that his correspondents wanted to hear about him rather than the weather. Writing to Baretti two years after the publication of *Rasselas,* in which he had a good deal to say about monastic life, he comments on the attractions of such a life: "Men will submit to any rule, by which they may be exempted from the tyranny of caprice and of chance." (I.365.) His own life, he thinks, has been too desultory.

In 1762, Johnson received his pension, after assurances that he was being rewarded for past services to literature, not hired to support the government. This was a sensitive point, considering Johnson's definition of *pension,* which he did not change.

Meanwhile, Boswell had finally met Johnson, after several failures. The scene in Tom Davies' bookshop is famous, and it is here that the biography begins to be great. From this point Boswell has his journal to rely on when he is in London, but it is most remarkable how relatively poor the journal is on the evening of their first meeting. It begins fairly well, with Davies introducing the two men, and Boswell's "Don't tell where I come from," followed by Davies' "From Scotland," Boswell's miserable "indeed I come from Scotland, but I cannot help it," and Johnson's hammer-blow: "that, I find, is what a very great many of your countrymen cannot help." (*London Journal*, p. 260.) In the *Life* Boswell makes this exchange less blunt by inserting "roguishly" after Davies' remark, and by prefacing Johnson's rejoinder by some explanation of what Boswell had intended, a joke rather than self-abasement.

In the *Journal* there is no further dialogue. Boswell gives a vivid description of the man who is not yet his hero, but in the *Life* he omits it at this point, since the elements of the picture had been established for the reader much earlier in the book. He then records what he remembers of the conversation, but all the subjects discussed occupy less than a page together, and they are only Johnson's remarks—on "uncommon parts" or intellectual superiority, Kames's *Elements of Criticism*, Wilkes and liberty, and Thomas Sheridan teaching oratory at Bath. So far as the *Journal* reveals, Boswell might have spent the rest of the evening in glum silence.

Of course this was not the case. In the margin of the journal Boswell wrote a reminder to himself about Garrick's refusing an order for a theater ticket for Miss Williams. The editors judge this memorandum to be nearly twenty-five years later than the main entry, but Boswell nevertheless expanded it into a second interchange between Johnson and himself in which he went down again, having objected that he could not think Garrick would grudge Johnson such a trifle. Johnson: "I have known David Garrick longer than you have done: and I know no right you have to talk to me on the subject." (I.392.) The brilliance of this expansion hardly needs comment, and Boswell has surpassed himself with the line which prefaces the interchange: "Eager to take any opening to get into conversation with him, I ventured to say. . . ." This shows us as much about Boswell as we have seen about Johnson, and the whole evening displays how Boswell trained himself to use a phrase to recollect what had happened many years before. His artistry then fitted the pieces together so that the reader is caught up into the interchange as almost a participant.

At 10 p.m., according to the diary, Boswell leaves regretfully; in the *Life* the episode comes to a cheerful end, as Davies, saying good night, tells him, "Don't be uneasy. I can see he likes you very well." (I.395.)

In the following week Boswell ventured to call on Johnson in his lodgings. He recorded little of interest in the way of talk, but the reader is hardly aware of this, inasmuch as just before the visit we are told of Johnson's retort to Blair's question whether any man alive could have written the Ossianic poems, "Yes, Sir, many men, many women, and many children." (I.396.) And apropos of Christopher Smart, who was mentioned, Boswell introduces into his narrative a remark made by Johnson at another time concerning the poet's insanity: "Another charge was, that he did not love clean linen; and I have no passion for it." (I.397.) So we are left with the impression of a lively visit, but Boswell has made it so by skillful insertion of materials garnered on other occasions.

Not long afterward, Goldsmith appears for the first time. Boswell did not like him much, thinking him vain, which he was, and a second-rate imitation of Johnson, which he was not. Nevertheless, Goldsmith's presence at any time made for liveliness, as, like Boswell, he was never content to be a silent observer. He liked to advance large generalizations: "knowledge was . . . often a source of unhappiness" (I.417), for example. This comment afforded Johnson an easy mark in attacking "often," and we now have conversation and dialogue, not mere pontificating. Boswell takes part, not brilliantly. But he is disarming in his frank statement that he is still, in the summer of 1763, something less than expert in recording and recalling the details and the nuances of their talk. He was twenty-two.

A few weeks later, Boswell's diary shows how he is moving the focus from himself to Johnson: in the *Life* we read "Talking of a young man" (I.454), whereas the original entry is "We then talked of Me." (*London Journal*, p. 326.) The content is the same, but Boswell has been able to turn a personal remark into a generalization about a man who is midway between being ignorant and well-informed.

In a short time Boswell left for a year's study in Holland, followed by an extended Grand Tour. The most important event in Johnson's life during this period was his meeting with Mr. and Mrs. Thrale and the rapid growth of their friendship. This friendship provided a badly needed emotional stability to Johnson's life: "The vivacity of Mrs. Thrale's literary talk roused him to cheerfulness and exertion, even when they were alone. But this was not often the case; for he found here a constant succession of what gave him the highest enjoyment: the society of the learned, the witty, and the eminent in every way, who were assembled in numerous companies, called forth his wonderful powers, and gratified him with admiration, to which no man could be insensible." (I.495–96.) Moreover, Mrs. Thrale was a diarist, and from her *Anecdotes of the late Samuel Johnson* Boswell obtained much material, particularly on the lighter, social side of Johnson's life. He would have preferred to have Mrs. Thrale merely turn over her materials to him; but using her published book was much better than nothing.

When Boswell returned from the Continent in 1766 he went to see Johnson before going home. Boswell was still worrying about how little he knew, but this time he enters the dialogue under his own name, rather than anonymously: "Do I know history? Do I know mathematicks? Do I know law?" (II.9.) Johnson reassures him as usual, and the conversation turns to Corsica and Boswell's intention to publish a book about it. Johnson's advice shows what keen insight he has already achieved into the young man's nature and capability: "You cannot go to the bottom of the subject; but all that you tell us will be new to us. Give us as many anecdotes as you can." (II.11.)

On another occasion Goldsmith was present. He complained of Johnson's lack of interest in the theater: " 'You give yourself no more concern about a new play, than if you had never had any thing to do with the stage.' JOHNSON. 'Why, Sir, our tastes greatly alter. The lad does not care for the child's rattle, and the old man does not care for the young man's whore.' " (II.14.) Goldsmith's interest in the theater was quickening, and he was soon to bring forth *The Good-Natur'd Man*, for which Johnson wrote the Prologue, and *She Stoops to Conquer*, which is dedicated to him, so that the flagging of his interest might be called temporary. At any rate, Boswell has preserved a lively exchange. I might mention that since reliable biographical information on Goldsmith is scarce, such glimpses as this are particularly welcome.

In 1767 Johnson had his famous interview with George III in the King's library, the account of which occupies several pages in the biography. This is one of the high points of the book, and, as I have mentioned, it was published separately before the book appeared, probably to fend off piracy. The interview was arranged in advance, and Johnson's friends gathered at Reynolds' house to hear his account of the conversation on his return. The report is circumstantial, partly in direct discourse, and the telling of it at Reynolds' is quite dramatic, with Joseph Warton pressing Johnson for details and Goldsmith remaining "unmoved upon a sopha at some distance, affecting not to join in the least in the eager curiosity of the company." (II.42.) Shortly, however, "the frankness and simplicity of his natural character prevailed," and he congratulated Johnson on how he had acquitted himself during the interview.

It is a fine set-piece. The casual reader, however, will not realize that Boswell was not there, but in Scotland. All of his materials were secondhand. Our admiration for this virtuoso performance need not be tempered with the notion that Boswell is merely reporting an event in which he participated. In the best sense, he has created the event.

Boswell's method of keeping his journal was to try to write something each night before going to bed. Usually this was a series of short notes, often in an abbreviated speedwriting, which would serve to remind him of the fuller conversation when, a day or a week later, he had time to expand them into a connected account. By the nature of this method, however, the entries tended to abruptness. This quality Boswell frequently tried to smooth out by qualifications. Typical is a comment on Lord Monboddo, a Scottish jurist, literary critic, and anthropologist, who never tired of seeking men with tails to provide the missing link between the apes and man: "I am *afraid*, (chuckling and laughing,) Monboddo does *not* know that he is talking nonsense." (II.74.) The two parenthetical modifiers smooth out the roughness of the remark, and add a pictorial quality to it as well.

When Johnson entered into political controversy with his four pamphlets of the 'seventies, he used, says Boswell, what he considered a most effective instrument—contempt. Boswell cites the sardonic comment on George Grenville which I have already discussed in the chapter on Johnson's political tracts: "He had powers not universally possessed: if he could have got the money, he could have counted it." Boswell regrets that this jibe at the late Chancellor of the Exchequer was reduced to "a mere flat unmeaning expression." (II.135.)

In 1772 Boswell was in London, and Johnson criticized Goldsmith's *Life of Parnell* for its lack of materials: Goldsmith had not lived in "social intercourse" with Parnell. This gave Boswell an admirable opening, which, as usual, he seized at once: "I said, that if it was not troublesome and presuming too much, I would request him to tell me all the little circumstances of his life; what schools he attended, when he came to Oxford, when he came to London, &c. &c. He did not disapprove of my curiosity as to these particulars; but said, 'They'll come out by degrees as we talk together.'" (II.166.) Note that Boswell does not explicitly ask for this information as a future biographer, but his intent is clear, and no doubt it was clear to Johnson also. Boswell was only thirty-one, but his main literary aim was coming into focus. It is not accidental that Johnson went on to discuss Ruffhead's *Life of Pope*, of which he had a poor opinion.

Johnson's occasional violence in conversation has been often remarked on. On one occasion he was asked if he had read a certain recent book: "JOHNSON. 'I have looked into it.' 'What (said Elphinston,) have you not read it through?' Johnson, *offended at being thus pressed*, . . . answered tartly, 'No, Sir; do *you* read books *through*?'" (II.226.) The phrase which I have italicized is Boswell's shrewd analysis. Johnson did not like to be cornered and responded by attacking.

A few days later Boswell records a literary judgment on an author Johnson *had* read, John Bunyan: "His *Pilgrim's Progress* has great merit, both for invention, imagination, and the conduct of the story; and it has had the best evidence of its merit, the general and continued approbation of mankind." (II.238.) This is worth remarking on, for while Bunyan's masterpiece had had a sort of underground fame for a century, it had not yet received much critical acclaim. Johnson had read it without being hindered by his dislike of religious enthusiasm or doubts about dissenters and their lack of education.

Not all of their conversations turned on books. Langton had made a will and Johnson thought he was being pompous about it:

> "I dare say, he thinks he has done a mighty thing. He won't stay till he gets home to his seat in the country, to produce this wonderful deed: he'll call up the landlord of the first inn on the road; and, after a suitable preface upon mortality and the uncertainty of life, will tell him that he should not delay making his will; and here, Sir, will he say, is my will, which I have just made, with the assistance of one of the ablest lawyers in the kingdom; and he will read it to him. . . ." He then burst into such a fit of laughter, that he appeared to be almost in a convulsion; and, in order to support himself, laid hold of one of the posts at the side of the foot pavement, and sent forth peals so loud, that in the silence of the night his voice seemed to resound from Temple-bar to Fleet-ditch. (II.261–62.)

Boswell, as a lawyer, is not at all sure that making a will should ever be the subject of levity; but as an author he has sketched a scene which leaves us in his debt.

One of Boswell's attractive qualities is his refusal to submerge his differences of opinion with Johnson. One of these was on the American question, where Boswell sided with the Colonies. *Taxation no Tyranny*, he thought, was an unfortunate sequel to *Falkland's Islands*, in which Johnson had opposed going to war over a trifle. Boswell, in fact, exercised unusual restraint in avoiding argument with Johnson on the Americans. Of *Taxation no Tyranny*, his opinion is unequivocal: "Positive assertion, sarcastical severity, and extravagant ridicule, which he himself reprobated as a test of truth, were united in this rhapsody." (II.313.)

During the 'seventies, Johnson made three extended tours. The first of these, to Edinburgh, the Highlands, and the Hebrides, was made the subject of Boswell's *Tour of the Hebrides,* but the reader of the *Life* is hardly aware that so large a piece of Boswell's journal has been extracted for use elsewhere. He has skillfully covered the gap by using a few letters and by comments on Johnson's book on the trip. In 1774 Johnson toured North Wales with the Thrales; Boswell again uses two letters to cover the summer's journey, unaware that Johnson had kept a diary for the period.

In the following year, however, Johnson spent several weeks in France with the Thrales, and in this instance Boswell had a large part of Johnson's diary, all of which he prints. It is a highly characteristic diary, condensed, largely factual in content, and extensive enough to give the reader a real feeling for Johnson's reaction to his only trip abroad. When Boswell visited Johnson in London in the following spring he heard more about France, particularly the virtual absence of a middle class, a matter of real political significance: "The great in France live very magnificently, but the rest very miserably. There is no happy middle state as in England." (II.402.)

There was talk of another tour, to Italy, but meantime Johnson planned to visit Oxford, Birmingham, Lichfield, and Ashbourne, and invited Boswell to go with him. To the future biographer, this was irresistible, for in all these places early friends of Johnson still lived who might be cajoled into yielding up anecdotes of the dim days of his youth, as indeed they did. Boswell says, disarmingly, "I was ready to accompany him; being willing even to leave London to have the pleasure of his conversation." (II.428.) I suggest that the reader ponder the force of Boswell's "even." The journey was a great success, both from the anecdotes generated by the visit and from those recollected by Johnson's early friends.

After their return to London they had dinner with Reynolds and others, and drinking was discussed. Johnson had had to choose between abstinence and drunkenness, since he found that he could not drink moderately. Reynolds defended drinking in the evening because it relieved the fatigue of the day and thereby animated conversation. Johnson: "No, Sir; wine gives not light, gay, ideal hilarity; but tumultuous, noisy, clamorous merriment." (III.41.) Sir Joshua retorted that Johnson was envious, and Johnson said that he was perhaps, on the contrary, contemptuous. But at this rather dangerous point, Johnson shifted the argument from personalities to literature; Boswell's lawyer friend Forbes thought a man might be warmed and made brisk by wine, as a bottle of beer is made livelier by being put before a fire; Johnson's genial laughter at the witticism blew away any irritation. Boswell observed that wine harmed some people, but that "the experience of mankind" was in favor of moderate drinking. (III.42.) In this remarkable exchange, particularly remarkable in the eighteenth century when heavy drinking was commonplace, Johnson was allowed the last word: "Sir, I do not say it is wrong to produce self-complacency by drinking; I only deny that it improves the mind. When I drank wine, I scorned to drink it when in company. I have drunk many a bottle by myself; in the first place, because I had need of it to raise my spirits; in the second place, because I would have nobody to witness its effects upon me." (III.42.) This is the sort of self-revelation that Johnson rarely made, and that he made it in Boswell's company shows the confidence he had in Boswell, who was now his declared biographer.

During the same visit to London, Boswell stage-managed his greatest production, a dinner party at which John Wilkes and Johnson met. The project was mad in concept, tricky in execution, and triumphant in outcome. Wilkes had been a friend of Boswell's for many years. Originally a liberal Whig, he had caused the government so much embarrassment by his opposition paper *The North Briton*, written with Churchill, that his lodgings were raided to find incriminating material. At his first trial the case was dismissed by a judge who declared unconstitutional the general search warrant under which the arrest had been made. In the second attempt, the government obtained proof sheets of Wilkes' indecent poem *Essay on Woman* and found a judge favorable to the case. Wilkes fled to Paris, was outlawed, eventually returned, was jailed, elected to Parliament, ejected, reelected, and finally seated. He had been attacked by Johnson, who disapproved of him totally. Naturally Boswell wanted to bring such opposites together to see the conflagration.

His publisher friends the Dillys were giving a dinner for Wilkes, Boswell, and others: " 'Pray (said I,) let us have Dr. Johnson.'—'What, with Mr. Wilkes? not for the world, (said Mr. Edward Dilly:) Dr. Johnson would never forgive me.'—'Come, (said I,) if you'll let me negociate for you, I will be answerable that all shall go well.' " (III.65.) Boswell builds up his readers' interest by imagining Johnson's reply to a direct approach: "Dine with Jack Wilkes, Sir! I'd as soon dine with Jack Ketch." So he conveyed the invitation without mentioning other guests, and, when Johnson started to accept, interrupted: "Provided, Sir, I suppose, that the company which he is to have, is agreeable to you." Johnson is naturally insulted at this imputation of boorishness and walks into the trap:

> "What do you mean, Sir? What do you take me for? Do you think I am so ignorant of the world, as to imagine that I am to prescribe to a gentleman what company he is to have at his table?" BOSWELL. "I beg your pardon, Sir, for wishing to prevent you from meeting people whom you might not like. Perhaps he may have some of what he calls his patriotick friends with him." JOHNSON. "Well, Sir, and what then? What care *I* for his *patriotick friends?* Poh!" BOSWELL. "I should not be surprized to find Jack Wilkes there." JOHNSON. "And if Jack Wilkes *should* be there, what is that to *me*, Sir? My dear friend, let us have no more of this. I am sorry to be angry with you; but really it is treating me strangely to talk to me as if I could not meet any company whatever, occasionally." BOSWELL. "Pray forgive me, Sir: I meant well. But you shall meet whoever comes, for me." (III.66.)

On the day appointed, Boswell called for Johnson and found that he had forgotten the appointment and agreed to dine with his blind pensioner Anna Williams. Boswell expostulated and Johnson referred him to Miss Williams. At first she was peevish, but Boswell tried reason and then the charm which he usually saved for amorous conquests. She capitulated, and he bore off Johnson, exulting "as much as a fortune-hunter who has got an heiress into a post-chaise . . . for Gretna Green." (III.68.)

The date of the dinner was 15 May 1776, more than a year after the outbreak of the American Revolution. The first of the "patriots" Johnson saw was Arthur Lee, an American, later minister to Spain; the next was Wilkes. Johnson was disconcerted, muttered something to himself, picked up a book and looked at it, and recovered with the call to dinner.

> Mr. Wilkes placed himself next to Dr. Johnson, and behaved to him with so much attention and politeness, that he gained upon him insensibly. No man eat more heartily than Johnson, or loved better what was nice and delicate. Mr. Wilkes was very assiduous in helping him to some fine veal. "Pray give me leave, Sir:—It is better here—A little of the brown—Some fat, Sir—A little of the stuffing—Some gravy—Let me have the pleasure of giving you some butter—Allow me to recommend a squeeze of this

> orange;—or the lemon, perhaps, may have more zest."—"Sir, Sir, I am obliged to you, Sir," cried Johnson, bowing, and turning his head to him with a look for some time of "surly virtue," but, in a short while, of complacency. (III.68–69.)

I know of no passage in eighteenth-century drama in which speech and action are so realistic, so suggestive of character, and yet so condensed as in that little scene. In the conversation that follows, Boswell's name does not appear for two pages. He is concentrating on his principals, though two unassigned remarks are probably his. Wilkes leads off with a mention of Foote, which induces Johnson to say that Foote was a poor mimic and then to tell a wonderful story of Foote as a beer salesman. He had persuaded his friend Fitzherbert to buy the beer, but it was so bad that the servants resolved that they would drink it no longer. They delegated a little black boy to tell their master, but when he went to deliver the message Foote was there, telling stories. The boy was so entranced that when he returned to the kitchen he told his fellow-servants: "This is the finest man I have ever seen. I will not deliver your message. I will drink his small-beer." (III.70.) The reader will try in vain to recall in a novel prior to this any child's conversation which is so immediately convincing. Moreover, it is probably the most sincere tribute Foote ever received as an actor.

The conversation turned to Garrick, and Boswell leads Johnson to talk of his old friend; then to Johnson's asking Cibber for anecdotes of Dryden, Wilkes on Shakespeare, Wilkes and Johnson on Horace, on the City Poets of the seventeenth century, and finally on the Scots. Here they unite to tease Boswell, and in this union their friendship may have been sealed. Boswell, bleeding freely, nevertheless tells all: "JOHNSON. (to Mr. Wilkes) 'You must know, Sir, I lately took my friend Boswell and shewed him genuine civilised life in an English provincial town. I turned him loose at Lichfield, my native city, that he might see for once real civility: for you know he lives among savages in Scotland, and among rakes in London.' WILKES. 'Except when he is with grave, sober, decent people like you and me.' JOHNSON. (smiling) 'And we ashamed of him.' " (III.77.)

Mrs. Macaulay, the historian of republican leanings, was mentioned, and Johnson told of asking her to have her footman sit down with them. After dinner Mrs. Knowles the Quakeress came in, and Wilkes later told Boswell that her bosom had the same effect on Johnson that the breasts of the actresses had had in the greenroom of the theater years earlier. On this characteristically boyish note the evening ended. Johnson's acquaintance with Wilkes, nevertheless, ripened into lasting friendship.

Next year Boswell again visited Johnson's boyhood friend Taylor at Ashbourne in Derbyshire. Unlike the earlier tour into the scenes of Johnson's youth, this was fairly unproductive of anecdotal matter. It may be that Taylor did not furnish an adequate foil. He was principally interested in his farm, and both Boswell and Johnson were bored, though Johnson was beginning to work hard on the *Lives of the Poets*. For the most part, Boswell reports subjects of conversation, rather than giving dialogue. The reader moves quickly on.

In 1778 Boswell, in London again, was present at a dinner at The Club. In the long conversation which he reported, he suppressed the names of all the speakers except his and Johnson's, using initials instead: C. (chemist) = Fordyce; E. = Edmund Burke; F. = Fitzpatrick; P. (painter) = Reynolds; R. = R. B. Sheridan; J. (used in the eighteenth century interchangeably with I., infidel) = Gibbon. Boswell has even submerged the information that the conversation took place at a meeting of The Club, although in the last paragraph "this society" is mentioned. (III.238.) The obfuscation is unusual for Boswell in that it serves no artistic purpose. All of those present appear elsewhere under their full names. The reason appears to be that at the time of writing his book, Boswell had some longings for a political career; more particularly, he seems to have hoped that Burke would help him achieve that aim. Burke is, indeed, treated in a very gingerly fashion throughout the *Life*. At this dinner there was an extended debate on speechmaking in Parliament in which Burke and Sheridan participated (Sheridan was not elected M. P. until two years later), and Boswell probably felt that unusual discretion was demanded of him. Such discretion is rare in this book, and in some others Boswell wrote. Moreover, at the time Boswell was writing the *Life*, both Sheridan and Burke were even more famous than at the moment of the dinner: they were managing the impeachment of Warren Hastings in the longest and most famous trial of the century.

The young Sheridan (he was twenty-six) sounds a little like Boswell as he says to Burke, "I don't mean to flatter, but when posterity reads one of your speeches in Parliament, it will be difficult to believe that you took so much pains, knowing with certainty that it could produce no effect, that not one vote would be gained by it." Burke: "Waving your compliment to me, I shall say in general, that it is very well worth while for a man to take pains to speak well in Parliament. A man, who has vanity, speaks to display his talents; and if a man speaks well, he gradually establishes a certain reputation and consequence in the general opinion, which sooner or later will have its political reward. Besides, though not one vote is gained, a good speech has its effect." (III.233.) Johnson remarks on the gratification of speaking well, and Burke resumes, with an acute analysis of the House of Commons, "a mixed body. (I except the Minority, which I hold to be pure, [smiling] but I take the whole House.) It is a mass by no means pure; but neither is it wholly corrupt, though there is a large proportion of corruption in it. There are many members who generally go with the Minister, who will not go all lengths." Johnson elaborates on this, ending, "In the House of Commons there are members enough who will not vote what is grossly unjust or absurd. No, Sir, there must always be right enough, or appearance of right, to keep wrong in countenance." (III.234.) Boswell is sure that there are always many Bad Guys in politics and that they are easily identified: "There is surely always a majority in parliament who have places, or who want to have them, and who therefore will be generally ready to support government without requiring any pretext." (III.234.) Burke and Gibbon make contributions somewhat less than profound, Boswell is glad that there are some moderates in politics, Reynolds suggests that the House of Commons resembles "a private company" (meaning club?), and Sheridan wonders what would happen if a minister, sure of a majority, "should resolve that there should be no speaking at all upon his side." Burke rises to his manifest duty, and crushes this subversive notion: "He must soon go out. That has been tried; but it was found it would not do." (III.235.)

As Boswell records the conversation, Burke then turned to a discussion of the Irish language, an excellent topic, since neither he nor anyone else present had any expertness to hinder a general conversation. The topics which followed were equally harmless—

travel books, the benevolence of men or their lack of it, the careless leaving of money in view of servants, with the irresistible temptation to theft, lending money to friends, and so on. The evening ended on a relaxed note.

A week later, Boswell boasted that he could take down in speedwriting "the substance and language" of any conversation well enough so that he could reproduce it "very completely" soon afterwards. Johnson invariably responded to a boast with a challenge, and so he read aloud "slowly and distinctly" a passage from Robertson's *History of America* while Boswell took notes. (III.270.) The result was very imperfect. Fortunately, Boswell was not discouraged, and, indeed, the experiment was beside the point. For what Boswell did in his journals was to get down the substance of a conversation in words *like* those a speaker probably used, in an arrangement *suggestive* of the speaker's known style. In this he was superb. It involves a quite exceptional ear and the exercise of a certain art in recording; it is not at all mere skill in stenography. A remark Johnson made a little later is not wholly inapplicable: "I think every man whatever has a peculiar style, which may be discovered by nice examination and comparison with others: but a man must write a great deal to make his style obviously discernible." (III.280.) To which it might be added that one must listen to an oral style carefully and on many occasions before being able to catch its characteristic features.

After a few days, there was another dinner at Dilly's with some of his "patriotic" friends, during which Johnson exploded on the subject of the American Revolution. On this occasion, however, Boswell has not given us enough of the surroundings to make the speeches convincing: they are thrown at us without preparation: "I am willing to love all mankind, *except an American*: . . . Rascals—Robbers—Pirates. . . ." Anna Seward, the Lichfield poetess, added a comment: "Sir, this is an instance that we are always most violent against those whom we have injured." Johnson's roars, says Boswell, "one might fancy could be heard across the Atlantick." (III.290.) The scene, however, is only a sketch, undeveloped and unrealized.

Quite the opposite is true of the meeting with Oliver Edwards. Here Boswell not only has the good luck of Johnson's entry in his diary on this encounter but, with uncanny rightness, he uses it to introduce his account: "In my return from church, I was accosted by Edwards, an old fellow-collegian, who had not seen me since 1729. He knew me, and asked if I remembered one Edwards; I did not at first recollect the name, but gradually as we walked along, recovered it, and told him a conversation that had passed at an alehouse between us. My purpose is to continue our acquaintance." (III.302.) Boswell, who was present, immediately begins to flesh out this skeletal outline: they were walking along Butcher-row; Edwards was "decent-looking," "elderly"; he was familiar in his greeting; Johnson, formal in his first response, soon remembered him as a fellow-student at Oxford and gave him a conventional invitation to his lodgings. Boswell, in a whisper, urged Edwards to come now, which he did. He was a retired lawyer, living outside London, sixty-five and senile. Suddenly Johnson places him: "Do you remember our drinking together at an alehouse near Pembroke gate?" and he reminds him of a line of Latin verse which Edwards had talked of, forty-nine years before, and another which Johnson had cited at the same time. Edwards does not even pretend to remember: he starts to reply with a platitude, but slides, unexpectedly, into one of the greatest lines of the century: "You are a philosopher, Dr. Johnson. I have tried too in my time to be a philosopher; but, I don't know how, cheerfulness was always breaking in." (III.304–05.) One stops in awe that Boswell should have *heard* this and, so unerringly for the character of Edwards, should have set it down in the right words.

Everything else in the portrait of Edwards is in keeping. He says of himself: "For my part, I must have my regular meals, and a glass of good wine. I find I require it. . . . Don't you eat supper, Sir? . . . For my part, now, I consider supper as a turnpike through which one must pass, in order to get to bed." In good time he leaves, inviting Johnson to visit him at his farm and reverting to the subject of their old age. Johnson: "I shall be sixty-eight next birthday." Actually, he would be sixty-nine, but he feels younger, and Boswell does not correct him. (III.305–06.) Edwards had the great virtue of being willing to sit and talk, in his own mode, and Johnson had the satisfaction of meeting someone from his young manhood who remembered him with pleasure and with respect.

In the summer Boswell was back in Scotland and had again to fill out his biography with letters. In one of these, Johnson closes in a highly characteristic manner—short, terse sentences, in contrast with his usual style, with a kind of wry comment very close to humor: "Mrs. Thrale, poor thing, has a daughter. [Her only son had died.] Mr. Thrale dislikes the times, like the rest of us. Mrs. Williams is sick; Mrs. Desmoulins is poor. I have miserable nights. Nobody is well but Mr. Levett. I am, dear Sir, Your most, &c. Sam. Johnson." (III.363.) A little later Boswell quotes a similar passage from a letter to Mrs. Thrale: "Williams hates every body; Levett hates Desmoulins, and does not love Williams; Desmoulins hates them both; Poll loves none of them." (III.368.) Boswell has already made it plain that Johnson was fond of all these pensioners who lived in his house; we are brought very close to them, and to his own tolerant irritation at them, by these comments. In this unquiet household he was trying to finish *The Lives of the Poets.*

A little more than a year later one of Johnson's younger friends died, Beauclerk, who with Langton had once roused him in the middle of the night for a tour of the town. Again Boswell draws on a letter for a remarkable obituary: "Poor dear Beauclerk. . . . His wit and his folly, his acuteness and maliciousness, his merriment and reasoning, are now over. Such another will not often be found among mankind." (III.420.) Johnson's love of his friends, his clear-sightedness, and his insistence on plain-speaking, are here seen at their best.

From about this point many readers will feel a falling-off in the movement of the biography. In 1780 Boswell did not come to London, and he fills in by including a large mass of recollections by Langton. These twenty or thirty pages are not arranged by subject, chronology, or, apparently, by free association; although some are individually interesting, the total effect is static. However lively Langton may have been as an Oxford undergraduate, he had long since subsided into a fairly conventional country gentleman, and Boswell has done nothing with these anecdotes except to print them.

Almost the same comment must be made on the next section, of about the same length, on *The Lives of the Poets.* Boswell's introduction to the subject and his comments on individual biographies tend to be perfunctory. He had, however, a large mass of the working manuscripts of the *Lives,* with hundreds of corrections in Johnson's hand. He reproduces a very large number of these, but unfortunately does nothing except reproduce them, in a context of a few words, with the reading finally adopted. Thus one of six reproduced from Milton is: "[Perhaps no] *scarcely any* man ever wrote so much, and praised so few"; the italicized words replace those in brackets. (IV.44.) He does not comment or even suggest anything Johnson might be aiming at in these changes, or make any attempt, indeed, to engage the reader's interest. The result is stupefying.

Early in 1781 Boswell wrote to Johnson announcing his intention to come to London, though he was still worrying himself about such insoluble problems as the conflict between liberty and necessity. After nearly two decades Johnson was beginning to tire of the subject and replied with typical abruptness: "I hoped you had got rid of all this hypocrisy of misery. What have you to do with Liberty and Necessity? Or what more than to hold your tongue about it? Do not doubt but I shall be most heartily glad to see you here again, for I love every part about you but your affectation of distress." (IV.71.) A few days later Boswell was in London.

Thrale died in April, and Johnson was busied with selling the great brewery: "We are not here to sell a parcel of boilers and vats, but the potentiality of growing rich, beyond the dreams of avarice." (IV.87.)

At church Boswell again saw Johnson's old college friend, the cheerful failed philosopher Oliver Edwards. Johnson remarked afterwards that he had not seen much of him since their chance encounter, "But (said he, smiling) he met me once, and said, 'I am told you have written a very pretty book called *The Rambler.*' I was unwilling that he should leave the world in total darkness, and sent him a set." (IV.90.) It is a worthy last appearance of Edwards.

In May, Dilly gave another dinner where Johnson and Wilkes were both present. This time both men were at ease. As before, they had a few jokes on Scotland at Boswell's expense. They talked, without heat, about contested elections, and apropos of nothing in particular Johnson told a story of Bet Flint, a woman of the town who, like many of his friends, wanted some literary assistance:

"Bet (said he) wrote her own Life in verse, which she brought to me, wishing that I would furnish her with a Preface to it. (Laughing.) I used to say of her that she was generally slut and drunkard;—occasionally, whore and thief. She had, however, genteel lodgings, a spinnet on which she played, and a boy that walked before her chair. Poor Bet was taken up on a charge of stealing a counterpane, and tried at the Old Bailey. Chief Justice ———, who loved a wench, summed up favourably, and she was acquitted. After which Bet said, with a gay and satisfied air, 'Now that the counterpane is *my own*, I shall make a petticoat of it.'" (IV.103.)

As usual Boswell has caught the picture with great skill. Later in the evening Wilkes said to Boswell, loudly enough for Johnson to overhear, "Dr. Johnson should make me a present of his 'Lives of the Poets,' as I am a poor patriot, who cannot afford to buy them." Johnson thought this over awhile and then, equally loudly, asked Dilly to send a set, with his compliments. (IV.107.)

Boswell's journalizing during much of this London visit was sporadic ("I neglected to keep any regular record . . ." [IV.110]) and as a result he gives in one place a series of anecdotes without connection, a method much less interesting than using them in the context of a dinner party or an extended conversation.

In 1782 Boswell did not come to London, partly because he could not afford to, and as a result the brief space he devotes to the year is made up largely of letters. In 1783 he did pay his usual visit, dined with Johnson at Mrs. Thrale's, and saw him at his house. There was some good conversation, partly inhibited by Johnson's increasingly bad health, but there is also another section of unrelated anecdotes. One of these, however, gives so much of Beauclerk's character that it is worth excerpting: "He thought Mr. Beauclerk made a shrewd and judicious remark to Mr. Langton, who, after having been for the first time in company with a well known wit about town, was warmly admiring and praising him, 'See him again,' said Beauclerk." (IV.197.)

There seems to be increasing lack of revision as the *Life* draws to its end. In part this may be due to the absence of Malone's critical supervision; Boswell, it will be recalled, had read to him "almost" all of his manuscript, and Malone had seen proofs of about half of the book (Advertisement). Perhaps Malone would have suggested that Boswell's flattery of Richard Owen Cambridge (IV.196) was fatuous, and that letters should not be tossed into the text without any introduction or connection (IV.219–20). The book had taken Boswell several years longer than he had expected, and these defects may be simply signs of haste to conclude.

There remain, nevertheless, superb passages. Boswell asks if Johnson has not been vexed by the turbulence of politics. Johnson says that he has not lost sleep nor appetite from such things, and that if Boswell thinks *he* has, it is cant: "My dear friend, clear your *mind* of cant. You may *talk* as other people do: you may say to a man, 'Sir, I am your most humble servant.' You are *not* his most humble servant. You may say, 'These are sad times; it is a melancholy thing to be reserved to such times.' You don't mind the times. You tell a man, 'I am sorry you had such bad weather the last day of your journey, and were so much wet.' You don't care six-pence whether he was wet or dry. You may *talk* in this manner; it is a mode of talking in Society: but don't *think* foolishly." (IV.221.)

In 1784, Boswell visited Johnson in London again and made a brief trip to Oxford with him, where there was much moral and theological discussion. On their return to London, Boswell, in concert with Reynolds, made an attempt to persuade the government to increase Johnson's pension enough for him to spend the winter in Italy, in hope of arresting his illness. The attempt eventually failed, but Johnson was naturally moved when Boswell told him what had been done: " 'This is taking prodigious pains about a man.'—'O! Sir, (said I, with most sincere affection,) your friends would do every thing for you.' He paused,—grew more and more agitated,—till tears started into his eyes, and he exclaimed with fervent emotion, 'God bless you all.' I was so affected that I also shed tears." (IV.337.) It was the last time Boswell was in Johnson's house.

After Boswell left for Scotland, the news of Mrs. Thrale's marriage to Piozzi came out. Boswell quotes a disapproving letter of Johnson's and then launches into an attack of several pages on what he considers the inaccuracy of her *Anecdotes*. Regardless of whether the attack is justified (for the most part it is trivial), his putting it at this point of his book is a serious artistic blunder. In a preface, a postscript, or even a long footnote, it would not have interrupted the narrative of Johnson's last months.

In July Johnson left for his last visit to Lichfield and Ashbourne. Here Boswell uses a number of letters, arranged according to the recipient. There is a good deal of overlapping. Yet there are passages that one would not miss: "I am favoured with a degree of ease that very much delights me, and do not despair of another race upon the stairs of the Academy." (IV.355.) "I have no company here, and shall naturally come home hungry for conversation." (IV.357.) "The town is my element; there are my friends, there are my books, to which I have not yet bidden farewell, and there are my amusements. Sir Joshua told me long ago, that my vocation was to publick life, and I hope still to keep my station, till God shall bid me *Go in peace*." (IV.358–59.)

When Johnson returned to London in November, he had only a few weeks to live. Boswell gives some samples of imitations of Johnson's prose style, which have no relevance here, and then moves to his deathbed. Leaving out some unpleasant details, he concentrates on Johnson's fear of death, his insistence on knowing from his doctors the prognosis of his illness, and his religious resignation. His will is given in full, along with the painful fact that Boswell is not mentioned in it, although a good many friends are. He is able to use memoranda of friends who called on Johnson during his last illness: Burke is afraid that so many people in the room "may be oppressive. . . ." " 'No, Sir, (said Johnson,) it is not so; and I must be in a wretched state, indeed, when your company would not be a delight to me.' Mr. Burke, in a tremulous voice, expressive of being very tenderly affected, replied, 'My dear Sir, you have always been too good to me.' " (IV.407.) But the sickroom is not all uninterrupted piety and friendship; the patient is sometimes irritable. One night an unfamiliar attendant stayed with him; on being asked how he liked the man, Johnson answered, "Not at all, Sir: the fellow's an ideot; he is as aukward as a turnspit when first put into the wheel, and as sleepy as a dormouse." (IV.411.)

After Johnson's death and his burial in Westminster Abbey, Boswell comes to his conclusion, three sentences of which seem to me to penetrate, with real acuity, into Johnson's nature:

> The solemn text, "of him to whom much is given, much will be required," seems to have been ever present to his mind, in a rigorous sense, and to have made him dissatisfied with his labours and acts of goodness, however comparatively great; so that the un-

> avoidable consciousness of his superiority was, in that respect, a cause of disquiet. (IV.427.). . . But his superiority over other learned men consisted chiefly in what may be called the art of thinking, the art of using his mind; a certain continual power of seizing the useful substance of all that he knew, and exhibiting it in a clear and forcible manner; so that knowledge, which we often see to be no better than lumber in men of dull understanding, was, in him, true, evident, and actual wisdom. (IV.427–28.). . . Exulting in his intellectual strength and dexterity, he could, when he pleased, be the greatest sophist that ever contended in the lists of declamation; and, from a spirit of contradiction, and a delight in shewing his powers, he would often maintain the wrong side with equal warmth and ingenuity; so that, when there was an audience, his real opinions could seldom be gathered from his talk; though when he was in company with a single friend, he would discuss a subject with genuine fairness. . . . (IV.429.)

This is a masterpiece. I have invited the reader to "taste and see," hoping that Boswell's art (and sometimes his artlessness) would engage him, for better or for worse, not only in the life of a great man of letters, but in the art of biography itself.

It may be still too soon to assess Boswell's ultimate place in English literature, for his journals are still in process of publication. There is, however, no reason to think that those which remain are different in kind from those now before us. We will have, at last, a more finished picture of the man than we have now, but the outlines and the colors are very clear. He was an ardent egoist, a romantic, a passionate lover of life, and always and at the same time a man dedicated to recording it with honesty and, usually, with completeness. He learned early, and Johnson reinforced this in him, the importance of the small revelatory detail and the personal anecdote. At the same time he was never overwhelmed by the greatness of the lions he tracked into their lairs—Voltaire, Rousseau, Paoli, Johnson. He was sometimes brash and thoughtless, and he was roughly handled, occasionally, for this behavior. But he was not cowed into sycophancy. Nor was he overwhelmed by these great men or absorbed by them. Even in such a comparatively superficial thing as his prose style, he shows no resemblance whatever to Johnson. In short, he was in the end his own man. He achieved his own style. He wrote his own great book.

Critical List of Editions and Studies

JOHNSON

STANDARD EDITIONS

Works, ed. Sir John Hawkins. 11 vols. London, 1787; four supplementary volumes edited by others, 1788–89.
The first collected edition.

Works. 11 vols. Oxford, 1825.
A convenient edition, without textual value.

The Yale Edition of the Works of Samuel Johnson, in progress. The following volumes have appeared:
I. *Diaries, Prayers, and Annals*, ed. E. L. McAdam, Jr., with D. and M. Hyde. New Haven, 1958.
II. *The Idler* and *The Adventurer*, ed. W. J. Bate, J. M. Bullitt, and L. F. Powell. 1963.
VI. *Poems*, ed. E. L. McAdam, Jr., with G. Milne. 1964.
VII, VIII. *Johnson on Shakespeare*, ed. Arthur Sherbo, 1968.

Dictionary. 2 vols. London, 1755, 1756, 1766, 1773; except for a facsimile, 1968, it has not been reprinted in its original form since the Eighteenth Century, but see *Johnson's Dictionary, A Modern Selection*, ed. E. L. McAdam, Jr. and G. Milne, New York, 1963.

Journey to the Western Islands and Boswell's *Tour to the Hebrides*, ed. R. W. Chapman. London, 1924.
A good text, with excellent annotation and appendices, which later editions omit.

Letters, ed. R. W. Chapman. 3 vols. Oxford, 1952.

Lives of the Poets, ed. G. B. Hill. 3 vols. Oxford, 1905.
Valuable explanatory notes.

BIBLIOGRAPHIES

Courtney, W. P., and D. Nichol Smith. *A Bibliography of Samuel Johnson*. Oxford, 1915.
This valuable work is primarily a description of the first printing of each of Johnson's works, along with some account of the composition of major works and their subsequent history.

Chapman, R. W., and A. T. Hazen. "Johnsonian Bibliography, a Supplement to Courtney," *Proceedings of the Oxford Bibliographical Society*, 1938, pp. 119–66.
Contains much important new information, including works not known to Courtney.

Clifford, J. L. *Johnsonian Studies, 1887–1950*. Minneapolis, 1951.
A critical survey of books and articles published since Hill's edition of Boswell's *Johnson*.

Clifford, J. L., and D. J. Greene. "A Bibliography of Johnsonian Studies, 1950–1960," *Johnsonian Studies*, ed. Magdi Wahba, Cairo, U.A.R., 1962.
Continues the preceding item.

Also valuable: (1) The annual critical bibliography of English Literature, 1660–1800, in *P.Q.*, which contains short reviews of important books; (2) Volume II of *C.B.E.L.*, 1940, with its *Supplement* of 1957, for a selective list; (3) The annual bibliography of *PMLA; (4) The Johnsonian Newsletter* publishes short notes on new books and articles and some news of work in progress.

BIOGRAPHIES

Boswell, *Life of Johnson*, ed. G. B. Hill, revised by L. F. Powell. 6 vols. Oxford, 1934–50.
The standard edition, with very full annotation and a remarkable index.

Clifford, J. L. *Young Sam Johnson*. New York, 1955.
A thorough, modern work, carrying Johnson's life to 1749. A second volume is expected.

Krutch, J. W. *Samuel Johnson*. New York, 1944.
A good one-volume life, valuable for Krutch's discussion of Johnson's literary criticism.

CRITICAL STUDIES

Bate, W. J. *The Achievement of Samuel Johnson*. New York, 1955.
A sensitive and balanced analysis of Johnson's major literary work.

Brown, J. E. *Critical Opinions of Samuel Johnson*. Princeton, 1926.
A dictionary of Johnson's critical ideas and his criticisms of authors.

Greene, D. J. *The Politics of Samuel Johnson*. New Haven, 1960.
The only reliable study of this intricate subject.

Hagstrom, J. H. *Johnson's Literary Criticism*. Minneapolis, 1952.

Hazen, A. T. *Johnson's Prefaces and Dedications*. New Haven, 1937.
The pioneering but still standard treatment of these anonymous works.

Hoover, B. B. *Johnson's Parliamentary Reporting*. Berkeley, 1953.

McAdam, E. L., Jr. *Dr. Johnson and the English Law.* Syracuse, N.Y., 1951.
Contains Johnson's extensive contributions to the law lectures of Robert Chambers at Oxford, not available elsewhere.

Sherbo, A. *Samuel Johnson, Editor of Shakespeare.* Urbana, 1956.
An original, brilliant, controversial study.

Sledd, J. H., and G. J. Kolb. *Dr. Johnson's Dictionary.* Chicago, 1955.
Essays illustrating the genesis of the *Dictionary*, and relating it to lexicographical tradition.

Wimsatt, W. *Philosophic Words: A Study of Style and Meaning in The Rambler and Dictionary.* New Haven, 1948.
———. *The Prose Style of Johnson.* New Haven, 1941.

BOSWELL

STANDARD EDITIONS

No collected edition of Boswell's works exists or is in prospect. The following list covers his major works; for the location of his minor publications, see Professor Pottle's *Literary Career* (below).

Private Papers from Malahide Castle, ed. G. Scott and F. A. Pottle. 18 vols. Mount Vernon, N.Y., 1928–34. *Index*, 1937.
Limited edition, except for the invaluable *Index* and the *Hebrides* (below). This does not include the papers found at Fettercairn, or later at Malahide. It will in time be largely superseded by the Yale edition now in progress.

The Yale Boswell. New Haven, 1950– .
Of Boswell's archives now at Yale, two editions are planned. One volume of the *research* edition, which will be very inclusive, has appeared, *The Correspondence of James Boswell and John Johnston*, ed. R. S. Walker, New York, 1966. The *trade* edition, in modern spelling, gives a selection expected to have general interest. Some things not by Boswell are included, such as Reynolds' *Portraits*.
The following volumes have appeared:

I. *Boswell's London Journal, 1762–1763*, ed. F. A. Pottle. New York, 1950.
II. *Boswell in Holland, 1763–1764*, ed. F. A. Pottle. 1951.
III. *Portraits*, by Sir Joshua Reynolds, ed. F. W. Hilles. 1952.
IV. *Boswell on the Grand Tour: Germany and Switzerland, 1764*, ed. F. A. Pottle. 1953.
V. *Boswell on the Grand Tour: Italy, Corsica, and France, 1765–1766*, ed. F. Brady and F. A. Pottle. 1955.

VI. *Boswell in Search of a Wife, 1766–1769,* ed. F. A. Pottle and F. Brady. 1956.

VII. *Boswell for the Defence, 1769–1774,* ed W. K. Wimsatt and F. A. Pottle. 1959.

VIII. *Boswell: The Ominous Years, 1774–1776,* ed. F. A. Pottle and C. Ryscamp. 1963.

The Hypochondriack, ed. Margery Bailey, 2 vols. Palo Alto, Calif., 1928.

Boswell's seventy contributions to *The London Magazine.* Reprinted as *Boswell's Column,* London, 1951.

Journal of a Tour to Corsica and Memoirs of Pascal Paoli, ed. M. Bishop. London, 1951.

Letters, ed. C. B. Tinker, 2 vols. Oxford, 1924.

Published just before Tinker's discovery of the Boswell archives, which will in time make this collection obsolete.

Life of Johnson and *Tour to the Hebrides,* ed. G. B. Hill, revised by L. F. Powell. 6 vols. Oxford, 1934–50.

The standard edition, a reprint of Boswell's third edition (1799), collated against the first and second. Full annotation, elaborate index.

Journal of a Tour to the Hebrides (with Johnson's *Journey to the Western Islands*), ed. R. W. Chapman. London, 1924.

Good text, with excellent annotation and appendices, which later editions omit.

Journal of a Tour to the Hebrides, ed. F. A. Pottle and C. H. Bennett. New York, 1936; reprinted with additions, 1961.

The unrevised manuscript, later reworked into the published *Tour* of 1785.

BIBLIOGRAPHIES

Pottle, F. A. *The Literary Career of James Boswell,* New Haven, 1929; reissued 1965.

A descriptive bibliography of each of Boswell's published works and a detailed history of his literary career. Indispensable.

Also valuable: (1) The annual critical bibliography of English Literature, 1660–1800, in *P.Q.,* which contains short reviews of important books; (2) Volume II of *C.B.E.L.,* 1940, with its *Supplement* of 1957, for a selective list; (3) The annual bibliography of *PMLA;* (4) *The Johnsonian Newsletter* publishes short notes on new books and articles and some news of work in progress.

BIOGRAPHIES AND CRITICAL STUDIES

The principal effort of Boswell scholars for the past forty years has very properly gone into editing the vast Boswell archives, and into biography connected with these labors. Criticism has been less bulky, and it is often to be found in the introductions to the volumes cited in the preceding section. It is not the less important for its relative slimness.

Pottle, F. A. *James Boswell, The Earlier Years.* New York, 1966.
The first volume of the definitive biography, by the world's leading authority.

Tinker, C. B. *Young Boswell.* Boston, 1922.
Sympathetic and delightful.

Wyndham Lewis, D. B. *The Hooded Hawk.* New York, 1946.
A lively biography, being superseded by Professor Pottle's work.

Index

SJ = Johnson; JB = Boswell

Aberbrothick, SJ and JB visit, 84
Aberdeen, SJ and JB visit, 83, 85, 210 f.
Accademia della Crusca, 21
Account of Corsica, 203 ff.
Adams, Dr. William, on *Dictionary,* 227; on first performance of *Irene,* 228; praises *Tour,* 218
Addison, Joseph, *Life,* 140 ff.; biography, no contemporary, 123; Blackmore, praise of, 156; Blenheim, poem on, 143; *Cato,* 32; character, 147; compared with Swift, 161; Congreve introduces to Montague, 142 f.; criticism vs. Dryden's, 150; death, 147; Dennis' criticism, 145; dictionary, projected, 146; Dryden admires, 142; examples from Tillotson for dictionary, 146; *Guardian,* 145; in Ireland, 143 f.; Italian opera, opposition to, 149, 151; pension to travel, 143; SJ's translation of, 3; political tracts, 70; and Pope, 147 f.; on Pope's and Philips' *Pastorals,* 165; Pope and Tickell, 166; Pope believed malicious, 165; Pope, praise of, 165; schoolboy prank, 142; secretary to Lord Wharton, 143 f.; on Smith, 135; and Steele, 142; Steele attacked, 146 f.; Steele on his humor, 147; succeeds Locke, 143; sycophancy, 143; *Tatler,* contributes to, 144; Tickell his editor, 160; Tickell's *Iliad* preferred to Pope's, 166; vacillation, 146; wine, addiction to, 148; wit, description of, 104; Yalden a college mate, 159
"Address to Reader," in *Gentleman's Magazine,* 10
Adventurer essays, 38 ff.
Ainsworth, Robert, *Thesaurus linguae Latinae* used by SJ, 19
Akenside, Mark, *Life,* 180 f.
Alexander the Great, 28 f.
Alfred, King, 7
Amadis of Gaul, SJ reads, 51, 221
American Colonies, Anna Seward defends, 244; JB's sympathy for, 237; compared with Ireland, 80; disputes with, 78 ff.; SJ's antipathy to, 244
Anacreon, *Dove,* 97
Andrewes, Dr. Lancelot, Bishop of Winchester, 94
Anne, Queen, reads *Spectator,* 144; touched SJ for king's evil, 220
Anoch, innkeeper's daughter at, 86
Anson, George Anson, Baron, *Voyage* and Falkland Islands, 73 f.
Arbuthnot, Dr. John, SJ's sketch of, 168; letters compared with Pope's, 167
Argyle, Duke of, entertains SJ and JB, 91
Ascham, Roger, SJ's Dedication to *English Works,* 46
Aston sisters, SJ's friendship with, 222
Auchinleck, SJ and JB visit, 83, 91, 215

Bacon, Sir Francis, cited in Preface to *Dictionary,* 22; marked volume of, used in *Dictionary,* 19
Bacon, Roger, 28
Bailey, Nathaniel, *Dictionary* used by SJ, 19 f.
Baretti, Giuseppe, his copy of letter to Chesterfield, 230; SJ writes to, 197, 231
Barretier (or Baretier or Baratier), Philip, *Life,* 10
Bathurst, Dr. Richard, dead before JB met SJ, 224; died at Havana, 75
Beattie, Dr. James, JB's advice to, 206; urged SJ go to Scotland, 208

Beauclerk, Topham, advice on a wit, 248; corespondent in divorce, 230; SJ on his death, 246; night jaunt with SJ, 229 f.
Behn, Mrs. Aphra, address to Nell Gwyn, 130; cited in *Drury Lane Prologue,* 23
Bell, John, prints edition of English poets, 92; publishers' cartel fights, 92
Bennet, James, SJ helps with *Ascham,* 46
biography, JB's "genius" for, 206; JB's interest in and method, 205; JB's plan to write SJ's life, 205; JB quotes *Rambler* on, 219; conversation and letters in, 217; SJ and JB discuss, 205; SJ's formula in *Waller,* 100; SJ on, 147; tradition in England, 217
Birch, Dr. Thomas, SJ's poem to, 7
Birmingham, SJ visits Hector and finds a wife at, 223
Blackmore, Sir Richard, *Life,* 156 f.; SJ adds to *Poets,* 92
Blackstone, Sir William, lectures, 48 f.
Blair, Rev. Hugh, SJ answers question on Ossianic poems, 233
Blake, Admiral Robert, *Life,* 9
blank verse, Akenside's praised, 180; Congreve's praised, 155; SJ's attitude to, 114; Mallet's use of, 180
Blount, Martha, friendship with Pope, 169
Boece, Hector, praised by SJ, 85
Boerhaave, Dr. Herman, *Life,* 9
Boethius SJ dictates translation of, to Mrs. Thrale, 5
Boileau-Despréaux, Nicolas, SJ prefers Pope to, 173; and Rochester, 118
Bolingbroke, Henry St. John, Viscount, friendship with Pope, 169; his *Patriot King,* 168 f.; ridicules Pope for *Essay on Man,* 167 f; trust in Prior, 163
Boothby, Miss Hill, SJ's friendship with, 222
Boswell, Alexander, JB's father, 187 f.; entertains SJ and JB, 215; forbids JB to go beyond Germany, 193; permits JB to go to Italy, 196
Boswell, James, accuracy, eagerness for, 218, 230; adaptability, 196; admitted to bar 202; advised on *Corsica* by SJ, 204 f.; American colonies, sympathy with, 237; arranges meeting of SJ and Wilkes, 239 ff.; asks Rousseau's help, 193; attacks Mrs. Piozzi, 249; authenticity, claim to, 218; and Baretti in Venice, 197; biography, discusses with SJ, 236, interest in, 205 f.; brash and thoughtless, 251; brings raw materials to life, 227 f.; challenged to duel, 209; character sketch of SJ, 208; Chesterfield, publishes letter to, 47; chides Smollett, 204; The Club, suppress names of speakers at, 242 ff.; comments on Roman antiquities, 197; compared with Gray, Pennant, and Gilpin, 212; compares copies of letter to Chesterfield, 230; compares self to Emile, 192; comparison with SJ in *Tour,* 208; on concubinage, 193; conservative, 187; contributions to periodicals, 205; Corsica, SJ encourages to write on, 234; Corsica, visit to, 197 ff.; country life, dislike of, 211; cruelty to dog, 201; curiosity, 231; death of mother, 201; defends Garrick, rebuked by SJ, 189, 232; diaries, 203, 206, method of keeping, 235, new kind of, 190 f.; diary basis of *Life,* 203; digressions, 212; diligence in obtaining data, 221; Dilly writes about *Poets,* 92; dines with SJ at Mrs. Thrale's, 248; disagreement with SJ, 183 f.; discretion, shows unusual, 242; ear, and recording ability, 244; editing inability, 211 f.; education, 187, 192 f.; expansion of notes, 232 f.; facility in languages, 196; father, relations with, 187 f., 192 ff.; father wants legal career for, 187; "feudal" attitudes, 187, 193; first call on SJ, 190; Frederick the Great, JB tries to meet, 191 f.; and Genoese spies, 201; in Germany, 191; Gold-

smith, dislikes, misjudges, 233; on Grand Tour, 191 ff.; Gray, "Sketch" of, 204; *Harleian Catalogue,* on SJ's contributions, 14; Hawkins, charged with inaccuracy, 218; helps Col on shipboard, 213 f.; hereditary melancholy, 192; heritage, pride in, 187; in Holland, 191, 234; honesty in self-assessment, 189 f.; hopes for Burke's help in politics, 212; "Hypochondriack" essays, 205; infatuation with Louisa, 188 f., 193; ingratiates self with reader, 190 f.; in Italy, 196 f.; SJ accompanies to Harwich, 190; SJ as father-figure to, 184, 190; and SJ's *Journey,* 207; SJ knew his intention to write life, 147; SJ's life, plans to write, 197, 205; on SJ's love for his wife, 228; on SJ's political pamphlets, 237; SJ reassures on return from Continent, 234; on SJ's religious scruples, 221 f.; on SJ's style, 45 f.; SJ tells he had "imitations" of all of Juvenal in his head, 8; SJ and Wilkes tease, 241, 247; *Journals,* 187 ff.; law studies, 187, 190 f.; liberty vs. necessity, 247; *Life,* models for, 217; *Life,* copyrighted parts of, 230; *Life,* wishes SJ had written, 218; literary ambition, 204; literary criticism weak, 230; in love with Girolama Piccolomini, 197; Mason acknowledged as model for *Life,* 218; meets SJ, 189 f., 231 ff.; meets Rousseau, 192 ff.; meets Wilkes, 189; a mimic, 194; mistakes length of SJ's stay at Oxford, 221; modifies SJ's statement on greenroom, 228; Monboddo, arranges meeting with, 85, 209 f.; and Mountstuart, in Italy, 197; needs reassurance, 190; no sycophant, 251; not a lion-hunter, 191; not in SJ's will, 250; opinion, independence of, 226, 237; originality of travel diary, 216; partner in *London Magazine,* 205; Mrs. Piozzi credited for anecdote, 220, uses her book, 237; plays Scots airs to Corsicans, 200; political hopes, 242; Lucy Porter, obtains information from, 224; prints derogatory remarks, 209; prints jottings for *Rambler, Adventurer,* 5; prods SJ into talk, 206; prose style his own, 251; protects image of SJ, 229; purgatory, presses SJ on, 206; *Rambler* quoted on biography, 37; on the *Rambler,* 228; reacted to SJ's ideas, 183 f.; reaction to Paoli, 200; rebels against father, 187 f.; reflected glory, 211; relevance, judgment on, 231; religion, conversion, 188, 192; reserved in *Life,* 218; sees Rousseau, 193; and Rousseau in London, 202; Rousseau sends letter of introduction, 197; Savage, disbelieves, 226; seasick in Hebrides, 213; seduces Rousseau's mistress, 201 f.; seeks army career, 188; seeks increased pension for SJ, 249; self-consciousness, lack of, 190 f., 211; self-portrait, 209; sense of drama, 190 f.; sexual adventures, 188 ff.; shocked by Rousseau 196; skill in expanding raw materials, 191; softens SJ's blunt remarks, 232, 238; stage manages SJ, 209 f., 214 f.; stenographic skill, test of, 244; suppresses evidence, 229; suppresses SJ's religious doubts, 221 f.; in Switzerland, 191 ff.; Temple writes to about Gray, 181; theater, interest in, 187; thinks in theatrical terms, 195 f.; topography, no interest in, 212; use of second and third hand materials, 226 ff., 235; visits Oxford, Birmingham, Lichfield, and Ashbourne, 238; and Voltaire, 194 f.; Walton's *Lives* recommended by SJ, 217; Miss Williams persuaded to let SJ dine with Wilkes, 240; writes in French, Italian, or English, 196; writes Temple on Voltaire, 195; writes Wilkes re SJ, 197; writing technique, 198 f.; wrote for an audience, 191

Boswell, Mrs. James, incurious about SJ's diary, 209

Boyle, Robert, 22

Brooke, Henry, *Gustavus Vasa* defended by SJ in *Compleat Vindication,* 12
Broome, William, *Life,* 164; help with Pope's *Odyssey,* 166 f.
Brown, Tom, SJ's teacher, 220
Brunswick succession, attacked in *Marmor,* 12
Buchan, Bullers of, SJ and JB visit, 85
Buckingham, George Villiers, 1st Duke of, 28
Buckingham, George Villiers, 2nd Duke of, *Rehearsal* ridicules Dryden, 128
Bunyan, John, SJ's opinion of *Pilgrim's Progress,* 236 f.
Burke, Edmund, JB hopes for political help from, 212; JB mentions freely in *Tour,* 212; complimented by Sheridan, 243; on House of Commons, 243; SJ denies he has wit, 65, 209, 212; SJ praises his eloquence, 212; at SJ's deathbed, 250; manages impeachment of Hastings, 242; name concealed by JB, 242; position opposed to SJ, 80; on speaking well in Parliament, 243
Burman, Peter, *Life,* 10
Burnet, Gilbert, Bishop of Salisbury, SJ uses in *Blake,* 9; his praise of Sarpi, 9
Burney, Fanny, Paoli tells he thought JB a spy, 199
Bute, John Stuart, Earl of, fall from power, 72
Butler, Samuel, *Life,* 115 ff.; compared to Rabelais, 116; debt to Cervantes, 115; Dryden on, 117
Byng, Admiral John, JB's overemphasis on, 231

Cambridge, Richard Owen, JB's praise of, 249
Cameron, Archibald, executed, 226
Carmichael, Poll, 246
Caroline, Queen, pensions Savage, 16
Carter, Elizabeth, SJ addresses poem to, 7; translates Crousaz, 13
Casa, Giovanni della, courtesy books, 144
Cave, Edward, SJ's Latin ode to, 7; SJ offers services to, 6; SJ's projects for, 8, 13; SJ's relationship with, 225; memorialized in *Dictionary,* 7, 14; published *Observations on Macbeth,* 18
Cervantes Saavedra, Miguel de, Butler indebted to, 115
Chambers, Ephraim, *Cyclopaedia* used by SJ, 19
Chambers, Robert, attends SJ to Newcastle, 208; SJ's law lectures for, 5, 47 ff.
Chapman, George, Waller's remarks on, 96 f.
Charles I, 28, 95
Charles II, celebrated by Dryden, 123, by Waller, 96; character of, in *King Arthur,* 127; defends Dryden's plagiarism, 125; preferred Dryden use rime, 124
Charles XII of Sweden, 28 f.
Charles Albert, Elector of Bavaria, 29
Chatterton, Thomas, use of obscenity, 190
Chesterfield, Philip Dormer Stanhope, Earl of, JB's opinion of his son, 191; "dedicator" and "patron," 27 f.; Hurgo Castroflet in *Debates,* 11; ignores SJ, 21; insistence on graces, 144; SJ's letter to, 47, 230; *Plan of Dictionary* addressed to, 18; praises *Dictionary,* 230
Churchill, Charles, writes *North Briton* with Wilkes, 189, 239
Cibber, Colley, anecdotes of Dryden, 241; hero of *Dunciad,* 168; Poet Laureate, 181; quarrel with Pope, 168; rejected Fenton's *Mariamne,* 157, Gay's *Beggar's Opera,* 158
Cibber, Theophilus, *Poets* written by Shiels, 160
Clarendon, Edward Hyde, Earl of, character of Waller, 96; in *Vanity of Human Wishes,* 28; SJ credits for data, 95; SJ uses in *Blake,* 9; Waller helps prosecute, 96
classical imitations, 7
Clifford, Martin, attack on Dryden, 126

The Club, JB suppresses names of speakers at, 242 ff.
Col, Isle of, SJ and JB visit, 88, 91, in storm off, 213; primitive life on, 214
Col, or Coll, "Young," Donald Maclean, 213 f.
Coleridge, Samuel Taylor, *Lyrical Ballads,* 172; on power of imagination, 140; "suspension of disbelief," 50; unities of drama, 65
Collier, Jeremy, controversy with Congreve 156; SJ's vignette of, 156
Collins, William, *Life,* 177 f.
Commons, House of, exclusion of Wilkes, 70 ff.; a resolution not law, 71
Compleat Vindication of Licensers of the Stage, 12 f.
Comus, Prologue, 112
Congreve, William, *Life,* 154 ff.; controversy with Collier, 156; education, 155; introduces Addison to Montague, 142 f.; political preferment, 155; Pope dedicates *Iliad* to, 166; praise of Dryden, 129; precocity, 155
contempt, SJ's use of, in political tracts, 71 f., 75 ff., 235 f.
conversation, use of, in biography, 217
Coote, Sir Eyre, SJ praises conversation, 86
Corbet, Andrew, on Addison, 142
Corneille, Pierre, 21
correspondence, use of, in biography, 217
Corsica, Account of, 203 ff.; artistic errors in, 205; based on JB's diary, 204; JB's expansion of notes for, 197 f.; dedication to Paoli (perhaps by Johnson), 204; SJ's advice on, 204 f.; success of, 205
Courayer, Pierre Francois Le, translation of Sarpi, 8 f.
Cowell, John, *Interpreter,* 19
Cowley, Abraham, *Life,* 100 ff.; Addison ranks Montague with, 143; arrested as spy, 101; best of metaphysical poets, 103; compared with Donne, 103, with Reynolds, 100 f., with Suckling and Dryden, 104; encoder to the King, 101; expelled from Cambridge, 101; SJ's favorite *Life,* 100; Latin verse, 101, 108; Milton's opinion of, 112; precocity, 101; receives M.D., 101; his religious poetry, 105 ff.; Spenser's influence, 100; translation commended, 107
Crabbe, George, SJ revises *Village,* 43
Croft, Herbert, Jr., wrote biographical part of *Young,* 179
Cromwell, Oliver, Dryden and Waller compete over, 123; permits Waller's return, 96; Sprat praises, 137; Waller praises, 96
Crousaz, Abbé Jean Pierre de, attacks Pope's *Essay on Man,* 168; Cave commissions translations of, 13; convinced SJ of faults in Pope's *Essay,* 173
Curll, Edmund, publishes Pope's letters, 167

Davies, Thomas, 189 f., 231 ff.
Davis, Captain, discovers Falkland Islands, 73
Day, Thomas, JB thanks for help, 204
Defoe, Daniel, SJ did not appreciate, 183; political tracts, 70
Delany, Dr. Patrick, praise of Swift, 163
Democritus, "Laughing Philosopher," *Vanity of Human Wishes,* 27
Denham, Sir John, *Life,* 107 f.
Denis, Mme., Voltaire's niece, 194
Dennis, John, attacked in *Dunciad,* 167; attacks Addison's *Cato,* 145, 149 f.; attacks Pope, 165; SJ credits for data on Cowley, 100; objections to Shakespeare, 63; Pope's hostility to, 165; praise of Blackmore, 156
Derrick, Samuel, SJ's retort on, 134 f.
Desmoulins, Mrs., 224 f., 246
dialogue, SJ's ear for, 157
Dictionary, 18 ff.; Addison's examples, 146; Chesterfield praises, 230; *Gentleman's Magazine* cited, 7;

method of compiling, 19 f.; *Plan* of, addressed to Chesterfield, 18; Pope's list of writers, 18; prejudice in definitions, 20; proposed by Dodsley, 18, 227; sources for word lists, 19
Dilly, Charles and Edward, give dinner for SJ and Wilkes, 239 ff., 247 f.; SJ explodes at dinner at, 244
Dilly, Edward, on *Lives of Poets,* 92
Diodati, memorialized by Milton, 109
Dodsley, Robert, includes *London* in his *Collection,* 8; SJ writes Preface for his *Preceptor,* 24 f.; Pope helps start as publisher, 169; proposes *Dictionary* project to SJ, 227; publishes *London,* 7
Donaldson, Alexander, challenges Shakespeare copyright, 18
Donne, John, compared with Cowley, 103
Dorando, 203
Dorset, Charles Sackville, Earl of, *Life,* 121
Douglas affair, basis of *Dorando,* 203
Douglas, Archibald, supported by JB, 203
Downes, John, SJ credits for data on Cowley, 100
Drake, Admiral Robert, *Life,* 9
dramatists, only masters of common life before Addison and Steele, 144
Drury-Lane Prologue, 22 ff.
Dryden, John, *Life,* 123 ff.; Addison ranks Montague with, 143; admired Addison, 142; attacked by Clifford, 126, by Settle, 126, 128; attacks Settle 125 f., 128; on Butler, 117; celebrates Restoration, 123; character, 129 f.; chronology of publications not easy, 124, 128; collaboration with Davenant, 125; compared with Cowley, 104, with Pitt, 174, with Pope, 169 f.; competed with Waller, 123; Congreve's praise of, 129; convert to Catholicism, 129; as critic, 125, 127 f., 130 f.; death and funeral, 129; faults, 132 ff.; finances, 130; gave name to an age, 183; immorality in his plays, 125, 131; SJ asks Cibber for anecdotes of, 241; SJ's error on *Mac Flecknoe,* 129; SJ's translation of lines on Milton, 42; lies about reasons for printing, 126 f.; no contemporary biography, 123; over-praise of Roscommon, 119; Pitt competed with, 174; plagiarism, 125; poetical diction, 131; Poet Laureate, 125, removed as, 129; Pope compares Fenton to, 157; praised power of imagination, 140; praises Cromwell, 123; Prior's satire on, 152; prologues compared with SJ's, 24; prose style, 131; publishing by subscription, 166; ridiculed, 128; rime, use of, 124; Shakespearean criticism expanded by Pope, 166; on source of Waller's smoothness, 95; Swift's hatred of, 161; sycophancy, 119, 121, 126 f., 130; on translation, 128, 131 f.; on unities of drama, 65
Dublin, piracy of *Lives of Poets,* 93
Duckett, George, attacked in *Dunciad,* 167
duelling, SJ and Goldsmith differ on, 206
Duke, Richard, *Life,* 136
Dunvegan, SJ enjoys, 88
Durfey, Thomas, cited in *Drury-Lane Prologue,* 23
Dyer, John, *Life,* 178

Edial, SJ's school at, 223 f.
Edinburgh, SJ and JB visit, 83, 91, 208 f., 215
education, SJ on sibling rivalry, 220 f.
Edwards, Oliver, SJ meets after 49 years, 244 f.; SJ sends set of *Rambler,* 247; on philosophy, 245
Edwards, Thomas, Shakespearean critic, 67
Elegy on Robert Levet, 44 f.
Elgin, cathedral at, SJ and JB visit, 86
Elphinston, James, on reading books through, 236
Englishman, founded by Steele, 145
Epilogue for Philips' *Distrest Mother,* 30

Ernulfus, Bishop of Rochester, curse of, 17

Fairfax, Edward, *Tasso* source of Waller's smoothness, 95; Waller surpasses, 99
Falkland Islands, in *The Patriot*, 78
Falkland's Islands, Thoughts on . . ., 73 ff.; JB's opinion of, 237
False Alarm, The 70 ff.
father-figure, JB and SJ, 184, 190, 221, 229; Jorden and SJ 221
Felixmarte de Hircania, SJ reads, 221
Fenton, Elijah, *Life*, 157; share in Pope's *Odyssey*, 157, 166 f.; wooden dialogue, 157
Fermor, Arabella, "Belinda" in *Rape of the Lock*, 165
Fielding, Henry, *Tom Jones, Joseph Andrews*, 34 f.
Fielding's theater, Haymarket, 12
fish, in Hebridean economy, 88
Fitzpatrick, John, Earl of Upper Ossory, name concealed by JB, 242
Fleetwood, Dr. William, *Sermons* reprinted in *Spectator*, 144
Flint, Bet, asks SJ for Preface to her Life, 248; SJ's anecdote of, 247 f.
Foote, Samuel, as beer salesman, 241; SJ calls poor mimic, 241; mimics SJ, 206
Forbes, Sir William, on drinking, 238
Ford, Cornelius, opinion of Broome, 164
Fordyce, George, name concealed by JB, 242
Fort Augustus, SJ and JB visit, 83, 86
Fort George, SJ and JB visit, 86
Francis, Sir Philip, perhaps Junius, 75 f.
Frederick the Great, JB tries to meet, 191 f.
Freeholder, Addison's humor, 146
French Academy, tries to fix French language, 21

Garrick, David, JB defends, 189, 232; describes SJ at Edial, 223 f.; describes Mrs. Johnson, 224; and *Drury-Lane Prologue*, 22 ff.; goes to London with SJ, 224; invites SJ to greenroom, 228; and *Irene*, 31, 227; SJ borrowed Shakespeare quartos, 61; SJ's Prologue to his *Lethe*, 24; SJ talks of, at dinner with Wilkes, 241; SJ's tribute to, 136, 222; on *London* and *Vanity of Human Wishes*, 8, 227; "performing at home," 227 f.; pupil with brother Peter at SJ's Edial school, 223 f.; refuses ticket to Miss Williams, 232
Garth, Sir Samuel, *Life*, 139; Pope's opinion of *Dispensary*, 139
Gataker, Thomas, defends gaming, 117
Gay, John, *Life*, 157 ff.; *Beggar's Opera*, subscription edition of poems, pastorals, 158; *Rural Sports*, 157
Gazetteer, SJ contemptuous of, 153
Genest, John, on *Drury-Lane Prologue*, 24
genius, SJ's definition of, 100 f., 173
Gentleman's Magazine, description of, 6 f.; gave new meaning to "magazine," 7; SJ becomes editor, 13 f., 225; SJ begins regular work on, 10, 26; SJ offers services to, 6; SJ's works in: *Barretier*, 10; *Blake*, 9; *Boerhaave*, 9; *Burman*, 10; *Cave*, 14; Crousaz on Pope, 13; *Drake*, 9; "Essay on Epitaphs," 13; *Parliamentary Debates*, 10 ff.; *Roscommon*, 24; *Sydenham*, 10, 13
George II, SJ protests brutality of, 226; mentioned, 7, 27 f.
George III, SJ compliments, 73; SJ's interview with, 235; let Bute go, 72
Gibbon, Edward, entered Oxford at 15, 221; name concealed by JB, 242
Glasgow, SJ and JB visit, 83, 91
Glasgow newspaper, account of SJ and JB on Skye, 215
Godolphin, Sidney Godolphin, Earl of, and Addison's *Campaign*, 143
Goldsmith, Oliver, JB dislikes and misjudges, 233; death hastened by James's "Powders," 15; on duelling, 206; "frankness and simplicity," 235; *Good-Natur'd Man*, 42; jealousy, 235; SJ attacks, 233; SJ

gives literary help, 43; SJ's Prologue to *Good-Natur'd Man,* 24, 234; liked generalizations, 233; *Parnell,* 138, 236; preferred Parnell to Gray, 138; says SJ lacks interest in theater, 234; *She Stoops to Conquer* dedicated to SJ, 234
Gordon, Alexander Gordon, Duke of, SJ and JB pass property of, 86
Grand Tour I, 192 ff.
Grand Tour II, 196 ff.
Granville, George, Baron Lansdowne, *Life,* 159
Gray, Thomas, *Life,* 181 ff.; JB's "Sketch" of, 205; SJ misses parody, 182; SJ prints matter not in poems, 93; journeys to Scotland, Westmoreland, Cumberland, 181; *Life* controversial, 181, 183; on *London,* 8; Mason's *Memoirs* of, 217; quarrel with Walpole, 181; refused Poet Laureateship, 181; Temple's "character" of, 205
Grenville, George, attacked in *Falkland's Islands,* 76, 236
Guardian, Addison in, 165; Steele and Addison produce, 145
Guthrie, William, his *Parliamentary Debates* in *Gentleman's Magazine,* 11
Gwyn, Nell, addressed by Aphra Behn, 130

Hailes, Sir David Dalrymple, Lord, JB thanks for help, 204
Halifax, Charles Montague, Earl of, *Life,* 137; and Addison's *Campaign,* 143; Addison ranks with Cowley and Dryden, 143; overrated because a peer, 137, 152; patron of Congreve, 155; and Pope's *Iliad,* 166; and Stepney, 121
Hammond, James, *Life,* 160
Hanmer, Sir Thomas, *Shakespeare,* 17, 61
Hanover, House of, attacked in *Marmor,* 12
Hanway, Jonas, *Essay on Tea,* 45
Harleian Catalogue, SJ's work on, 14 f., 226
Harleian Miscellany, SJ's introduction to, choice of items for, 17
Harley, Edward: see Oxford, Earl of
Hastings, Warren, impeachment, 242
Hawkesworth, John, *Adventurer,* 38 f.; *Swift,* 161
Hawkins, Sir John, *Johnson,* charges against, 218, the official *Life,* 224; on SJ's work on *Harleian Catalogue,* 14; SJ's *Works,* 11
Hawkins, Sir Richard, sights Falkland Islands, 73
Hazen, Allen T., SJ's *Prefaces and Dedications,* 46
Heath, Benjamin, Shakespeare critic, 67
Heath, James, SJ uses in *Blake,* 9
Hector, Edmund, on SJ's mother, 219; SJ visits 4, 223; takes SJ's dictation, 5, 223
Henry VIII, 28
Hervey, Rev. Henry, SJ's sermon for, 47
Highlands, social structure and economy, 88 ff.
Hill, Aaron, in *Dunciad,* 167
Hogarth, William, description of SJ, 226
Holland, JB's journal in, lost, 191; JB's legal studies in, 190 f.
Hooker, Richard, cited in Preface to *Dictionary,* 22
Horace, SJ and Wilkes discuss, 241; Pope's "imitations" of, 7
Howard, Sir Robert, and Dryden, 124
Hughes, John, *Life* 151 f.
Hume, David, SJ attacks, 208 f.; Rousseau and, 201
Hunt, Edward, 23
Hunter, Rev. John, SJ's schoolmaster, 220
Hyde, Mrs. Donald F., portrait of Mrs. Johnson, 224
Hypochondriack, JB's essays, 205

Idler, 39 ff.; on debtors' prisons, 40 f.; "Essay on Epitaphs" in, 13; on literary criticism, 41 f.; persona established, 39; on war, 39 f.
imagination, power of, praised, 140
Inverness, SJ and JB visit, 83
Iona, Isle of, SJ visits, 91

Ireland, taxation of, 80
Irene, Adams on opening night, 228; based on Knolles, 30 f.; blank verse in, 31; cast in premiere, 31; financial success, 30; SJ finishes draft of, 6, 30, 225; Garrick produces, asks changes in, 30 ff., 228; vs. other contemporary tragedies, 32
irony, in *The False Alarm*, 71 f.; in *Rasselas*, 51 f.; in *Taxation no Tyranny*, 79
Isham, Lt. Col. Ralph H., on JB and Thérèse, 201 f.

James I, morality of court of, 94
James, Dr. Robert, SJ's tribute to, 136, 222; *Medicinal Dictionary*, "Powders," SJ's work on, 15
Johnson, Elizabeth Jervis Porter, SJ's wife, appearance, 224; comment on *Rambler*, 228; SJ leaves in Lichfield, 224; SJ's love for, 229; SJ meets, marries, 223; SJ takes to London, 225
Johnson, Michael, SJ's father, 219; bookshop, 221; dies, 222
Johnson, Samuel, accepts JB as biographer, 205; accepts pro-Pope sources, 147 f., 165 f.; accompanies JB to Harwich, 190; vs. Addison on Smith, 135; advice to JB on Corsica, 204 f.; on American Revolution, 244; anger in *Idler*, 40; appearance, 221, 223 f., 226; attacks Hume, 208 f.; "balances" beauties and defects, 41; beats Osborne, 226; Beauclerk and Langton on night jaunt, 229 f.; believes novel should instruct youth, 34 f.; on biography, 37, 147, 205, 236; biography, method of writing, 8 f.; book reviews in *Literary Magazine*, 45; JB and Reynolds seek increased pension for, 249; with JB at Oxford, Birmingham, Lichfield, Ashbourne, 238; JB drives to rudeness, 214 f.; on JB's worry over liberty vs. necessity, 247; on brutality of George II, 226; burial, 250; Burke at deathbed, 250; on Burke's eloquence, 212; on cant, 249; and Cave, 225; Chambers, lectures for, 47 ff.; character sketch of, in *Tour*, 208; charges Garrick with selfishness, 189, 232; compared to a whale, 215; compares France with England, 238; comparison with JB, 208; composed in his head, 8, 16; composed rapidly, 11, 16; confidence in JB, 239; consciousness of intellectual superiority, 250 f.; contempt, use of, 71 f., 75 ff., 235 f.; considers tour to Italy, 238; credits Corbet for data on Addison, 142, Goldsmith for Parnell, 138, Percy for Clifford vs. Dryden, 126, Spence for Gay, 158, Tonson for Dryden 130, Walmesley for Smith, 135, Warburton and Langton for Pope 164,—other credits to Clarendon, Whitelock, 95, Wood, Dennis, Downes, 100, —and 95, 100, 126, 130, 135, 138, 142, 158, 164; and Dame Oliver, 220; death, fear of, 250; Dedication to *Ascham*, 46; delight in showing intellectual powers, 251; denies Burke's wit, 209, 212; dines with Wilkes, 239 ff.; dislike of country life, 211; dislikes wordplay, 64 f., 209; dislikes writing, 5; on drinking, 238 f.; Dryden on Milton, translation of, 42; early years in London, 224; earnings from *Irene*, 30, *Lives of Poets*, 92; edits *Gentleman's Magazine*, 13 f., 225; education, 220 ff.; Edwards, remembered after 49 years, 244 f., sees again, 247, sends set of *Rambler*, 247; encourages JB to write on Corsica, 234; enters Oxford at 19, 221; errs in date of *Mac Flecknoe*, 129; fails to credit source of *King*, 137; father-figure to JB, 184, 190, 221, 229; in father's bookstore, 221; favors dictation, 5; on female dress, 220; first book, 223; on Bet Flint, 248; on freedom of speech, 12 f.; friendship, diversity of 229 f.; friendship with Aston sisters and Hill Boothby, 222, with Thrales, 234; gave name to an age, 183; goes to London with Garrick,

224; and Goldsmith on duelling, 206; on Goldsmith's *Parnell*, 236; and the greenroom, 228; and Hector at Birmingham, 223; on home study and self education, 24 f.; independence of, 70; insults Scotland, 90 f.; interest in legal career, 48 f.; interview with George III, 235; and Ivy Lane Club, 224; and Jacobites, 12, 226; Jorden a surrogate father to, 221; on Juvenal, 155 f.; on Kames, 232; knew JB to write his life, 147; and Mrs. Knowles, 242; on Langton's will, 237; leaves wife in Lichfield, 224; letter to Chesterfield, 47, 230; letter to Langton, 231; literary aid to friends, Bennet, 46, JB, 204, Chambers 48, Crabbe, 43, Goldsmith, 43, Hawkesworth, 161, Charlotte Lennox, 62, Hannah More, 43, Percy, Reynolds, 45, Anna Williams, 43, —others, 15, 38 f., 43, 45 ff., 62, 161, 204; on love, patience, and faith, 29 f.; on Mrs. Macaulay's republicanism, 241 f.; marriage, 6, 223; meets JB, 189 f., 231 ff.; melancholia, 221 f.; on metaphysics, 132; methods of composition, 5; on Milton's school-teaching, 109; on monastic life, 231; on Monboddo, 235, dislikes, 209 f., visits, 210; not to be categorized, 183; offended by Lady Lochbuy, 214 f.; open mind, 183; on Ossianic controversy, 210 f., 233; parodies of Percy, 43; parodies attacked by Wordsworth, 43; pension, 231, 249; pensioners, 246; perhaps wrote Dedication for *Corsica*, 204; physical infirmities, 226; on *Pilgrim's Progress*, 236 f.; plans to visit Italy, 249; playfulness, 231; poetic justice in drama, 150; poor vision, 219 f.; poverty, 3, 222; praise of blank verse, 155; precocity, 3; procrastination, 223; prodded into talk, 206; prose style, 5, 11, 14 f., 22, 45 f.; on public opinion, 149; on purgatory, 206; Rambler a moralist, 35; reaction to overpraise, 134 f.; reacted to JB's ideas, 183 f.; read JB's Scottish tour diary, 207; read romances as a boy, 221; reassures JB after Grand Tour, 234; rebukes JB, 189, 232; religious doubts, 221 f.; religious resignation, 250; reply to Hanway on *Essay on Tea*, 45; retort on Elphinston, 236; ridicules Warton, 44; on Ruffhead's *Pope*, 236, said to lack interest in theater, 234; satire in *London*, *Vanity of Human Wishes*, and *Rasselas*, 29 f.; school at Edial, 223 f.; on Scotland and Scots, 20, 84, 86, 215; seasick in Hebrides, 213; seeks second wife (JB ignores), 229; sermon on wife, other sermons, 47; Shakespeare, Oxford ed., 17 f.; Shakespeare, edition abandoned, 18; on Thomas Sheridan, 232; *She Stoops to Conquer* dedicated to, 234; on simple life on Col, 214; skepticism, 6, 10, 122, 141, 147 f., 158; skepticism, lack of, on Pope vs. Addison, 147 f.; on Smart's insanity, 233; Adam Smith's remark on, 15, 222; social education, 222; as sophist, 251; stage managed by JB, 209 f., 214 f.; at Stourbridge School, 221; suggests JB read Walton's *Lives*, 217; takes wife to London, 225; teachers, 220 ff.; teaches at Market Bosworth, Leicestershire, 222 f.; thinks to travel abroad, 222; on Mrs. Thrale's remarriage, 249; Toryism moderated in old age, 145 f.; touched for king's evil, 220; translates Pope's *Messiah*, 221; on translation, 128, 131 f.; 141; on treatment of natives by Europeans, 6; violence in conversation, 236; vocabulary not Latinate, 6; "vocation to publick life," 250; in Wales and France with Thrales, 237 f.; Walpole, Sir Robert, attitude toward, 153; war, hatred of, 29, 39 f., 73 ff., 78, 82; on Wilkes, 232; and Wilkes form friendship, 242; and Wilkes tease JB, 241; on wine, 148

Johnson, Sarah, SJ's mother, 219

Johnston, John, JB writes diary for, 188, 191
Jonson, Ben, cited in *Drury-Lane Prologue*, 23; on Shakespeare, 66
Jorden, Rev. William, SJ's tutor, 221
Journal of a Tour to the Hebrides: see *Tour to the Hebrides*
Journey to the Western Islands, 83 ff.; JB disagreed with, 207; contrast with JB's *Tour,* 83
Junius, 75 f.
Juvenal, and SJ, 8; SJ's "imitation" of *Third Satire,* 7, 26; of *Tenth Satire,* 26; qualities SJ admires in, 155 f.

Kames, Henry Home, Lord, *Elements of Criticism,* 232
Keats, John, *Endymion,* 133
Kelly, Hugh, SJ's Prologue to *Word to the Wise,* 24, 42 f.
Kingsborough, SJ meets Flora Macdonald at, 88, 212
King's evil (scrofula), SJ touched for, 220
King, William, *Life,* 137
Knolles, Richard, *History of the Turks,* 30 f.
Knowles, Mrs. Mary, 242

La Bruyère, Jean de, 144
Lade, Sir John, satirized by SJ, 44
Langton, Bennet, Beauclerk's advice to, 248; gave SJ data on Pope, 164; SJ writes to, 231; night jaunt with SJ, 229 f.; recollections, 227, 246; his will, 237
Laud, Archbishop William, 28
Law, William, *Serious Call,* 221
Lee, Arthur, SJ meets, 240
Le Grand, Joachim, 4 ff.
Lennox, Charlotte, *Shakespear Illustrated,* 62
Letter to the People of Scotland, 207
Le Vasseur, Thérèse, Rousseau's mistress, 193 f.; JB seduces, 201 f.
Levet, Robert, SJ's Elegy on, 44 f.; mentioned, 246
liberty of conscience, SJ on, 77
Licensing Act, 12
Lichfield, SJ's birthplace, 3 f., 180, 221 f.
Life of Johnson, 217 ff.; authenticity, 218; JB copyrights parts, 230; JB's diary basis of, 203; JB's models for, 217; JB more reserved in, 218; JB's sources, 224 f.; JB wishes SJ had written, 218; Burke not freely mentioned in, 212; compared with Hawkins and Mrs. Piozzi, 218; conversation, letters in, 217; dedicated to Reynolds, 218; differs from SJ's *Lives,* 217; Malone's help with, 207; uniqueness, 218 f.
Literary Magazine, SJ's book reviews for, 45; SJ reports Seven Years' War in, 153
Lives of the Poets (see individual poets), 92 ff.; JB's treatment of, in *Life,* 246; commissioned to crush competition, 92; compared with *Irene,* 30; Dilly writes JB about, 92; foreshadowed by early biographies, 9 f.; SJ adds names, 92; SJ's greatest achievement, 183; SJ's responsibility for contents, 93; *Life of Savage* in, 17; pirated in Dublin, 93; separate publication in London, 93
Lobo, Father Jerome, *Abyssinia* suggested locale and name of *Rasselas,* 50; SJ translates *Abyssinia,* 4 ff., 223
"local" poetry, Denham's introduction of, 107
Lochbuy, Lady (Mrs. Maclean), offends SJ, 214 f.
Locke, John, Addison succeeds as Commissioner of Appeals, 143
London, 7 f.; attributed to Pope, 225; compared with *Vanity of Human Wishes,* 26, 29 f.; faults, 8; Garrick's comment on, 227; issued by Dodsley, 7; quoted, 3; success of, 8, 225
London Chronicle, JB's contributions to, 205
London Journal, 188 ff.; characterized, 190 f.
London Magazine, JB a partner, his contributions to, 205

Louisa, JB's infatuation with, 188 f., 191, 193
Lyttelton, George Lyttelton, Baron, *Life*, 181

Macaulay, Mrs. Catharine, republican leanings, 241 f.
Macclesfield, Anne, Countess of, Savage claims as mother, 16, 226
Macdonald, Flora, SJ and JB visit, 88, 212
Maclean, Sir Allan, and SJ's breakfast, 215
Macleod, Norman, of Macleod, entertains SJ, JB, 88
Macpherson, James, *Fragments of Ancient Poetry*, 90 f.; SJ discusses, 210 f.
Mahomet, a rope dancer, in *Drury-Lane Prologue*, 23
Mahomet II, Sultan of Turkey, in *Irene*, 31
Maittaire, Michael, dedication *Harleian Catalogue*, 14
Mallet or Malloch, David, *Life*, 180
Malone, Edmond, assistance with *Tour* and *Life*, 207 f., 218, 248 f.; JB queries as to relevance, 231; *Tour* dedicated to, 208
Marlborough, John Churchill, Duke of, praised by Addison, 143, 149
Marlborough, Sarah, Duchess of, Addison's dedication to, 143
Martin, Martin, *Description Western Islands*, 207
Marmor Norfolciense, 12
Mason, Rev. William, character of Gray, 181; *Memoirs of Gray*, 217
metaphysical poets, Cowley best of, 103; designation invented by SJ, 101; failed in their purpose, 102 f.; SJ generally unfavorable, 102 ff.
metrical harmony of Waller, 95
Miller, Philip, *Gardener's Dictionary* used by SJ, 19
Milton, John, *Life*, 16, 77, 108 ff.; on amateur dramatics, 109; appearance, 112; JB reproduces SJ's variants, 247; character, 112; cited in Preface to *Dictionary*, 22; his common sense and SJ's, 77; compared with Cowley, 101, 108; *Comus* benefit for descendant, 24, 42, 112; daughters read to, 111; enters political controversy, 110; epigraph in *Patriot*, 76 f.; escapes persecution at Restoration, 111; finances, 112; on freedom of speech, 12 f.; and SJ, likenesses, 77; SJ unsympathetic to, 108 ff.; Latin pronunciation, 111; learning, 112; on licensing the press, 110; marriage difficulties, 110; musical verse, 122; *Paradise Lost*, sales of, 111; parodied by Philips, 122; as patriot, 109; qualities as a poet, 114; religious changes, 110; religious views, 112; resents obedience, 109; rusticated from Cambridge, 108; scheme of education, 109; as schoolteacher, 109; on Spenser, Shakespeare, Cowley, 112; and Tuscan poetry, 109
modulation, in Milton's verse, 122
monastic life, SJ's comment on, 231
Monboddo, James Burnet, Lord, JB softens SJ's remarks on, 235; JB thanks for help, 204; SJ and JB visit, 85, 210; dislike for SJ, 209 f.; magnetic conversation, 85; search for men with tails, 209 f.
Montague, Charles: see Halifax, Earl of
Montrose, inn at, 84
More, Hannah, SJ gives literary help to, 43
Morgann, Maurice, Shakespearean critic, 69
Mountstuart, John Stuart, Viscount, JB joins in Italy, 197
Muck, Isle of, smallpox inoculation, 88
Mull, Isle of, SJ and JB visit, 91, 214
music, Akenside's blank verse, 180; Collins' lines impeded with consonants, 178; Dryden, *Hind and Panther*, 133; Dryden's "inarticulate poetry," 173; SJ calls Fenton's lines wooden, 157; SJ praises Denham, 108; SJ's use of musical terms for poetry, 99; melody of Pope's meter, 173; modulation of Milton,

122; in Pope's *Iliad*, 172; Waller not all musical, 97; Waller's softness, smoothness, sweetness, 99
mythology, SJ objects to, 112, 132, 140, 158, 182

Neale (or Neile), Dr. Richard, Bishop of Durham, 94
Nichols, John, biography of King, 137
Norden, F. L., *Travels in Egypt and Nubia*, 51
North, Frederick Lord, ministry employs SJ, 70
North Briton, edited by Churchill and Wilkes, 189, 239

"Observations on *Macbeth*," 17 f.
Oldisworth, William, "character" of Smith, 135
Oldys, William, *British Librarian*, *Harleian Catalogue*, 14
Oliver, Dame, SJ's first teacher, 220
Olympiodorus, cited by SJ, 17
onomatopoeia, Pope's use of, 171
oriental tales in *Rambler*, 50
Ormond, Duchess of, gift to Dryden, 130
Orrery, Roger Boyle, 1st Earl of, copied by Dryden, 124
Orrery, John Boyle, 5th Earl of, gives SJ data on Dorset, 121
Osborne, Thomas, hires SJ, 14; SJ beats, 15, 226; publishes *Harleian Catalogue*, 14
Ossianic poems, SJ on, 233
Otway, Thomas, *Life*, 119 f.
Oviedo, Patriarch of, zeal for conversion, 6
Oxford, Robert Harley, 1st Earl of, downfall, *Vanity of Human Wishes*, 28; trust in Prior, 153
Oxford, Edward Harley, 2nd Earl of, library purchased by Osborne, 14

Paoli, General Pasquale, JB and, 198 ff.; Pitt compliments, 201; Smollett wrong on age, 204; thinks JB a spy, 199; writes JB, 201
Parliament, on disputed elections, 78; powers of, re colonies, 78; represents only small number of Britons, 80; right to tax, 78, 80
Parliamentary Debates, in *Gentleman's Magazine*, 10 ff.
Parnell, Thomas, *Life*, 138
parody, of Congressional Address, 81; SJ misses, in Gray, 182
Passerat, Jean, compared with Rochester, 118
pastoral, SJ's dislike of, 101, 109, 112, 159, 176
Patriot, The, 76 ff.
Pennant, Thomas, *Tour in Scotland*, 207
Percy, Dr. Thomas, gives help on *Dryden*, 126; *Hermit of Warkworth* parodied, 43; SJ helps, 45; on SJ and Scotland, 84; *Reliques*, 43
Petrarch, Francis, compared with Waller, 98, 100
plagiarism, SJ and, 118
Plan of a Dictionary, appeared, 226 f.
Philips, Ambrose, *Life*, 176; SJ's Epilogue for *Distrest Mother*, 30; pastorals preferred to Pope's, 158, 176
Philips, John, *Life*, 122 f.
Phillips, Edward, *New World of English Words*, 19
Piccolomini, Girolama, in love with JB, 197
Pindar, Cowley's version of odes, 105
Piozzi, Gabriel Mario, marries Mrs. Thrale, 249
Piozzi, Mrs. (see also Thrale, Mrs.), *Anecdotes* chronologically inexact, 218; on SJ and Queen Anne, 220
Pitt, Christopher, *Life*, 174
Pitt, William, "the elder," Earl of Chatham, attacked in *Falkland's Islands*, 74 f.; compliments Paoli, 201
poetry, SJ's definition of, 113
Politian, SJ's proposals for, 4
Political Tracts, 70 ff.
Poll (Carmichael), 246

Pomfret, John, *Life*, 120 f.; SJ adds to *Poets*, 92

Pope, Alexander, *Life*, 164 ff.; and Addison, 147 f.; Addison praises, 165; Addison prefers Tickell's *Iliad*, 166; admired Prior's *Alma*, 154; asked to see Dryden, 164; attacks Theobald, Dennis, Duckett, and Hill in *Dunciad*, 167; and Martha Blount, 169; and Bolingbroke, 167 ff.; borrowed from Tickell to revise *Iliad*, 160; Cibber made hero of *Dunciad*, 168; compares Fenton with Dryden, 157; compared with Dryden, 169 f., with Blackmore, 156; critical ability, 170 f.; Crousaz attacks *Essay on Man*, 168; Curll's publication of letters, 167; declares Addison malicious, 165; dedicates *Iliad* to Congreve, 166; on Denham's strength, 108; Dennis attacks, 165; devious, 166; dispute over *Pastorals*, 165; Dunciad derived from *Mac Flecknoe*, 172; *Dunciad* tells success of *Beggar's Opera*, 158; expanded Dryden's character of Shakespeare, 166; on expletives, 99; Fermors considered *Lock* an insult, 165; friendship, 169; frugality, 169; on Garth, 139; Gay dedicates *Rural Sports* to, 157; genius, 169, 173; gratitude to Warburton, 168; Halifax and *Iliad*, 166; helps Dodsley start as publisher, 169; *Iliad* compared with Tickell's, 160; *Iliad* published by subscription, 165 f.; incites Gay to write pastorals, 158; investments, 166; on SJ, 7; SJ believes pro-Pope sources, 165; SJ prefers to Boileau, 173; SJ translates *Messiah*, 4, 221; SJ uses his list of writers in *Dictionary*, 18; letters compared with Arbuthnot's, Swift's, 167; liberality, 169; *London* published same day as *One Thousand Seven Hundred and Thirty Eight*, 7; melody of his verse, 173; *Odyssey* criticized by Spence, 167; *Odyssey* partly by Broome and Fenton, 157, 164, 166 f.; *Pastorals* written at sixteen, 164; personality, 169; pretended contempt of world, 169; on Prior, 153; Prologue for Addison's *Cato*, 145; published Parnell's poems, 138; recommended SJ as teacher, 225; religion, 169; on Roscommon, 119; and Savage, 16, 169; *Shakespeare*, 61, 67, 166; snob, 164; Spence's *Anecdotes*, 164; thought Addison made Tickell's translation, 166; thought author of *London*, 225; trick on Bolingbroke, 168 f.; use of onomatopoeia, 171; Walsh encouraged, 123, 165; Warburton defends *Essay on Man*, 168; Wycherley encouraged, 165

Porter, Lucy, SJ's stepdaughter, 224

Preface for Dodsley's *Preceptor*, 24 f.

Prefaces, Biographical and Critical . . . English Poets: see *Lives of the Poets*

Prologues, to Garrick's *Lethe*, Milton's *Comus*, Goldsmith's *Good-Natur'd Man*, Kelly's *Word to the Wise*, 24

Prior, Matthew, *Life*, 152 ff.; character, 153; compared with Cowley, 154; and Halifax, 152; in politics, 152 f.; Pope's opinion of, 153; would fix English language, 153

Pritchard, Hannah, as Irene, 228

Public Advertiser, Junius letters in, 75

puns, SJ's opinion of, 209

purgatory, JB presses SJ for views on, 206

Puritans, animosity to holidays, gaming, 116 f.

Quincy, John, used by SJ in *Dictionary*, 19

Quixote, Don, in *Rambler*, 34

Raasay, Isle of, SJ and JB visit, 87 f.

Rabelais, François, compared to Butler, 116

Racine, Jean, *Distrest Mother* adapted from, 30

Rambler, 32 ff.; on biography, 37 f.; on contradiction, 36 f.; on criticism, 34; defence of unusual words, 21; farewell essay, 38; on fiction, 34 f.; on hero of fiction, 69; SJ sends set to Edwards, 247; on marriage, 35 f.; mottoes translated, 43; on optimism, 35; persona of, 33 ff.; persona of, not separate from SJ, 38; in tradition of *Tatler* and *Spectator,* 32; on writers, 33 ff.

Rapin-Thoyras, Paul de, used in *Blake,* 9

Rasselas, 50 ff.; composed in a week, 5, 50; contrasted with *London* and *Vanity of Human Wishes,* 30; exotic setting, 51; first oriental tale in English, 50; location, name from Lobo's *Abyssinia,* 50; novel without an ending, 60; poetic function described, 53 f.; success of, 50; written to pay mother's funeral expenses, 50

recognition, as pleasure in literature, 178

religious poetry, Cowley failed in, 105 ff.; Denham and Waller failed in, 107

Reynolds, Sir Joshua, JB meets, 229; commended *Tour,* 218; compared with Cowley, 100 f.; compares House of Commons to private company, 243; defends drinking, 238; *Discourses,* 101; and Hogarth's description of SJ, 226; influenced by Richardson, 100; SJ attracted to, 229; SJ considers a genius, 100 f.; SJ's help with *Discourses,* 45; *Life* dedicated to, 218; met SJ in fifties, 224; name concealed by JB, 242; original mind, 229; reads *Savage,* 226; seeks increased pension for SJ, 249; tells SJ his "vocation to publick life," 250

Rich, John, produces *Beggar's Opera,* 158

Richelieu, Armand J. du Plessis de, Cardinal, cited, 21

Richardson, Jonathan, the elder, influenced Reynolds, 100

Richardson, Samuel, *Clarissa,* 34 f., 140; SJ at house of, 226; and sycophants, 229

Rivers, Richard Savage, Earl, claimed as father by Savage, 15 f.; 226

Robertson, Dr. William, *History of America,* 244; urged SJ visit Scotland, 208

Rochester, John Wilmot, Earl of, *Life,* 117 f.; compared with Passerat and Boileau, 118

Roscommon, Wentworth Dillon, Earl of, *Life,* 24, 118 f.; correctness of, 119; Dryden's and Pope's opinion of, 119; on reformation of language, 118; on translation, 119

Rousseau, Jean-Jacques, JB meets, 191 ff.; JB seduces his mistress, 201 f.; JB sees in London, 202; JB writes, 201; discussions with JB, 193 f.; driven from Switzerland, 201; *Emile,* 192, 194; and Hume, 201; illegitimate children, 193, 196; primitivism disproved, 89; sends JB letter of introduction for Corsica, 197; and Voltaire, 194

Rowe, John, father of Nicholas, on royal prerogative, 139

Rowe, Nicholas, *Life,* 139 ff.; Addison and Pope on, 141; eulogy by Welwood, 141; *Shakespeare,* 61, 141

Ruffhead, Owen, SJ criticizes *Pope,* 236; Pope's "Unfortunate Lady," 165

Rymer, Thomas, objections to Shakespeare, 63

Sacheverell, Dr. Henry, SJ heard preach, 219

St. Andrews, SJ and JB visit, 83 f., 209

St. Chrysostom, cited by SJ, 17

sarcasm, in *False Alarm,* 72

Sarpi, Father Paul, *Life,* 8; SJ's proposals, *Council of Trent,* 8 f.; praised by Burnet and Wotton, 9

Savage, Richard, *Life,* 12, 15 ff., 226; *Life,* success of, 17; JB disbelieves his story, 226; character, 15; dead before JB met SJ, 224; friendship with SJ, 15; SJ's poem on, 7; not model for Thales in *London,* 7 f.; Pope and his pension, 169

schoolmasters, SJ salutes, 141 f.

Scotland and Scots, SJ's comments on, 71, 84, 90 f., 232
Settle, Elkanah, and Dryden, 125 f., 128; *Empress of Morocco*, 125; works uncollected, 128
Seven Years' War, JB avoids service in, 188; SJ reports in *Literary Magazine*, 153; unheralded by poetry, 153
Seward, Anna, defends American colonists, 244
Shadwell, Thomas, succeeded Dryden as Laureate, 129
Shaftesbury, Anthony Ashley, Earl of, *Ascham* dedicated to, 46
Shakespeare, cited in *Drury-Lane Prologue*, 22 f.; Milton's opinion of, 112; Oxford edition, 17; Rowe's imitation of, 141
Shakespeare, 61 ff.; first variorum edition, 62; published by group headed by Tonson, 18
Sheffield, John, Duke of Buckingham, *Life*, 152
Shenstone, William, *Life*, 178 f.
Sheridan, Richard Brinsley, compliments Burke, 243; name concealed by JB, 242; *Pizarro*, 32
Sheridan, Thomas, teaching oratory, 232
Shiels, Robert, wrote Cibber's *Poets*, 160
"Short Song of Congratulation," 44
Sidney, Lady Dorothy, "Sacharissa," pursued by Waller, 95
Sidney, Sir Philip, 37
similes, defined by SJ, 149, 171
Skye, Isle of, SJ and JB visit, 87, 212
Slanes Castle, SJ and JB visit, 85
Smart, Christopher, insanity of, 233; SJ's retort on, 134 f.; *Song to David*, 98
Smith, Adam, JB attended lectures of, 187; on SJ's knowledge, 15, 222; review of *Dictionary*, 22, 187; *Wealth of Nations*, 41, 187
Smith, Edmund, *Life*, 134 ff., 222; Oldisworth's "Character" of, 135
Smollett, Tobias, errs on Paoli's age, 204; *Roderick Random*, 34
Somervile, William, *Life*, 161
sonnet, SJ says unsuccessful in English, 113
Spectator, Addison and Steele begin, 144 f.; prepares audience of *Cato*, 145
Spence, Joseph, *Anecdotes*, 164, 167; criticized Pope's *Odyssey*, 167; SJ uses unpublished *Anecdotes*, 152
Spenser, Edmund, influence on Cowley, 100; Milton on, 112; versification, 66
Sprat, Thomas, *Life*, 137; SJ credits his *Cowley*, 100
Steele, Sir Richard, and Addison, 142, 146 f.; *Englishman*, 145; *Guardian*, 145; packs theater for *Cato*, 145; political tracts, 70; *Spectator*, 144 f.; *Tatler*, 144 f.; in tradition of courtesy books, 144 f.
"Stella" (Esther Johnson), married Swift, 162
Stepney, George, *Life*, 121 f.
Sterne, Laurence, curse of Ernulfus in *Tristram*, 17
Stewart, Francis, amanuensis on *Dictionary*, 18
Stourbridge School, SJ at, 3, 221
Strafford, Thomas Wentworth, Earl of, *Vanity of Human Wishes*, 28
Strong, Capt. John, probably named Falkland Islands, 73
Suckling, Sir John, compared with Cowley, 104
supernatural, SJ's interest in, 90, 118
Swift, Jonathan, *Life*, 161 ff.; attacked *Whig Examiners*, 145 f.; and his archbishop, 162; birthplace in question, 161; comparison with Addison, 161; Delany praised, 163; dictated political opinions of nation, 163; diction, 163; disliked by SJ, 161 f.; economies, 161; educated self, 161; forces withdrawal of debased coinage, 162; friend of Oxford, 28; on *Beggar's Opera*, 158; hatred of Dryden, 161; Hawkesworth's biography of, 161; and Ireland, 162 f.; SJ's mixed admiration for, 183; letters compared with Pope's, 167; political

tracts, 70; proposals for fixing language, 153, 162; represents Irish clergy, 161; resentment of the world, 169; selfishness, 163; and Stella, 162; "tainted" mind, 163; and Vanessa, 162
Sydenham, Dr. Thomas, *Life*, 10, 13

Talisker, SJ and JB at, 88
Tatler, 144 f.
Taxation no Tyranny, 78 ff.; JB's opinion of, 237
Taylor, Dr. John, SJ and JB visit, 242; SJ's sermons for, 47; on *Plan of Dictionary*, 227; talk "of bullocks," 89
Temple, Rev. William Johnson, JB writes, 195; "character" of Gray, 181, 205
Theobald, Lewis, attacked Pope's *Shakespeare*, 61, 166; first hero of *Dunciad*, 167; *Shakespeare*, 61
Thomson, James, *Life*, 174 f.; SJ perhaps adds to *Poets*, 92
Thoughts on Falkland's Islands: see *Falkland's Islands*
Thrale, Henry, death, 247; dislikes the times, 246; friendship with SJ, 234; SJ as executor, 247
Thrale, Mrs. Hester Lynch (afterwards Mrs. Piozzi), *Anecdotes of Johnson* useful to JB, 234; attacked by JB, 249; has daughter, 246; SJ and JB dine with, 248; on SJ's anonymous writings, 45 ff.; SJ dictates translation to, 5; SJ's friendship with, 234; on SJ and JB's Scottish tour, 208; marries Piozzi, 249
Thyer, Robert, editor of Butler, 115
Tickell, Thomas, *Life*, 160; ignores Addison-Steele controversy, 147; *Iliad* compared with Pope's, 160, 166; would fix English language, 153
Tillotson, Dr. John, Addison's examples collected for dictionary, 146
Tonson, Jacob, the elder, and Dryden, 130
Tonson, Jacob, the younger, and SJ's *Shakespeare*, 18
Tories, SJ criticizes, 73
Tour to the Hebrides, 207 ff., 237; contrast with SJ's *Journey*, 83; dedicated to Malone, 208; Malone's help with, 207 f.; no previous model for, 216; praised by Adams, 218
translation, Cowley's, 107; Denham's, 107 f.; Dryden on, 128; Roscommon on, 119
Tusser, Thomas, *Husbandrie* used by SJ, 19

Ulinish, Skye, SJ and JB visit, 88
U.S. *Constitution*, anticipated in *Taxation no Tyranny*, 79
Universal Chronicle, *Idler* in, 39

"Vanessa" (Esther Vanhomrigh), and Swift, 162
Vanity of Human Wishes, The, 26 ff.; compared with *London*, 26, 29 f.; draws on SJ's own experience, 28; echoed in *Rasselas*, 53, 56; first work to bear SJ's name, 26; Garrick on, 227; SJ's ending and Juvenal's, 29; moderation of, 8; moral pointed, 28
Vergil, imitated by Philips, 122 f.; SJ and Monboddo on, 210
Vernon, Admiral Edward, *Blake* reflects on, 9
"Vision of Theodore," 24
Voltaire, JB and, 191, 194 f.; JB gets to speak English, 194; on JB's Scottish tour, 208; on British constitution, 195; *Candide*, 56; contrast to Rousseau, 194; objections to Shakespeare, 63; *Philosophical Dictionary*, 195; pretended illness, 195; on religion, 195
Voyage to Abyssinia, 223

Waller, Edmund, *Life*, 94 ff., one of first written, 93; on Chapman's *Homer*, 96 f.; and Charles I, 95; on Charles II, 96; compared with Petrarch, 98, 100; on Cromwell, 96; defends Episcopacy, 95; de-

scendant at Aberdeen, 210; and Dryden, 123; and Fairfax, 95, 99; fined and exiled, 96; parliamentary career, 96; plot against Parliament, 95; poetic faults and virtues, 97 ff.; prosecutes Clarendon, 96; softness, smoothness, sweetness, 99; some poems not musical, 97
Walmesley, Gilbert, SJ's tribute to, 136, 222; source of data on Smith, 135
Walpole, Horace, quarrel with Gray, 181
Walpole, Sir Robert, attacked in *Gustavus Vasa,* 12, and in *Marmor,* 12; his London and Alfred's, 7; SJ's attitude toward, 153; and Licensing Act, 12; and Prior, 153; success of *London* due to opposition to, 8; and Whig opposition, 11
Walsh, William, *Life,* 123; encouraged Pope, 123, 165
Walton, Izaak, *Lives* read by JB, 217
Warburton, Dr. William, defends Pope against Crousaz, 168; gave data on Pope's *Odyssey,* 164; heir to Pope's works, 168; Pope helps make a bishop, 168; praises SJ in his *Shakespeare,* 18; *Shakespeare,* 61, 67
Warren, Thomas, SJ works for, 4 ff.
Warton, Dr. Joseph, and SJ's interview with George III, 235
Warton, Rev. Thomas, SJ ridicules *Poems,* 44
Warwick, Earl of, at Addison's deathbed, 147
Watts, Isaac, *Life,* 175 f.; added to *Poets* by SJ, 92, 175
Welwood, James, eulogy on Rowe, 141
West, Gilbert, *Life,* 176 f.
Wharton, Thomas Wharton, Marquis of, Addison secretary to, 143 f.
Whig Examiners, 145 f.
Whitelocke, Bulstrode, SJ credits for data on Waller, 95
Wilkes, John, attentions to SJ, 240 f.; barred from Commons, 70 ff.; JB writes about SJ, 197; career, 239; and Churchill, 189, 239; convicted of sedition and impiety, 71; dinner with SJ, 239 ff., 247 f.; *Essay on Woman,* 239; in *False Alarm,* 70 ff.; friend of JB, 71, 189, 196; friendship with SJ, 242; hints for set of *Poets,* 248; SJ disapproves of, 70 f., 239; SJ remarks on, and liberty, 232; and SJ tease JB, 241; and *North Briton,* 189, 239; on Shakespeare, 241; use of obscenity, 190
Williams, Anna, 246; Garrick refuses theater ticket to, 232; gives data to JB, 224 f.; SJ's literary help to, 43; lets SJ dine with Wilkes, 240
wine, SJ's remarks perhaps autobiographical, 148
Wolsey, Thomas, Cardinal, in *Vanity of Human Wishes,* 28
Wordsworth, William, attacks SJ's parody, 43; attack on poetic diction, 106; *Lyrical Ballads,* 172; on proper language of poetry, 64
Wood, Anthony à, on Cowley, 100
Wotton, William, on Sarpi, 9

Xerxes, 29

Yalden, Thomas, *Life,* 159 f.; SJ adds to *Poets,* 92
York, Anne, Duchess of, Dryden's dedication to, 126 f.
York, Edward Augustus, Duke of, and JB, 191
Young, Edward, *Life,* 179

Zelide: see the following
Zuylen, Belle or Isabella de, JB and, 191

ABCDEFGHIJ—R—73210/69